Global Strategies

The Harvard Business Review Book Series

Global Strategies

Insights from the World's Leading Thinkers

With a Preface by
Percy Barnevik

Afterword by
Rosabeth Moss Kanter

A Harvard Business Review Book

The *Harvard Business Review* articles in this collection are available as individual reprints. Discounts apply to quantity purchases. For information and ordering contact Operations Department, Harvard Business School Publishing, Boston, MA 02163. Telephone: (617) 495-6192, 9 a.m. to 5 p.m. Eastern Time, Monday through Friday. Fax: (617) 495-6985, 24 hours a day.

The paper used in this publication meets the requirements of the American National Standard for Permanence of Paper for Printed Library Materials Z39.48-1984

Library of Congress Cataloging-in-Publication Data

Global stratagies: insights from the world's leading thinkers/with a preface by Percy Barnevik; afterword by Rosabeth Moss Kanter.
    p.   cm. — (The Harvard business review book series)
    Articles originally published in the Harvard business review since 1982.
    Includes index.
    ISBN 0-87584-561-4
    1. International business enterprises.   2. Strategic planning.
    3. Competion, International.   I. Harvard business review.   II. Series.
HD2755.5.G554   1994
    658'.049—dc20   94-16424
                                                                       CIP

Contents

Board of Management speaks candidly about rapid
changes in Europe and advocates a philosophy of
competition among companies, not countries.

David Whitwam contends that many companies
pursue an international—but not a global—strategy,
planting flags around the world but neglecting to
leverage their resources to create the powerful,
cohesive, world leaders they could be. Whirlpool's
ongoing transformation from international to global
involves a commitment to change throughout the
organization.

Part II   Developing a Global Strategy

To compete successfully, a global company needs
three strategic capabilities: global-scale efficiency, local
responsiveness, and the ability to leverage learning
worldwide. These capabilities require the leadership of
specialists, who are made, not born. Profiles of several
managers illustrate the skills required to achieve
organizational integration and global leadership.

Multinationals can no longer rely on sheer size and
geographic reach to dominate the volatile global
arena. By integrating far-flung plants into tightly
connected yet flexible production systems, companies
can seize the opportunity for a new manufacturing
scale advantage.

headquarters and subsidiaries should oversee global marketing efforts.

Vitro's current challenges and opportunities are common to companies around the world.

Preface

Percy Barnevik

This collection of fourteen essays on global strategies published by the *Harvard Business Review* over the past decade represents a mix of theories and concepts with practical experiences of companies and managers. Both approaches provide useful insights for the many companies today that are developing and implementing strategies to achieve global competitiveness.

Strategy and Execution

In my experience as the leader of a "global" company, I have found that execution, not strategy per se, is primarily what differentiates the winners from the losers, whether they operate on a global or a local scale. Certainly it is important to be guided by a good strategy, or rather a good *set* of strategies, adapted to the particular product and regional and competitive circumstances. Likewise, it is important to communicate clear strategic objectives so that employees subscribe to the company's mission. But pushing technically doomed products or pursuing global standardization in highly customized domestic markets in the name of "strategy" can be ruinous. When you study a thriving company you're bound to find execution as the key to its success. By "execution," I mean the ways top management motivates and mobilizes the company's many managers and front-line employees and how management communicates with employees to achieve consensus. In these days of surplus in products and services, the customer reigns. While every company wants to be customer-oriented—and many espouse slogans to that effect—few are truly customer-driven on the shop floor or deep inside the research labs.

Why do we spend so much time analyzing the strategies of successful companies and so little studying the execution of these strategies? This state of affairs reminds me of the story of the drunkard who has lost his key; instead of searching for it in the darkness where it fell, he looks under the light of a street lamp. Companies readily talk about their strategies but are not as likely to reveal the true inner workings of their operations. Developing and articulating a strategy is often more intellectually exciting than doing the daily, repetitive work of making a company and its employees function better. When asked to explain the reason for a successful endeavor, I often disappoint the questioner by admitting that it can be attributed to no spectacular, hidden strategy but to the execution.

It is often easy to be dazzled by flashy concepts and slick managerial jargon. The much touted "international matrix organization," for example, can be a disaster or a triumph, depending on how the model is implemented, how individuals understand their roles and relationships within the organization, how procedures are specified, how managers can contain overhead costs. As the English say, "the devil is in the details."

When I am asked how I split my time between strategy formulation and execution, I answer 10 percent and 90 percent, respectively. Of the 10 percent devoted to strategy, most involves taking uncomfortable positions, such as cancelling a project we once believed in, or trying to look around the corners where no market research is available, such as when considering investments in the former Soviet republics or in China.

The strategies proposed and described in this book are not intended to offer a simple solution to the challenge of competing in an increasingly borderless world. On the contrary, they represent a wide range of conceptual and practical approaches to meeting this challenge, anticipating and creating opportunities, and designing successful programs. Company case studies and first-person accounts by executives and managers illustrate the variety of approaches being explored in the rapidly changing competitive environment and the pitfalls of attempting to globalize without a solid strategy. I would argue, in fact, that the common thread among successful companies is their leaders' combination of vision, leadership, communication, and execution. My comments below offer less a road map to reading this collection than some thoughts on the state of globalization inspired by a review of the articles.

The Advantages of Globalization

Essays such as Hamel and Prahalad's "Strategic Intent," Hout, Porter, and Rudden's "How Global Companies Win Out," and McGrath and Hoole's "Manufacturing's New Economies of Scale" illustrate the advantages of having a global outlook. For highly standardized products, the economies of scale realized by integrating production globally—running fewer plants worldwide, buying inputs from fewer suppliers, and reducing duplication in engineering—can lower unit costs by 20 to 30 percent. If combined with reallocation of manufacturing to low-cost countries, the unit costs drop even further. Thus, a company can gain *offensive* advantages by increasing volume through globalization or, if already operating globally, by applying a broad integrative strategy to existing, country-specific operations.

This degree of integration requires strong internal leadership. And while it may be difficult to rationalize plants, shift production, and close some facilities, it is even more difficult to persuade engineers in different countries to agree on a common design. At the same time, having a presence in many markets can offer a *defensive* advantage by enabling a company to retaliate against attackers on its home ground. Many Western companies wish they had a presence in Japan for this very reason, especially when they compete for public procurement contracts in that country, where prices can be 20 to 30 percent above world market levels. Another defensive advantage comes from not depending too heavily on one market, even a large one like the United States.

A third advantage of globalization is the *economy of scope* that broad-based global competitors may gain over local niche players. For example, a plant builder that produces the whole range of products included in the plant can offer lower costs and shorter delivery times to customers, thereby dominating local producers of specialized parts. Similarly, offering a broad assortment of standard products can yield advantages to a company in lower distribution costs and to its customers in lower prices.

As many of the cases illustrate, the final product need not be globally standardized. In fact, it can appear highly differentiated, despite a high degree of component standardization. The case of Electrolux, described by Christopher Bartlett and Sumantra Ghoshal in "What Is a Global Manager?," is an excellent example. Even with food and beverage products, where different national tastes require individualized products and packaging, global companies can gain important advantages through the interaction of their product managers around the world.

Domestic or Global?

There has long been discussion over which dimension in the country versus product matrix should have the upper hand. This debate is explored here from several perspectives, including organizational design, product development, and marketing strategies. The fact is that no one model is superior. Some companies have successfully applied a strict global product organization without a single country manager. Others have applied the opposite extreme with highly independent country managers who may even compete against each other. Of course many companies' positions lie between these extremes. Some large, well-known multinationals such as N.V. Philips (profiled in Nan Stone's interview with former president and chairman Wisse Dekker) have emphasized one dimension in the matrix (country) at one time and the other (product) at a later stage. Successful companies are found in all camps—Motorola is noted for its strong global product leadership and Nestlé for its strong country management.

One explanation for companies' achieving success through a variety of organizational solutions is that products, customers, and competitive characteristics differ substantially from one business to another. Companies with a few highly standardized and independent product lines favor strong global product leadership. On the other hand, companies that have many interacting product lines, share customers across product lines, or require strong local added value and close cooperation with networks of local suppliers and distributors tend to demand strong country-level management. I maintain that whatever organizational structure is chosen, the key to its success is the quality of execution and the degree to which top management can create and encourage an atmosphere of cooperation, shared commitment, and mutual understanding.

The tendency in recent years is for multinationals to increase the power of global product management in relation to country management. One reason is intensified competition across borders, in which domestic competition is often replaced by low-priced import competition. In response, global companies must restructure, optimizing global production and supply. These efforts require strong global management along product lines. Meanwhile, the regional economic integration of Western Europe and North America, including attempts to standardize public regulations, hastens the threat of cross-border competition.

An additional challenge—not explored explicitly in these essays—is managing the risk of rising overhead costs and increasing bureaucracy as companies globalize. A good rule of thumb is that the combined costs of country holding companies or country-based management and staff, together with global group headquarters, should not exceed 1 to 1.5 percent of invoicing. When these costs approach 2 to 3 percent an alarm bell should sound. At 4 to 5 percent—or more—companies are destined for trouble, not only because the costs are pulling them down, but because the bureaucratic paper shuffling tends to inhibit the entrepreneurship and productivity of operating units and promote an inward-looking company atmosphere.

In conclusion, I would say that the product/country matrix can be weighted along either dimension and work well. The decisive factors are the characteristics of the company's business and competitive environment, and, above all, the way the matrix is implemented and understood. Overhead costs, always a looming threat, should be kept to a minimum.

Competitors in Focus

Many of the articles rightly point out that the competitive situation of the business must play an important role in shaping its global strategy. I like to say to my employees: "Focus on the best competitors in benchmarking and the worst ones when you go for market share—not the reverse."

Many companies focus too closely on the old and resource-rich competitors while neglecting the newer, faster, smaller, more nimble ones. The history of Western companies is rife with such underestimations, first of Japanese, then of other Asian, competitors. The lessons of the past should be useful now that China and Eastern Europe are emerging as international competitors. Hamel and Prahalad offer some interesting examples of newcomers zooming in on weak spots in a domestic market, such as the United States, to establish a presence—what the authors call the "loose brick" strategy. The major domestic players sometimes mistook this approach for a niche strategy, when it was actually the beginning of a broad attack.

As a substantial middle class emerges in countries such as China, India, Thailand, and Indonesia, we will see a consumer-driven increase in demand. Western companies that establish themselves as insiders in these markets will have to learn how to meet new competitors in a rapidly evolving environment. In "Local Memoirs of a Global Manager," Procter & Gamble executive Gucharan Das offers valuable insights into the marketing environment in India, and more broadly, in the developing world.

Changing Europe

The interview with Wisse Dekker highlights the declining competitiveness of many European companies in recent decades, the costs of rigidity in the labor market, and the expectations surrounding the creation of a unified European market. Since the publication of the interview in 1989, a dramatic change has occurred—the opening of Central and Eastern Europe. With the inclusion of the former Soviet republics and the former Warsaw Pact countries, a continent of 400 million people is now one of 800 million. What will be the implications of 60 million well-trained industrial workers in Eastern Europe earning a mere 5 to 10 percent of what their 40 million Western counterparts earn?

These conditions may represent a threat to some industries in the West (such as agriculture, textiles, and basic metals), but they also imply opportunities for others (such as computers and telecommunications equipment) and for Europe as a whole. One opportunity is the enormous potential for new and expanding markets for infrastructure, investment goods, and consumer products, as these troubled East European countries gradually emerge from their present economic and political chaos. Another opportunity lies in the economic integration between high-wage Western Europe and low-wage Eastern Europe that could increase Europe's competitiveness against the other two major regions, the Americas and Asia Pacific. Interestingly, these two regions face similar opportunities: high-wage North America integrating with low-wage Latin America, and high-wage Japan integrating with low-wage developing countries in Asia.

Proactive companies that adopt aggressive strategies to exploit these new opportunities will be the winners; defensive companies that cling to protection will be the losers.

Strategic Alliances

Two essays—Kenichi Ohmae's "Global Logic of Strategic Alliances" and Howard Perlmutter and David Heenan's "Cooperate to Compete Globally"—extol the virtues of strategic alliances, or global strategic partnerships (GSPs). While strategic alliances can sometimes be useful, I would advise readers to exercise caution when considering alliances as a means to achieve global leadership.

There are obviously merits to some strategic alliances. With the right external conditions and the dedication of the participating parties, these alliances can breed success, as evidenced by Hewlett-Packard's experiences with partners in Japan and General Electric's with SNECMA in France. Strategic alliances can be powerful tools for penetrating new markets, allowing one partner to build on the other's experience and achieve substantial savings by using the partner's distribution networks. When the product and market range are well defined and the partners have few conflicting interests, strategic alliances can help participants achieve short- and long-term success.

Nevertheless, entering into strategic alliances can be dangerous as a general strategy for globalization. Acquiring and merging with companies in other countries, and going on to establish a common corporate culture and agenda is demading, even with a common set of shareholders and board members and a single top management team. Add to this the challenges of optimizing the global structure by reallocating export markets, closing plants, and transferring production when national loyalties come into play. And keep in mind that these changes become even more difficult to effect when minority interests need to be protected or an equal partner needs to be placated.

Further, the rewards from a common global strategy—whether it is applied by equal partners in an alliance or by wholly owned companies in a group—are often shared unequally. A global strategy can mean heavy market investments in one country, temporarily burdening its P&L while benefiting a supplier in another country. When price wars are waged as a strategy for gaining market share, the local partner may be hurt badly while other companies in other countries belonging to the same group may benefit.

One of the more common problems in alliances is agreeing on how a jointly owned company or each individual partner should behave in third-country markets. The problems for a joint venture of competing against wholly owned companies in third-country markets can be substantial and can, after some years, lead to the dissolution of the alliance. Limitations to competition can be set but may mean legal trouble for the partners, as local antitrust authorities tend to be more suspicious of joint ventures between competitors than of outright acquisitions or mergers. Given these inherent weaknesses, it is noteworthy that several of the alliances described by Perlmutter and Heenan in 1986 have since been dissolved.

Some strategic alliances are no more than poor substitutes for full acquisitions or mergers. Alliances may be chosen as the path of least resistance; separate company management structures and boards continue to exist, national pride is kept intact, shareholders need not exchange shares, employees and unions may be lulled into a false sense of security, and difficult decisions can be pushed into the future. These limitations, and the additional bureaucracy required to manage the alliance relationship, may outweigh the advantages. And alliance participants may be looking for an escape hatch that a full merger does not allow.

The two essays offer many practical guidelines for managing alliances. These principles can also be applied to managing acquisitions or mergers between companies in different countries. I would argue, in fact, that these guidelines are actually *more* difficult to apply in alliances for the reasons expressed above.

Company Executives and Global Managers

The insights offered in this collection by company executives and managers from all corners of the world are particularly valuable. Dutch-British Unilever, for example, has been a true multinational company since its founding in 1930. Through the years, it has changed its emphasis from country-based management to global product management, and more recently to a more balanced position between the two extremes. The focus is on execution as the company strives to combine a decentralized structure and a deep understanding of local markets with global optimization of resources and a degree of centralized control of finances and product lines. This is what Unilever calls "unity in diversity" and what we at ABB call being "global and local, big and small."

Floris Maljers describes how Unilever seeks to achieve consensus between global headquarters and national managers through "Extended Head Office" exercises and efforts to communicate through several layers deep down into the organization. The quality of this execution will determine Unilever's success.

Development of managers plays an important role in this process. At Unilever, Dutch and British managers have gradually been replaced by local managers in most countries. A bottleneck in most multinational companies today is the lack of truly global leaders—people who can understand different cultures and lead mixed-nationality teams. Such global leaders are not born but must be developed. At ABB we achieve this training by giving young managers both national and global assignments.

Maljers candidly admits that Unilever's development into one of the great transnationals has not been achieved by applying any particular theory. It has instead come through a messy evolution of trial and error, but with some consistent practices: emphasis on training high-quality managers and linking decentralized units through a common corporate culture.

It is the success of companies like Unilever that best illustrates my contention that excellent execution is the key to success in global markets.

Global Strategies

PART

I

The Global Challenge

1
Strategic Intent

Gary Hamel and C.K. Prahalad

Today managers in many industries are working hard to match the competitive advantages of their new global rivals. They are moving manufacturing offshore in search of lower labor costs, rationalizing product lines to capture global scale economies, instituting quality circles and just-in-time production, and adopting Japanese human resource practices. When competitiveness still seems out of reach, they form strategic alliances—often with the very companies that upset the competitive balance in the first place.

Important as these initiatives are, few of them go beyond mere imitation. Too many companies are expending enormous energy simply to reproduce the cost and quality advantages their global competitors already enjoy. Imitation may be the sincerest form of flattery, but it will not lead to competitive revitalization. Strategies based on imitation are transparent to competitors who have already mastered them. Moreover, successful competitors rarely stand still. So it is not surprising that many executives feel trapped in a seemingly endless game of catch-up—regularly surprised by the new accomplishments of their rivals.

For these executives and their companies, regaining competitiveness will mean rethinking many of the basic concepts of strategy.[1] As "strategy" has blossomed, the competitiveness of Western companies has withered. This may be coincidence, but we think not. We believe that the application of concepts such as "strategic fit" (between resources and opportunities), "generic strategies" (low cost vs. differentiation vs. focus), and the "strategy hierarchy" (goals, strategies, and tactics) have often abetted the process of competitive decline. The new global competitors approach strategy from a perspective that is fundamentally different from that which underpins Western management thought. Against such competitors, marginal adjustments to current orthodoxies are no more likely to produce competitive revitalization than are marginal improvements in operating efficiency. (The appendix describes our research and summarizes the two contrasting approaches to strategy we see in large, multinational companies.)

Few Western companies have an enviable track record anticipating the moves of new global competitors. Why? The explanation begins with the way most companies have approached competitor analysis. Typically, competitor analysis focuses on the existing resources (human, technical, and financial) of present competitors. The only companies seen as a threat are those with the resources to erode margins and market share in the next planning period. Resourcefulness, the pace at which new competitive advantages are being built, rarely enters in.

In this respect, traditional competitor analysis is like a snapshot of a moving car. By itself, the photograph yields little information about the car's speed or direction—whether the driver is out for a quiet Sunday drive or warming up for the Grand Prix. Yet many managers have learned through painful experience that a business's initial resource endowment (whether bountiful or meager) is an unreliable predictor of future global success.

Think back. In 1970, few Japanese companies possessed the resource base, manufacturing volume, or technical prowess of U.S. and European industry leaders. Komatsu was less than 35% as large as Caterpillar (measured by sales), was scarcely represented outside Japan, and relied on just one product line—small bulldozers—for most of its revenue. Honda was smaller than American Motors and had not yet begun to export cars to the United States. Canon's first halting steps in the reprographics business looked pitifully small compared with the $4 billion Xerox powerhouse.

If Western managers had extended their competitor analysis to include these companies, it would merely have underlined how dramatic the resource discrepancies between them were. Yet by 1985, Komatsu was a $2.8 billion company with a product scope encompassing a broad range of earth-moving equipment, industrial robots, and semiconductors. Honda manufactured almost as many cars worldwide in 1987 as Chrysler. Canon had matched Xerox's global unit market share.

The lesson is clear: assessing the current tactical advantages of known competitors will not help you understand the resolution, stamina, and inventiveness of potential competitors. Sun-tzu, a Chinese military strategist, made the point 3,000 years ago: "All men can see the tactics whereby I conquer," he wrote, "but what none can see is the strategy out of which great victory is evolved."

Companies that have risen to global leadership over the past 20 years invariably began with ambitions that were out of all proportion to their resources and capabilities. But they created an obsession with winning at all levels of the organization and then sustained that obsession over the 10- to 20-year quest for global leadership. We term this obsession "strategic intent."

On the one hand, strategic intent envisions a desired leadership position and establishes the criterion the organization will use to chart its progress. Komatsu set out to "Encircle Caterpillar." Canon sought to "Beat Xerox." Honda strove to become a second Ford—an automotive pioneer. All are expressions of strategic intent.

At the same time, strategic intent is more than simply unfettered ambition. (Many companies possess an ambitious strategic intent yet fall short of their goals.) The concept also encompasses an active management process that includes: focusing the organization's attention on the essence of winning; motivating people by communicating the value of the target; leaving room for individual and team contributions; sustaining enthusiasm by providing new operational definitions as circumstances change; and using intent consistently to guide resource allocations.

Strategic intent captures the essence of winning. The Apollo program—landing a man on the moon ahead of the Soviets—was as competitively focused as Komatsu's drive against Caterpillar. The space program became the scorecard for America's technology race with the USSR. In the turbulent information technology industry, it was hard to pick a single competitor as a target, so NEC's strategic intent, set in the early 1970s, was to acquire the technologies that would put it in the best position to exploit the convergence of computing and telecommunications. Other industry observers foresaw this convergence, but only NEC made convergence the guiding theme for subsequent strategic decisions by adopting "computing and communications" as its intent. For Coca-Cola, strategic intent has been to put a Coke within "arm's reach" of every consumer in the world.

Strategic intent is stable over time. In battles for global leadership, one of the most critical tasks is to lengthen the organization's attention span. Strategic intent provides consistency to short-term action, while leaving room for reinterpretation as new opportunities emerge. At Komatsu, encircling Caterpillar encompassed a succession of medium-term programs aimed at exploiting specific weaknesses in Caterpillar or building particular competitive advantages. When Caterpillar threatened Komatsu in Japan, for example, Komatsu responded by first improving quality, then driving down costs, then cultivating export markets, and then underwriting new product development.

Strategic intent sets a target that deserves personal effort and commitment. Ask the chairmen of many American corporations how they measure their contributions to their companies' success and you're likely to get an answer expressed in terms of shareholder wealth. In a company that possesses a strategic intent, top management is more likely to talk in terms of global market leadership. Market share leadership typically yields shareholder wealth, to be sure. But the two goals do not have the same motivational impact. It is hard to imagine middle managers, let alone blue-collar employees, waking up each day with the sole thought of creating more shareholder wealth. But mightn't they feel different given the challenge to "Beat Benz"—the rallying cry at one Japanese auto producer? Strategic intent gives employees the only goal that is worthy of commitment: to unseat the best or remain the best, worldwide.

Many companies are more familiar with strategic planning than they are with strategic intent. The planning process typically acts as a "feasibility sieve." Strategies are accepted or rejected on the basis of whether managers can be precise about the "how" as well as the "what" of their plans. Are the milestones clear? Do we have the necessary skills and resources? How will competitors react? Has the market been thoroughly researched? In one form or another, the admonition "Be realistic!" is given to line managers at almost every turn.

But can you *plan* for global leadership? Did Komatsu, Canon, and Honda have detailed, 20-year "strategies" for attacking Western markets? Are Japanese and Korean managers better planners than their Western counterparts? No. As valuable as strategic planning is, global leadership is an objective that lies outside the range of planning. We know of few companies with highly developed planning systems that have managed to set a strategic intent. As tests of strategic fit become more stringent, goals that cannot be planned for fall by the wayside. Yet companies that are afraid to commit to goals that lie outside the range of planning are unlikely to become global leaders.

Although strategic planning is billed as a way of becoming more future oriented, most managers, when pressed, will admit that their strategic plans reveal more about today's problems than tomorrow's opportunities. With a fresh set of problems confronting managers at the beginning of every planning cycle, focus often shifts dramatically from year to year. And with the pace of change accelerating in most industries, the predictive horizon is becoming shorter and shorter. So plans do little more than project the present forward incrementally. The goal of strategic intent is to fold the future back into the present. The important question is not "How will next year be different from this year?" but "What must we do differently next year to get closer to our strategic intent?" Only with a carefully articulated and adhered to strategic intent will a succession of year-on-year plans sum up to global leadership.

Just as you cannot plan a 10- to 20-year quest for global leadership, the chance of falling into a leadership position by accident is also remote. We don't believe that global leadership comes from an undirected process of intrapreneurship. Nor is it the product of a skunkworks or other techniques for internal venturing. Behind such programs lies a nihilistic assumption: the organization is so hidebound, so orthodox ridden that the only way to innovate is to put a few bright people in a dark room, pour in some money, and hope that something wonderful will happen. In this "Silicon Valley" approach to innovation, the only role for top managers is to retrofit their corporate strategy to the entrepreneurial successes that emerge from below. Here the value added of top management is low indeed.

Sadly, this view of innovation may be consistent with the reality in many large companies.[2] On the one hand, top management lacks any particular point of view about desirable ends beyond satisfying shareholders and keeping raiders at bay. On the other, the planning format, reward criteria, definition of served market, and belief in accepted industry practice all work together to tightly constrain the range of available means. As a result, innovation is necessarily an isolated activity. Growth depends more on the inventive capacity of individuals and small teams than on the ability of top management to aggregate the efforts of multiple teams towards an ambitious strategic intent.

In companies that overcame resource constraints to build leadership positions, we see a different relationship between means and ends. While strategic intent is clear about ends, it is flexible as to means—it leaves room for improvisation. Achieving strategic intent requires enormous creativity with respect to means: witness Fujitsu's use of strategic alliances in Europe to attack IBM. But this creativity comes in the service of a clearly prescribed end. Creativity is unbridled, but not uncorralled, because top management establishes the criterion against which employees can pretest the logic of their initiatives. Middle managers must do more than deliver on promised financial targets; they must also deliver on the broad direction implicit in their organization's strategic intent.

Strategic intent implies a sizable stretch for an organization. Current capabilities and resources will not suffice. This forces the organization to be more inventive, to make the most of limited resources. Whereas the traditional view of strategy focuses on the degree of fit between existing resources and current opportunities, strategic intent creates an extreme misfit between resources and ambitions. Top management then challenges the organization to close the gap by systematically building new advantages. For Canon this meant first understanding Xerox's patents, then licensing technology to create a product that would yield early market experience, then gearing up internal R&D efforts, then licensing its own technology to other manufacturers to fund further R&D, then entering market segments in Japan and Europe where Xerox was weak, and so on.

In this respect, strategic intent is like a marathon run in 400-meter sprints. No one knows what the terrain will look like at mile 26, so the role of top management is to focus the organization's attention on the ground to be covered in the next 400 meters. In several companies, management did this by presenting the organization with a series of corporate challenges, each specifying the next hill in the race to achieve strategic intent. One year the challenge might be quality, the next total customer care, the next entry into new markets, the next a rejuvenated product line. As this example indicates, corporate challenges are a way to stage the acquisition of new competitive advantages, a way to identify the focal point for employees' efforts in the near to medium term. As with strategic intent, top management is specific about the ends (reducing product development times by 75%, for example) but less prescriptive about the means.

Like strategic intent, challenges stretch the organization. To preempt Xerox in the personal copier business, Canon set its engineers a target price of $1,000 for a home copier. At the time, Canon's least expensive copier sold for several thousand dollars. Trying to reduce the cost of existing models would not have given Canon the radical price-performance improvement it needed to delay or deter Xerox's entry into personal copiers. Instead, Canon engineers were challenged to reinvent the copier—a challenge they met by substituting a disposable cartridge for the complex image-transfer mechanism used in other copiers.

Corporate challenges come from analyzing competitors as well as from the foreseeable pattern of industry evolution. Together these reveal potential competitive openings and identify the new skills the organization will need to take the initiative away from better positioned players. Exhibit I, "Building Competitive Advantage at Komatsu," illustrates the way challenges helped that company achieve its intent.

For a challenge to be effective, individuals and teams throughout the organization must understand it and see its implications for their own jobs. Companies that set corporate challenges to create new competitive advantages (as Ford and IBM did with quality improvement) quickly discover that engaging the entire organization requires top management to:

Create a sense of urgency, or quasi crisis, by amplifying weak signals in the environment that point up the need to improve, instead of allowing inaction to precipitate a real crisis. (Komatsu, for example, budgeted on the basis of worst case exchange rates that overvalued the yen.)

Develop a competitor focus at every level through widespread use of competitive intelligence. Every employee should be able to benchmark his or her efforts against best-in-class competitors so that the challenge becomes personal. (For example, Ford showed production-line workers videotapes of operations at Mazda's most efficient plant.)

Provide employees with the skills they need to work effectively—training in statistical tools, problem solving, value engineering, and team building, for example.

Give the organization time to digest one challenge before launching another. When competing initiatives overload the organization, middle managers often try to protect their people from the whipsaw of shifting priorities. But this "wait and see if they're serious this time" attitude ultimately destroys the credibility of corporate challenges.

Exhibit I.

Building Competitive Advantage At Komatsu

Corporate Challenge	Protect Komatsu's home market against Caterpillar		Reduce costs while maintaining quality	
Programs	early 1960s	Licensing deals with Cummins Engine, International Harvester, and Bucyrus-Erie to acquire technology and establish benchmarks	1965	C D (Cost Down) program
			1966	Total C D program
	1961	Project A (for Ace) to advance the product quality of Komatsu's small- and medium-sized bulldozers above Caterpillar's		
	1962	Quality Circles companywide to provide training for all employees		

Establish clear milestones and review mechanisms to track progress and ensure that internal recognition and rewards reinforce desired behavior. The goal is to make the challenge inescapable for everyone in the company.

It is important to distinguish between the process of managing corporate challenges and the advantages that the process creates. Whatever the actual challenge may be—quality, cost, value engineering, or something else—there is the same need to engage employees intellectually and emotionally in the development of new skills. In each case, the challenge will take root only if senior executives and lower level employees feel a reciprocal responsibility for competitiveness.

Make Komatsu an International enterprise and build export markets		Respond to external shocks that threaten markets		Create new products and markets	
early 1960s	Develop Eastern bloc countries	1975	V-10 program to reduce costs by 10% while maintaining quality; reduce parts by 20%; rationalize manufacturing system	late 1970s	Accelerate product development to expand line
1967	Komatsu Europe marketing subsidiary established			1979	Future and Frontiers program to identify new businesses based on society's needs and company's know-how
1970	Komatsu America established				
		1977	¥ 180 program to budget company-wide for 180 yen to the dollar when exchange rate was 240		
1972	Project B to improve the durability and reliability and to reduce costs of large bulldozers			1981	EPOCHS program to reconcile greater product variety with improved production efficiencies
1972	Project C to improve payloaders	1979	Project E to establish teams to redouble cost and quality efforts in response to oil crisis		
1972	Project D to improve hydraulic excavators				
1974	Establish presales and service department to assist newly industrializing countries in construction projects				

We believe workers in many companies have been asked to take a disproportionate share of the blame for competitive failure. In one U.S. company, for example, management had sought a 40% wage-package concession from hourly employees to bring labor costs into line with Far Eastern competitors. The result was a long strike and, ultimately, a 10% wage concession from employees on the line. However, direct labor costs in manufacturing accounted for less than 15% of total value added. The company thus succeeded in demoralizing its entire blue-collar work force for the sake of a 1.5% reduction in total costs. Ironically, further analysis showed that their competitors' most significant cost savings came not from lower hourly wages but from better work methods invented by employees. You can imagine how eager the U.S. workers were to make similar contributions after the strike and concessions. Contrast this situation with what happened at Nissan when the yen strengthened: top management took a big pay cut and then asked middle managers and line employees to sacrifice relatively less.

Reciprocal responsibility means shared gain and shared pain. In too many companies, the pain of revitalization falls almost exclusively on the employees least responsible for the enterprise's decline. Too often, workers are asked to commit to corporate goals without any matching commitment from top management—be it employment security, gain sharing, or an ability to influence the direction of the business. This one-sided approach to regaining competitiveness keeps many companies from harnessing the intellectual horsepower of their employees.

Creating a sense of reciprocal responsibility is crucial because competitiveness ultimately depends on the pace at which a company embeds new advantages deep within its organization, not on its stock of advantages at any given time. Thus we need to expand the concept of competitive advantage beyond the scorecard many managers now use: Are my costs lower? Will my product command a price premium?

Few competitive advantages are long lasting. Uncovering a new competitive advantage is a bit like getting a hot tip on a stock: the first person to act on the insight makes more money than the last. When the experience curve was young, a company that built capacity ahead of competitors, dropped prices to fill plants, and reduced costs as volume rose went to the bank. The first mover traded on the fact that competitors undervalued market share—they didn't price to capture additional share because they didn't understand how market share leadership could be translated into lower costs and better margins. But there is no more undervalued market share when each of 20 semiconductor companies builds enough capacity to serve 10% of the world market.

Keeping score of existing advantages is not the same as building new advantages. The essence of strategy lies in creating tomorrow's competitive advantages faster than competitors mimic the ones you possess today. In the 1960s, Japanese producers relied on labor and capital cost advantages. As Western manufacturers began to move production offshore, Japanese companies accelerated their investment in process technology and created scale and quality advantages. Then as their U.S. and European competitors rationalized manufacturing, they added another string to their bow by accelerating the rate of product development. Then they built global brands. Then they deskilled competitors through alliances and outsourcing deals. The moral? An organization's capacity to improve existing skills and learn new ones is the most defensible competitive advantage of all.

To achieve a strategic intent, a company must usually take on larger, better financed competitors. That means carefully managing competitive engagements so that scarce resources are conserved. Managers cannot do that simply by playing the same game better—making marginal improvements to competitors' technology and business practices. Instead, they must fundamentally change the game in ways that disadvantage incumbents—devising novel approaches to market entry, advantage building, and competitive warfare. For smart competitors, the goal is not competitive imitation but competitive innovation, the art of containing competitive risks within manageable proportions.

Four approaches to competitive innovation are evident in the global expansion of Japanese companies. These are: building layers of advantage, searching for loose bricks, changing the terms of engagement, and competing through collaboration.

The wider a company's portfolio of advantages, the less risk it faces in competitive battles. New global competitors have built such portfolios by steadily expanding their arsenals of competitive weapons. They have moved inexorably from less defensible advantages such as low wage costs to more defensible advantages like global brands. The Japanese color television industry illustrates this layering process.

By 1967, Japan had become the largest producer of black-and-white television sets. By 1970, it was closing the gap in color televisions. Japanese manufacturers used their competitive advantage—at that time, primarily, low labor costs—to build a base in the private-label business, then moved quickly to establish world-scale plants. This investment gave them additional layers of advantage—quality and reliability—as well as further cost reductions from process improvements. At the same time, they recognized that these cost-based advantages were vulnerable to changes in labor costs, process and product technology, exchange rates, and trade policy. So throughout the 1970s, they also invested heavily in building channels and brands, thus creating another layer of advantage, a global franchise. In the late 1970s, they enlarged the scope of their products and businesses to amortize these grand investments, and by 1980 all the major players—Matsushita, Sharp, Toshiba, Hitachi, Sanyo—had established related sets of businesses that could support global marketing investments. More recently, they have been investing in regional manufacturing and design centers to tailor their products more closely to national markets.

These manufacturers thought of the various sources of competitive advantage as mutually desirable layers, not mutually exclusive choices. What some call competitive suicide—pursuing both cost and differentiation—is exactly what many competitors strive for.[3] Using flexible manufacturing technologies and better marketing intelligence, they are moving away from standardized "world products" to products like Mazda's mini-van, developed in California expressly for the U.S. market.

Another approach to competitive innovation—searching for loose bricks—exploits the benefits of surprise, which is just as useful in business battles as it is in war. Particularly in the early stages of a war for global markets, successful new competitors work to stay below the response threshold of their larger, more powerful rivals. Staking out underdefended territory is one way to do this.

To find loose bricks, managers must have few orthodoxies about how to break into a market or challenge a competitor. For example, in one large U.S. multinational, we asked several country managers to describe what a Japanese competitor was doing in the local market. The first executive said, "They're coming at us in the low end. Japanese companies always come in at the bottom." The second speaker found the comment interesting but disagreed: "They don't offer any low-end products in my market, but they have some exciting stuff at the top end. We really should reverse engineer that thing." Another colleague told still another story. "They haven't taken any business away from me," he said, "but they've just made me a great offer to supply components." In each country, their Japanese competitor had found a different loose brick.

The search for loose bricks begins with a careful analysis of the competitor's conventional wisdom: How does the company define its "served market"? What activities are most profitable? Which geographic markets are too troublesome to enter? The objective is not to find a corner of the industry (or niche) where larger competitors seldom tread but to build a base of attack just outside the market territory that industry leaders currently occupy. The goal is an uncontested profit sanctuary, which could be a particular product segment (the "low end" in motorcycles), a slice of the value chain (components in the computer industry), or a particular geographic market (Eastern Europe).

When Honda took on leaders in the motorcycle industry, for example, it began with products that were just outside the conventional definition of the leaders' product-market domains. As a result, it could build a base of operations in underdefended territory and then use that base to launch an expanded attack. What many competitors failed to see was Honda's strategic intent and its growing competence in engines and power trains. Yet even as Honda was selling 50cc motorcycles in the United States, it was already racing larger bikes in Europe—assembling the design skills and technology it would need for a systematic expansion across the entire spectrum of motor-related businesses.

Honda's progress in creating a core competence in engines should have warned competitors that it might enter a series of seemingly unrelated industries—automobiles, lawn mowers, marine engines, generators. But with each company fixated on its own market, the threat of Honda's horizontal diversification went unnoticed. Today companies like Matsushita and Toshiba are similarly poised to move in unexpected ways across industry boundaries. In protecting loose bricks, companies must extend their peripheral vision by tracking and anticipating the migration of global competitors across product segments, businesses, national markets, value-added stages, and distribution channels.

Changing the terms of engagement—refusing to accept the front runner's definition of industry and segment boundaries—represents still another form of competitive innovation. Canon's entry into the copier business illustrates this approach.

During the 1970s, both Kodak and IBM tried to match Xerox's business system in terms of segmentation, products, distribution, service, and pricing. As a result, Xerox had no trouble decoding the new entrants' intentions and developing countermoves. IBM eventually withdrew from the copier business, while Kodak remains a distant second in the large copier market that Xerox still dominates.

Canon, on the other hand, changed the terms of competitive engagement. While Xerox built a wide range of copiers, Canon standardized machines and components to reduce costs. Canon chose to distribute through office-product dealers rather than try to match Xerox's huge direct sales force. It also avoided the need to create a national service network by designing reliability and serviceability into its product and then delegating service responsibility to the dealers. Canon copiers were sold rather than leased, freeing Canon from the burden of financing the lease base. Finally, instead of selling to the heads of corporate duplicating departments, Canon appealed to secretaries and department managers who wanted distributed copying. At each stage, Canon neatly sidestepped a potential barrier to entry.

Canon's experience suggests that there is an important distinction between barriers to entry and barriers to imitation. Competitors that tried to match Xerox's business system had to pay the same entry costs—the barriers to imitation were high. But Canon dramatically reduced the barriers to entry by changing the rules of the game.

Changing the rules also short-circuited Xerox's ability to retaliate quickly against its new rival. Confronted with the need to rethink its business strategy and organization, Xerox was paralyzed for a time. Xerox managers realized that the faster they downsized the product line, developed new channels, and improved reliability, the faster they would erode the company's traditional profit base. What might have been seen as critical success factors—Xerox's national sales force and service network, its large installed base of leased machines, and its reliance on service revenues—instead became barriers to retaliation. In this sense, competitive innovation is like judo: the goal is to use a larger competitor's weight against it. And that happens not by matching the leader's capabilities but by developing contrasting capabilities of one's own.

Competitive innovation works on the premise that a successful competitor is likely to be wedded to a "recipe" for success. That's why the most effective weapon new competitors possess is probably a clean sheet of paper. And why an incumbent's greatest vulnerability is its belief in accepted practice.

Through licensing, outsourcing agreements, and joint ventures, it is sometimes possible to win without fighting. For example, Fujitsu's alliances in Europe with Siemens and STC (Britain's largest computer maker) and in the United States with Amdahl yield manufacturing volume and access to Western markets. In the early 1980s, Matsushita established a joint venture with Thorn (in the United Kingdom), Telefunken (in Germany), and Thomson (in France), which allowed it to quickly multiply the forces arrayed against Philips in the battle for leadership in the European VCR business. In fighting larger global rivals by proxy, Japanese companies have adopted a maxim as old as human conflict itself: my enemy's enemy is my friend.

Hijacking the development efforts of potential rivals is another goal of competitive collaboration. In the consumer electronics war, Japanese competitors attacked traditional businesses like TVs and hi-fis while volunteering to manufacture "next generation" products like VCRs, camcorders, and compact disc players for Western rivals. They hoped their rivals would ratchet down development spending, and in most cases that is precisely what happened. But companies that abandoned their own development efforts seldom reemerged as serious competitors in subsequent new product battles.

Collaboration can also be used to calibrate competitors' strengths and weaknesses. Toyota's joint venture with GM, and Mazda's with Ford, give these automakers an invaluable vantage point for assessing the progress their U.S. rivals have made in cost reduction, quality, and technology. They can also learn how GM and Ford compete—when they will fight and when they won't. Of course, the reverse is also true: Ford and GM have an equal opportunity to learn from their partner-competitors.

The route to competitive revitalization we have been mapping implies a new view of strategy. Strategic intent assures consistency in resource allocation over the long term. Clearly articulated corporate challenges focus the efforts of individuals in the medium term. Finally, competitive innovation helps reduce competitive risk in the short term. This consistency in the long term, focus in the medium term, and inventiveness and involvement in the short term provide the key to leveraging limited resources in pursuit of ambitious goals. But just as there is a process of winning, so there is a process of surrender. Revitalization requires understanding that process too.

Given their technological leadership and access to large regional markets, how did U.S. and European companies lose their apparent birthright to dominate global industries? There is no simple answer. Few companies recognize the value of documenting failure. Fewer still search their own managerial orthodoxies for the seeds for competitive surrender. But we believe there is a pathology of surrender (summarized in "The Process of Surrender") that gives some important clues.

The Process of Surrender

In the battles for global leadership that have taken place during the last two decades, we have seen a pattern of competitive attack and retrenchment that was remarkably similar across industries. We call this the process of surrender.

The process started with unseen intent. Not possessing long-term, competitor-focused goals themselves, Western companies did not ascribe such intentions to their rivals. They also calculated the threat posed by potential competitors in terms of their existing resources rather than their resourcefulness. This led to systematic underestimation of smaller rivals who were fast gaining technology through licensing arrangements, acquiring market understanding from downstream OEM partners, and improving product quality and manufacturing productivity through companywide employee involvement programs. Oblivious of the strategic intent and intangible advantages of their rivals, American and European businesses were caught off guard.

Adding to the competitive surprise was the fact that the new entrants typically attacked the periphery of a market (Honda in small motorcycles, Yamaha in grand pianos, Toshiba in small black-and-white televisions) before going head-to-head with incumbents. Incumbents often misread these attacks, seeing them as part of a niche strategy and not as a search for "loose bricks." Unconventional market entry strategies (minority holdings in less developed countries, use of nontraditional channels, extensive corporate advertising) were ignored or dismissed as quirky. For example, managers we spoke with said Japanese companies' position in the European computer industry was nonexistent. In terms of brand share that's nearly true, but the Japanese control as much as one-third of the manufacturing value added in the hardware sales of European-based computer businesses. Similarly, German auto producers claimed to feel unconcerned over the proclivity of Japanese producers to move upmarket. But with its low-end models under tremendous pressure from Japanese producers, Porsche has now announced that it will no longer make "entry-level" cars.

Western managers often misinterpreted their rivals' tactics. They believed that Japanese and Korean companies were competing solely on the basis of cost and quality. This typically produced a partial response to those competitors' initiatives: moving manufacturing offshore, outsourcing, or instituting a quality program. Seldom was the full extent of the competitive threat appreciated—the multiple layers of advantage, the expansion across related product segments, the development of global brand positions. Imitating the currently visible tactics of rivals put Western businesses into a perpetual catch-up trap. One by one, companies lost battles and came to see surrender as inevitable. Surrender was not inevitable, of course, but the attack was staged in a way that disguised ultimate intentions and sidestepped direct confrontation.

It is not very comforting to think that the essence of Western strategic thought can be reduced to eight rules for excellence, seven S's, five competitive forces, four product life-cycle stages, three generic strategies, and innumerable two-by-two matrices.[4] Yet for the past 20 years, "advances" in strategy have taken the form of ever more typologies, heuristics, and laundry lists, often with dubious empirical bases. Moreover, even reasonable concepts like the product life cycle, experience curve, product portfolios, and generic strategies often have toxic side effects: They reduce the number of strategic options management is willing to consider. They create a preference for selling businesses rather than defending them. They yield predictable strategies that rivals easily decode.

Strategy "recipes" limit opportunities for competitive innovation. A company may have 40 businesses and only four strategies—invest, hold, harvest, or divest. Too often strategy is seen as a positioning exercise in which options are tested by how they fit the existing industry structure. But current industry structure reflects the strengths of the industry leader; and playing by the leader's rules is usually competitive suicide.

Armed with concepts like segmentation, the value chain, competitor benchmarking, strategic groups, and mobility barriers, many managers have become better and better at drawing industry maps. But while they have been busy map making, their competitors have been moving entire continents. The strategist's goal is not to find a niche within the existing industry space but to create new space that is uniquely suited to the company's own strengths, space that is off the map.

This is particularly true now that industry boundaries are becoming more and more unstable. In industries such as financial services and communications, rapidly changing technology, deregulation, and globalization have undermined the value of traditional industry analysis. Map-making skills are worth little in the epicenter of an earthquake. But an industry in upheaval presents opportunities for ambitious companies to redraw the map in their favor, so long as they can think outside traditional industry boundaries.

Concepts like "mature" and "declining" are largely definitional. What most executives mean when they label a business mature is that sales growth has stagnated in their current geographic markets for existing products sold through existing channels. In such cases, it's not the industry that is mature, but the executives' conception of the industry. Asked if the piano business was mature, a senior executive in Yamaha replied, "Only if we can't take any market share from anybody anywhere in the world and still make money. And anyway, we're not in the 'piano' business, we're in the 'keyboard' business." Year after year, Sony has revitalized its radio and tape recorder businesses, despite the fact that other manufacturers long ago abandoned these businesses as mature.

A narrow concept of maturity can foreclose a company from a broad stream of future opportunities. In the 1970s, several U.S. companies thought that consumer electronics had become a mature industry. What could possibly top the color TV? they asked themselves. RCA and GE, distracted by opportunities in more "attractive" industries like mainframe computers, left Japanese producers with a virtual monopoly in VCRs, camcorders, and compact disc players. Ironically, the TV business, once thought mature, is on the verge of a dramatic renaissance. A $20 billion-a-year business will be created when high-definition television is launched in the United States. But the pioneers of television may capture only a small part of this bonanza.

Most of the tools of strategic analysis are focused domestically. Few force managers to consider global opportunities and threats. For example, portfolio planning portrays top management's investment options as an array of businesses rather than as an array of geographic markets. The result is predictable: as businesses come under attack from foreign competitors, the company attempts to abandon them and enter others in which the forces of global competition are not yet so strong. In the short term, this may be an appropriate response to waning competitiveness, but there are fewer and fewer businesses in which a domestic-oriented company can find refuge. We seldom hear such companies asking: Can we move into emerging markets overseas ahead of our global rivals and prolong the profitability of this business? Can we counterattack in our global competitors' home markets and slow the pace of their expansion? A senior executive in one successful global company made a telling comment: "We're glad to find a competitor managing by the portfolio concept—we can almost predict how much share we'll have to take away to put the business on the CEO's 'sell list.'"

Companies can also be overcommitted to organizational recipes, such as strategic business units and the decentralization an SBU structure implies. Decentralization is seductive because it places the responsibility for success or failure squarely on the shoulders of line managers. Each business is assumed to have all the resources it needs to execute its strategies successfully, and in this no-excuses environment, it is hard for top management to fail. But desirable as clear lines of responsibility and accountability are, competitive revitalization requires positive value added from top management.

Few companies with a strong SBU orientation have built successful global distribution and brand positions. Investments in a global brand franchise typically transcend the resources and risk propensity of a single business. While some Western companies have had global brand positions for 30 or 40 years or more (Heinz, Siemens, IBM, Ford, and Kodak, for example), it is hard to identify any American or European company that has created a new global brand franchise in the last 10 to 15 years. Yet Japanese companies have created a score or more— NEC, Fujitsu, Panasonic (Matsushita), Toshiba, Sony, Seiko, Epson, Canon, Minolta, and Honda, among them.

General Electric's situation is typical. In many of its businesses, this American giant has been almost unknown in Europe and Asia. GE made no coordinated effort to build a global corporate franchise. Any GE business with international ambitions had to bear the burden of establishing its credibility and credentials in the new market alone. Not surprisingly, some once-strong GE businesses opted out of the difficult task of building a global brand position. In contrast, smaller Korean companies like Samsung, Daewoo, and Lucky Gold Star are busy building global-brand umbrellas that will ease market entry for a whole range of businesses. The underlying principle is simple: economies of scope may be as important as economies of scale in entering global markets. But capturing economies of scope demands interbusiness coordination that only top management can provide.

We believe that inflexible SBU-type organizations have also contributed to the deskilling of some companies. For a single SBU, incapable of sustaining investment in a core competence such as semiconductors, optical media, or combustion engines, the only way to remain competitive is to purchase key components from potential (often Japanese or Korean) competitors. For an SBU defined in product-market terms, competitiveness means offering an end product that is competitive in price and performance. But that gives an SBU manager little incentive to distinguish between external sourcing that achieves "product embodied" competitiveness and internal development that yields deeply embedded organizational competences that can be exploited across multiple businesses. Where upstream component manufacturing activities are seen as cost centers with cost-plus transfer pricing, additional investment in the core activity may seem a less profitable use of capital than investment in downstream activities. To make matters worse, internal accounting data may not reflect the competitive value of retaining control over core competence.

Together a shared global corporate brand franchise and shared core competence act as mortar in many Japanese companies. Lacking this mortar, a company's businesses are truly loose bricks—easily knocked out by global competitors that steadily invest in core competences. Such competitors can co-opt domestically oriented companies into long-term sourcing dependence and capture the economies of scope of global brand investment through interbusiness coordination.

Last in decentralization's list of dangers is the standard of managerial performance typically used in SBU organizations. In many companies, business unit managers are rewarded solely on the basis of their performance against return on investment targets. Unfortunately, that often leads to denominator management because executives soon discover that reductions in investment and head count—the denominator—"improve" the financial ratios by which they are measured more easily than growth in the numerator—revenues. It also fosters a hair-trigger sensitivity to industry downturns that can be very costly. Managers who are quick to reduce investment and dismiss workers find it takes much longer to regain lost skills and catch up on investment when the industry turns upward again. As a result, they lose market share in every business cycle. Particularly in industries where there is fierce competition for the best people and where competitors invest relentlessly, denominator management creates a retrenchment ratchet.

The concept of the general manager as a movable peg reinforces the problem of denominator management. Business schools are guilty here because they have perpetuated the notion that a manager with net present value calculations in one hand and portfolio planning in the other can manage any business anywhere.

In many diversified companies, top management evaluates line managers on numbers alone because no other basis for dialogue exists. Managers move so many times as part of their "career development" that they often do not understand the nuances of the businesses they are managing. At GE, for example, one fast-track manager heading an important new venture had moved across five businesses in five years. His series of quick successes finally came to an end when he confronted a Japanese competitor whose managers had been plodding along in the same business for more than a decade.

Regardless of ability and effort, fast-track managers are unlikely to develop the deep business knowledge they need to discuss technology options, competitors' strategies, and global opportunities substantively. Invariably, therefore, discussions gravitate to "the numbers," while the value added of managers is limited to the financial and planning savvy they carry from job to job. Knowledge of the company's internal planning and accounting systems substitutes for substantive knowledge of the business, making competitive innovation unlikely.

When managers know that their assignments have a two- to three-year time frame, they feel great pressure to create a good track record fast. This pressure often takes one of two forms. Either the manager does not commit to goals whose time line extends beyond his or her expected tenure. Or ambitious goals are adopted and squeezed into an unrealistically short time frame. Aiming to be number one in a business is the essence of strategic intent; but imposing a three- to four-year horizon on the effort simply invites disaster. Acquisitions are made with little attention to the problems of integration. The organization becomes overloaded with initiatives. Collaborative ventures are formed without adequate attention to competitive consequences.

Almost every strategic management theory and nearly every corporate planning system is premised on a strategy hierarchy in which corporate goals guide business unit strategies and business unit strategies guide functional tactics.[5] In this hierarchy, senior management makes strategy and lower levels execute it. The dichotomy between formulation and implementation is familiar and widely accepted. But the strategy hierarchy undermines competitiveness by fostering an elitist view of management that tends to disenfranchise most of the organization. Employees fail to identify with corporate goals or involve themselves deeply in the work of becoming more competitive.

The strategy hierarchy isn't the only explanation for an elitist view of management, of course. The myths that grow up around successful top managers—"Lee Iacocca saved Chrysler," "De Benedetti rescued Olivetti," "John Sculley turned Apple around"—perpetuate it. So does the turbulent business environment. Middle managers buffeted by circumstances that seem to be beyond their control desperately want to believe that top management has all the answers. And top management, in turn, hesitates to admit it does not for fear of demoralizing lower level employees.

The result of all this is often a code of silence in which the full extent of a company's competitiveness problem is not widely shared. We interviewed business unit managers in one company, for example, who were extremely anxious because top management wasn't talking openly about the competitive challenges the company faced. They assumed the lack of communication indicated a lack of awareness on their senior managers' part. But when asked whether they were open with their own employees, these same managers replied that while they could face up to the problems, the people below them could not. Indeed, the only time the work force heard about the company's competitiveness problems was during wage negotiations when problems were used to extract concessions.

Unfortunately, a threat that everyone perceives but no one talks about creates more anxiety than a threat that has been clearly identified and made the focal point for the problem-solving efforts of the entire company. That is one reason honesty and humility on the part of top management may be the first prerequisite of revitalization. Another reason is the need to make participation more than a buzzword.

Programs such as quality circles and total customer service often fall short of expectations because management does not recognize that successful implementation requires more than administrative structures. Difficulties in embedding new capabilities are typically put down to "communication" problems, with the unstated assumption that if only downward communication were more effective—"if only middle management would get the message straight"—the new program would quickly take root. The need for upward communication is often ignored, or assumed to mean nothing more than feedback. In contrast, Japanese companies win, not because they have smarter managers, but because they have developed ways to harness the "wisdom of the anthill." They realize that top managers are a bit like the astronauts who circle the earth in the space shuttle. It may be the astronauts who get all the glory, but everyone knows that the real intelligence behind the mission is located firmly on the ground.

Where strategy formulation is an elitist activity it is also difficult to produce truly creative strategies. For one thing, there are not enough heads and points of view in divisional or corporate planning departments to challenge conventional wisdom. For another, creative strategies seldom emerge from the annual planning ritual. The starting point for next year's strategy is almost always this year's strategy. Improvements are incremental. The company sticks to the segments and territories it knows, even though the real opportunities may be elsewhere. The impetus for Canon's pioneering entry into the personal copier business came from an overseas sales subsidiary—not from planners in Japan.

The goal of the strategy hierarchy remains valid—to ensure consistency up and down the organization. But this consistency is better derived from a clearly articulated strategic intent than from inflexibly applied top-down plans. In the 1990s, the challenge will be to enfranchise employees to invent the means to accomplish ambitious ends.

We seldom found cautious administrators among the top managements of companies that came from behind to challenge incumbents for global leadership. But in studying organizations that had surrendered, we invariably found senior managers who, for whatever reason, lacked the courage to commit their companies to heroic goals—goals that lay beyond the reach of planning and existing resources. The conservative goals they set failed to generate pressure and enthusiasm for competitive innovation or give the organization much useful guidance. Financial targets and vague mission statements just cannot provide the consistent direction that is a prerequisite for winning a global competitive war.

This kind of conservatism is usually blamed on the financial markets. But we believe that in most cases investors' so-called short-term orientation simply reflects their lack of confidence in the ability of senior managers to conceive and deliver stretch goals. The chairman of one company complained bitterly that even after improving return on capital employed to over 40% (by ruthlessly divesting lackluster businesses and downsizing others), the stock market held the company to an 8:1 price/earnings ratio. Of course the market's message was clear: "We don't trust you. You've shown no ability to achieve profitable growth. Just cut out the slack, manage the denominators, and perhaps you'll be taken over by a company that can use your resources more creatively." Very little in the track record of most large Western companies warrants the confidence of the stock market. Investors aren't hopelessly short-term, they're justifiably skeptical.

We believe that top management's caution reflects a lack of confidence in its own ability to involve the entire organization in revitalization—as opposed to simply raising financial targets. Developing faith in the organization's ability to deliver on tough goals, motivating it to do so, focusing its attention long enough to internalize new capabilities—this is the real challenge for top management. Only by rising to this challenge will senior managers gain the courage they need to commit themselves and their companies to global leadership.

Appendix

Over the last ten years, our research on global competition, international alliances, and multinational management has brought us into close contact with senior managers in America, Europe, and Japan. As we tried to unravel the reasons for success and surrender in global markets, we became more and more suspicious that executives in Western and Far Eastern companies often operated with very different conceptions of competitive strategy. Understanding these differences, we thought, might help explain the conduct and outcome of competitive battles as well as supplement traditional explanations for Japan's ascendance and the West's decline.

We began by mapping the implicit strategy models of managers who had participated in our research. Then we built detailed histories of selected competitive battles. We searched for evidence of divergent views of strategy, competitive advantage, and the role of top management.

Two contrasting models of strategy emerged. One, which most Western managers will recognize, centers on the problem of maintaining strategic fit. The other centers on the problem of leveraging resources. The two are not mutually exclusive, but they represent a significant difference in emphasis—an emphasis that deeply affects how competitive battles get played out over time.

Both models recognize the problem of competing in a hostile environment with limited resources. But while the emphasis in the first is on trimming ambitions to match available resources, the emphasis in the second is on leveraging resources to reach seemingly unattainable goals.

Both models recognize that relative competitive advantage determines relative profitability. The first emphasizes the search for advantages that are inherently sustainable, the second emphasizes the need to accelerate organizational learning to outpace competitors in building new advantages.

Both models recognize the difficulty of competing against larger competitors. But while the first leads to a search for niches (or simply dissuades the company from challenging an entrenched competitor), the second produces a quest for new rules that can devalue the incumbent's advantages.

Both models recognize that balance in the scope of an organization's activities reduces risk. The first seeks to reduce financial risk by building a balanced portfolio of cash-generating and cash-consuming businesses. The second seeks to reduce competitive risk by ensuring a well-balanced and sufficiently broad portfolio of advantages.

Both models recognize the need to disaggregate the organization in a way that allows top management to differentiate among the investment needs of various planning units. In the first model, resources are allocated to product-market units in which relatedness is defined by common products, channels, and customers. Each business is assumed to own all the critical skills it needs to execute its strategy successfully. In the second, investments are made in core competences (microprocessor controls or electronic imaging, for example) as well as in product-market units. By tracking these investments across businesses, top management works to assure that the plans of individual strategic units don't undermine future developments by default.

Both models recognize the need for consistency in action across organizational levels. In the first, consistency between corporate and business levels is largely a matter of conforming to financial objectives. Consistency between business and functional levels comes by tightly restricting the means the business uses to achieve its strategy—establishing standard operating procedures, defining the served market, adhering to accepted industry practices. In the second model, business-corporate consistency comes from allegiance to a particular strategic intent. Business-functional consistency comes from allegiance to intermediate-term goals, or challenges, with lower level employees encouraged to invent how those goals will be achieved.

Notes

1. Among the first to apply the concept of strategy to management were H. Igor Ansoff in *Corporate Strategy: An Analytic Approach to Business Policy for Growth and Expansion* (New York: McGraw-Hill, 1965) and Kenneth R. Andrews in *The Concept of Corporate Strategy* (Homewood, Ill.: Dow Jones-Irwin, 1971).

2. Robert A. Burgelman, "A Process Model of Internal Corporate Ven-

turing in the Diversified Major Firm," *Administrative Science Quarterly*, June 1983.

3. For example, see Michael E. Porter, *Competitive Strategy* (New York: Free Press, 1980).

4. Strategic frameworks for resource allocation in diversified companies are summarized in Charles W. Hofer and Dan E. Schendel, *Strategy Formulation: Analytical Concepts* (St. Paul, Minn.: West Publishing, 1978).

5. For example, see Peter Lorange and Richard F. Vancil, *Strategic Planning Systems* (Englewood Cliffs, N.J.: Prentice-Hall, 1977).

2
How Global Companies Win Out

Thomas Hout, Michael E. Porter, and Eileen Rudden

Hold that obituary on American manufacturers. Some not only refuse to die but even dominate their businesses worldwide. At the same time Ford struggles to keep up with Toyota, Caterpillar thrives in competition with another Japanese powerhouse, Komatsu. Though Zenith has been hurt in consumer electronics, Hewlett-Packard and Tektronix together profitably control 50% of the world's industrial test and measurement instrument market. American forklift truck producers may retreat under Japanese pressure, but two U.S. chemical companies—DuPont and Dow—dramatically outperform their competitors.

How do these American producers hold and even increase profitability against international competitors? By forging integrated, global strategies to exploit their potential; and by having a long-term outlook, investing aggressively, and managing factories carefully.

The main reason is that today's international competition in many industries is very different from what it has been. To succeed, an international company may need to change from a multidomestic competitor, which allows individual subsidiaries to compete independently in different domestic markets, to a global organization, which pits its entire worldwide system of product and market position against the competition.

The global company—whatever its nationality—tries to control leverage points, from cross-national production scale economies to the foreign competitors' sources of cash flow. By taking unconventional action, such as lowering prices of an important product or in key markets, the company makes the competitor's response more expensive and difficult. Its main objective is to improve its own effectiveness while eroding that of its competitors.

Not all companies can or should forge a global strategy. While the rewards of competing globally are great, so are the risks. Major policy and operating changes are required. Competing globally demands a number of unconventional approaches to managing a multinational business to sometimes allow:

Major investment projects with zero or even negative ROI.

Financial performance targets that vary widely among foreign subsidiaries.

Product lines deliberately overdesigned or underpriced in some markets.

A view of country-by-country market positions as interdependent and not as independent elements of a worldwide portfolio to be increased or decreased depending on profitability.

Construction of production facilities in both high and low labor-cost countries.

Not all international businesses lend themselves to global competition. Many are multidomestic in nature and are likely to remain so, competing on a domestic-market-by-domestic-market basis. Typically these businesses have products that differ greatly among country markets and have high transportation costs, or their industries lack sufficient scale economies to yield the global competitors a significant competitive edge.

Before entering the global arena, you must first decide whether your company's industry has the right characteristics to favor a global competitor. A careful examination of the economies of the business will highlight its ripeness for global competition.[1] Simply put, the potential for global competition is greatest when significant benefits are gained from worldwide volume—in terms of either reduced unit costs or superior reputation or service—and are greater than the additional costs of serving that volume.

Identifying potential economies of scale requires considerable insight. Advantages to increased volume may come not only from larger production plants or runs but also from more efficient logistics networks or higher volume distribution networks. Worldwide volume is also particularly advantageous in supporting high levels of investment in research and development; many industries requiring high levels of R&D, such as pharmaceuticals or jet aircraft, are global. The level of transport or importing costs will also influence the business's tendency to become global. Transport is a relatively small portion of highly traded optical goods, for example, while it is a barrier in trading steel reinforcing bars.

Many businesses will not be able to take the global step precisely because their industries lack these characteristics. Economies of scale may be too modest or R&D spending too closely tied to particular markets. Products may differ significantly across country boundaries, or the industry may emphasize distribution, installation, and other local activities. Lead times may be short, as in fashion-oriented businesses and in many service businesses, including printing. Also, transportation costs and government barriers to trade may be high, and distribution may be fragmented and hard to penetrate. Many consumer nondurable businesses or low-technology assembly companies fall into this category, as do many heavy raw-material processing industries and wholesaling and service businesses.

Our investigation into the strategies of successful global companies leads us to believe that a large group of international companies have global potential, even though they may not know it. Almost every industry that is now global—automobiles and TV sets, for example— was not at one time. A company must see the potential for changing competitive interaction in its favor to trigger a shift from multidomestic to global competition. And because there is no guarantee that the business can become global, the company must be willing to risk the heavy investment that global competition requires.

A company that recognizes its business as potentially global but not yet so must ask itself whether it can innovate effectively and must understand its impact on the competition to find the best answers to these three questions:

What kind of strategic innovation might trigger global competition?

Is it in the best position among all competitors to establish and defend the advantages of global strategy?

What kind of resources—over how long a period—will be required to establish the leading position?

The Successful Global Competitor

If your industry profile fits the picture we've drawn, you can better judge your ability to make these kinds of unconventional decisions by looking at the way three global companies have succeeded. These organizations (American, European, and Japanese) exemplify the global competitor. They all perceive competition as global and formulate strategy on an integrated, worldwide basis. Each has developed a strategic innovation to change the rules of the competitive game in its particular industry. The innovation acts as a lever to support the development of an integrated global system but demands a market position strong enough to implement it.

Finally, the three companies have executed their strategies more aggressively and effectively than their competitors. They have built barriers to competitive responses based on careful assessment of competitors' behavior. All three have the financial resources and commitment needed to compete unconventionally and the organizational structure to manage an integrated system.

We will take a careful look at each of these three and how they developed the strategic innovation that led, on the one hand, to the globalization of their industries and, on the other, to their own phenomenal success. The first company's innovation was in manufacturing; the second, in technology; and the third, in marketing.

THE CATERPILLAR CASE: WARRING WITH KOMATSU

Caterpillar Tractor Company turned large-scale construction equipment into a global business and achieved world leadership in that business even when faced with an able Japanese competitor. This accomplishment was difficult for a variety of reasons. For one thing, specifications of construction equipment varied widely across countries. Also, machines are expensive to transport, and field distribution—including user financing, spare parts inventories, and repair facilities—is demanding and best managed locally.

Navy Seabees who left their Caterpillar equipment in other countries following World War II planted the seeds of globalization. The company established independent dealerships to service these fleets, and this base of units provided a highly profitable flow of revenue from spare parts, which paid for inventorying new units. The Caterpillar dealers quickly became self-sustaining and to this day are larger, better financed, and do a more profitable parts business than their competitors. This global distribution system is one of Cat's two major barriers against competition.

The company used its worldwide production scale to create its other barrier. Two-thirds of the total product cost of construction equipment is in heavy components—engines, axles, transmissions, and hydraulics—whose manufacturing costs are capital intensive and highly sensitive to economies of scale. Caterpillar turned its network of sales in different countries into a cost advantage by designing product lines that use identical components and by investing heavily in a few large-scale, state-of-the-art component manufacturing facilities to fill worldwide demand.

The company then augmented the centralized production with assembly plants in each of its major markets—Europe, Japan, Brazil, Australia, and so on. At these plants Cat added local product features, avoiding the high transportation cost of end products. Most important, Cat became a direct participant in local economies. The company achieved lower costs without sacrificing local product flexibility and became a friend rather than a threat to local governments. No single "world model" was forced on the customer, yet no competitor could match Caterpillar's production and distribution cost.

Not that they haven't tried. The most recent—and greatest—challenge to Caterpillar has come from Komatsu (see Exhibit I for a financial comparison). Japan's leading construction equipment producer forged its own global strategy based on exporting high-quality products from centralized facilities with labor and steel cost advantages. Over the last decade Komatsu has gained some 15% of the world construction-equipment market, with a significant share of sales in nearly every product line in competition with Cat.

Caterpillar has maintained its position against Komatsu and gained world share. The two companies increasingly dominate the market vis-à-vis their competitors, who compete on a domestic or regional basis. What makes Caterpillar's strategy so potent? The company has fostered the development of four characteristics essential to defending a leading world position against a determined competitor:

1. *A global strategy of its own.* Caterpillar's integrated global strategy yields a competitive advantage in cost and effectiveness. Komatsu simply plays catch-up ball rather than pulling ahead. Facing a competitor that has consciously devised a global strategy, Komatsu is in a much weaker position than were Japanese TV and automobile manufacturers when they took off.

2. *Willingness to invest in manufacturing.* Caterpillar's top management appears committed to the kind of flexible automated manufacturing systems that allow full exploitation of the economies of scale from its worldwide sales volume.

Exhibit I.   *Financial Comparison of Caterpillar and Komatsu*

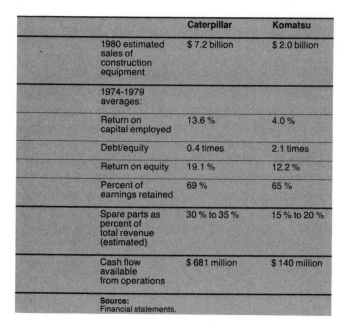

	Caterpillar	Komatsu
1980 estimated sales of construction equipment	$ 7.2 billion	$ 2.0 billion
1974-1979 averages:		
Return on capital employed	13.6 %	4.0 %
Debt/equity	0.4 times	2.1 times
Return on equity	19.1 %	12.2 %
Percent of earnings retained	69 %	65 %
Spare parts as percent of total revenue (estimated)	30 % to 35 %	15 % to 20 %
Cash flow available from operations	$ 681 million	$ 140 million
Source: Financial statements.		

3. *Willingness to commit financial resources.* Caterpillar is the only Western company that matches Komatsu in capital spending per employee; in fact, its overall capital spending is more than three times that of the Japanese company. Caterpillar does not divert resources into other businesses or dissipate the financial advantage against Komatsu by paying out excessive dividends. Because Komatsu's profitability is lower than Caterpillar's, it must exhaust debt capacity in trying to match Cat's high investment rates.

4. *Blocking position in the Japanese market.* In 1963, Caterpillar formed a joint venture in Japan with Komatsu's long-standing but weaker competitor, Mitsubishi. Operationally, the venture serves the Japanese market. Strategically, it acts as a check on the market share and cash flow of Komatsu. Japan accounts for less than 20% of the world market but yields over 80% of Komatsu's worldwide cash flow. The joint venture is number two in market position, serving to limit Komatsu's profits. Japanese tax records indicate that the Cat-Mitsubishi joint

venture has earned only modest profits, but it is of great strategic value to Caterpillar.[2]

L.M. ERICSSON: CAN SMALL BE BEAUTIFUL?

L.M. Ericsson of Sweden has become a successful global competitor by developing and exploiting a technological niche. Most major international telephone-equipment producers operated first in large, protected home markets that allowed the most efficient economies of scale. The additional profits helped underwrite R&D and provided good competitive leverage. Sweden's home market is relatively small, yet Ericsson translated the advent of electronic switching technology into a powerful global lever that befuddled competitors in its international market niche. In the electromechanical era of the 1960s, the telephone switching equipment business was hardly global. Switching systems combine hardware and software. In the electromechanical stage, 70% of total installed costs lay in hardware and 70% of hardware cost was direct labor, manufacturing overhead, and installation of the equipment.

Each country's telephone system was unique, economies of scale were low, and the wage rate was more important than the impact of volume on costs. In the late 1960s, major international companies (including Ericsson) responded by moving electroswitching production to LDCs not only to take advantage of cheaper labor but also to respond to the desire of government telephone companies to source locally.

Eventually, each parent company centrally sourced only the core software and critical components and competed on a domestic-market-by-domestic-market basis. For its part, Ericsson concentrated investment in developing countries without colonial ties to Europe and in smaller European markets that lacked national suppliers and that used the same switching systems as the Swedish market.

The telecommunications industry became global when, in the 1970s, electronic switching technology emerged, radically shifting cost structures and threatening the market position Ericsson had carved for itself. Software is now 60% of total cost; 55% of hardware cost is in sophisticated electronic components whose production is highly scale sensitive. The initial R&D investment required to develop a system has jumped to more than $100 million, which major international companies could have amortized more easily than Ericsson. In addition, the move to electronics promised to destroy the long-standing relationships Ericsson enjoyed with smaller government telephone companies. And it appeared that individual electronic switching systems would require a large fixed-cost software investment for each country, making the new technology too expensive for the smaller telephone systems, on which Ericsson thrived.

Ericsson knew that the electronic technology would eventually be adapted to small systems. In the meantime, it faced the possibility of losing its position in smaller markets because of its inability to meet the ante for the new global competition.

The company responded with a preemptive strategic innovation—a modular technology that introduced electronics to small telephone systems. The company developed a series of modular software packages that could be used in different combinations to meet the needs of diverse telephone systems at an acceptable cost. Moreover, each successive system required fewer new modules. As Exhibit II shows, the first system—Södertalje in Sweden—required all new modules, but by the third year, the Abo system in Finland required none at all. Thus the company rapidly amortized development costs and enjoyed economies of scale that steepened as the number of software systems sold increased. As a result, Ericsson was able to compete globally in small systems.

Ericsson's growth is accelerating as small telephone systems convert to electronics. The company now enjoys an advantage in software cost and variety that continually reinforces itself. Through this technology Ericsson has raised a significant entry barrier against other companies in the small-system market.

HONDA'S MARKETING GENIUS

Before Honda became a global company, two distinct motorcycle industries existed in the world. In Asia and other developing countries, large numbers of people rode small, simple motorcycles to work. In Europe and America, smaller numbers of people drove big, elaborate machines for play. Since the Asian motorcycle was popular as an inexpensive means of transportation, companies competed on the basis of price. In the West, manufacturers used styling and brand image to differentiate their products. No Western market exceeded 100,000

Exhibit II. Ericsson's Technology Lever: Reduction of Software Cost through Modular Design

	Representative systems	New modules required	Existing modules used
Year 1	Södertalje, Sweden	57	0
Year 2	Orleans, France	22	57
Year 3	Åbo, Finland	0	77

Source:
Boston Consulting Group, *A Framework for Swedish Industrial Policy* (Uberforlag, Stockholm, 1978).

units; wide product lines and small volumes meant slight opportunities for economies of scale. Major motorcycle producers such as Harley-Davidson of the United States, BMW of West Germany, and Triumph and BSA of the United Kingdom traded internationally but in only modest volumes.

Honda made its industry global by convincing middle-class Americans that riding motorcycles could be fun. Because of the company's marketing innovations, Honda's annual growth rate was greater than 20% from the late 1950s to the late 1960s. The company then turned its attention to Europe, with a similar outcome. Honda invested for seven full years before sustaining profitability in Europe, financing this global effort with cash flows earned from a leading market position at home and in the United States.

Three crucial steps were decisive in Honda's achievement. First, Honda turned market preference around to the characteristics of its own products and away from those of American and European competitors. Honda targeted new consumers and used advertising, promotions, and trade shows to convince them that its motorbikes were inexpensive, reliable, and easy to use. A large investment in the distribution network—2,000 dealerships, retail missionaries, generous warranty and service support, and quick spare-parts availability—backed up the marketing message.

Second, Honda sustained growth by enticing customers with the upper levels of its product line. Nearly half of new bike owners purchased larger, more expensive models within 12 months. Brand loyalty proved very high. Honda exploited these trends by expanding from its line of a few small motorcycles to one covering the full range of size and features by 1975. The result: self-sustaining growth in dollar volume and a model mix that allowed higher margins. The higher volume reduced marketing and distribution costs and improved the position of Honda and other Japanese producers who invaded the 750cc "super bike" portion of the market traditionally reserved for American and European companies. Here Honda beat the competition with a bike that was better engineered, lower priced, and whose development cost was shared over the company's wide product line.

The third step Honda took was to exploit economies of scale through both centralized manufacturing and logistics. The increasing volume of engines and bike assemblies sold (50,000 units per month and up) enabled the company to use less costly manufacturing techniques unavailable to motorcycle producers with lower volumes (see Exhibit III). Over a decade, Honda's factory productivity rose at an average annual rate of 13.1%—several times higher than European and American producers. Combined with lower transportation cost, Honda's increased output gave it a landed cost per unit far lower than the competition's. In turn, the lower production cost helped fund Honda's heavy marketing and distribution investment. Finally, economies of scale in marketing and distribution, combined with low production cost, led to the high profits that financed Honda's move into automobiles.

WHAT CAN WE LEARN?

Each of these successful global players changed the dynamics of its industry and pulled away from its major competitors. By achieving economies of scale through commonality of design, Caterpillar exploited both its worldwide sales volume and its existing market for parts revenues. Competitors could not match its costs or profits and therefore could not make the investment necessary to catch up. Ericsson created a cost advantage by developing a unique modular technology perfectly adapted to its segment of the market. Its global strategy turned electronics from a threat to Ericsson into a barrier to its competitors. Honda used marketing to homogenize worldwide demand and unlock the potential for economies of scale in production, marketing, and distribution. The competition's only refuge was the highly brand-conscious, small-volume specialty market.

In each case, the industry had the potential for a worldwide system of products and markets that a company with a global strategy could

Exhibit III. The Effect of Volume on Manufacturing Approaches in Motorcycle Production

Cost element	Low volume	High volume
Machine tools	Manual, general purpose	Numerical control, special purpose
Changeover time	Manual, slow (hours)	Automatic positioning, fast (minutes)
Work-in-process inventory	High (days of production)	Low (hours of production)
Materials handling	Forklift trucks	Automated
Assembly	Bay assembly	Motorized assembly line
Machine tool design	Designed outside the company, available throughout industry	Designed in-house, proprietary
Rework	More	Less

Source:
Strategy Alternatives for the British Motorcycle Industry,
a report prepared for the British Secretary of State for Industry
by the Boston Consulting Group, July 30, 1975.

exploit. Construction equipment offered large economies of scale in component manufacture, allowing Caterpillar to neutralize high transportation costs and government barriers through local assembly. Ericsson unlocked scale economies in software development for electronic switches. The modular technology accommodated local product differences and governments' desire to use local suppliers. Once Honda's marketing techniques raised demand in major markets for products with similar characteristics, the industry's economies of scale in production combined with low transportation costs and low tariff barriers to turn it into a global game.

In none of the cases did success result from a "world product." The companies accommodated local differences without sacrificing production costs. The global player's position in one major market strengthened its position in others. Caterpillar's design similarities and central component facilities allowed each market to contribute to its already favorable cost structure. Ericsson's shared modules led to falling costs each time a system was sold in a new country. Honda drew on scale economies from the centralized production of units sold in each market and used its U.S. marketing and distribution experience to succeed in Europe.

In addition to superior effectiveness and cost advantages, a winning global strategy always requires abilities in two other dimensions. The first is timing. The successful global competitor uses a production cost or distribution advantage as a leverage point to make it more difficult or expensive for the competitor to respond. The second is financial. The global innovator commits itself to major investment before anyone else, whether in technology, facilities, or distribution. If successful, it then reaps the benefits from increased cash flows from either higher volume (Honda and Ericsson) or lower costs (all three companies). The longer the competitor takes to respond, the larger the innovator's cash flows. The global company can then deploy funds either to increase investment or lower prices, creating barriers to new market entrants.

A global player should decide against which of its major competitors it must succeed first in order to generate broad-based success in the future. Caterpillar located in the Far East not only to source products locally but also to track Komatsu. (Cat increasingly sources product and manufacturing technology from Japan.) Ericsson's radical departure in technology was aimed squarely at ITT and Siemens, whose large original market shares would ordinarily have given them an advantage in the smaller European and African markets. Honda created new markets in the United States and Europe because its most powerful competitors, Yamaha and Kawasaki, were Japanese. By exploiting the global opportunity first, Honda got a head start, and it remained strong even when competitors' own international ambitions came to light.

Playing the Global Chess Game

Global competition forces top management to change the way it thinks about and operates its businesses. Policies that made sense when the company was multidomestic may now be counterproductive. The most powerful moves are those that improve the company's worldwide cost position or ability to differentiate itself and weaken key worldwide competitors. Let us consider two potential moves.

The first is preempting the leading positions in major newly industrializing countries (NICs). Rapid growth in, for example, Mexico, Brazil, and Indonesia has made them an important part of the worldwide market for many capital goods. If its industry has the potential to become global, the company that takes a leading position in these markets will have made a decisive move to bar its competitors. Trade barriers are often prohibitively high in these places, and a company that tries to penetrate the market through a *self-contained* local subsidiary is likely to fall into a trap.

The astute global competitor will exploit the situation, however, by building a specialized component manufacturing facility in an NIC which will become an integral part of a global sourcing network. The company exports output of the specialized facility to offset importing complementary components. Final assembly for the domestic and smaller, neighboring markets can be done locally. (Having dual sources for key items can minimize the risk of disruption to the global sourcing network.)

A good illustration of this strategy is Siemens's circuit breaker operation in Brazil. When the company outgrew its West German capacity for some key components, it seized the opportunity presented by Brazilian authorities seeking capital investments in the heavy electrical equipment industry. Siemens now builds a large portion of its common components there, swaps them for other components made in Europe, and is the lowest-cost and leading supplier of finished product in Brazil.

Another move that can be decisive in a global industry is to establish a solid position with your largest customers to block competitors. Many businesses have a few customers that dominate the global market. The global competitor recognizes their importance and prevents current or prospective competitors from generating any sales.

A good example is a British company, BSR, the world's largest producer of automatic record changers. In the 1970s, when Japanese exports of audio equipment were growing rapidly, BSR recognized that it could lose its market base in the United States and Europe if the Japanese began marketing record changers. BSR redesigned its product to Japanese specifications and offered distributors aggressive price discounts and inventory support. The Japanese could not justify expanding their own capacity. BSR not only stalled the entry of the Japanese into the record-changer market but it also moved ahead of its existing competitor, Garrard.

A global company can apply similar principles to block the competition's access to key distributors or retailers. Many American companies have failed to seize this opportunity in their unwillingness to serve large, private-label customers (e.g., Sears, Roebuck) or by neglecting the less expensive end of their product line and effectively allowing competitors access to their distributors. Japanese manufacturers in particular could then establish a toehold in industries like TV sets and farm equipment.

The decision on prices for pivotal customers must not be made solely on considerations of ROI. Equally important in global competition is the impact of these prices on prospective entrants and the cost of failing to protect and expand the business base. One way to control the worldwide chess game in your favor is to differentiate prices among countries.

Manage Interdependently

The successful global competitor manages its business in various countries as a single system, not a portfolio of independent positions. In the view of portfolio planning theory, a market's attractiveness and the strength of a company's position within it determine the extent of corporate resources devoted to it. A company should defend strong positions and try to turn weak ones around or abandon them. It will pursue high-profit and/or high-growth markets more aggressively than lower-profit or lower-growth ones, and it will decide on a stand-alone basis whether to compete in a market.

Accepting this portfolio view of international competition can be disastrous in a global industry. The global competitor focuses instead on its ability to leverage positions in one country market against those in other markets. In the global system, the ability to leverage is as important as market attractiveness; the company need not turn around weak positions for them to be useful.

The most obvious leverage a company obtains from a country market is the volume it contributes to the company's overall cost or effectiveness. DuPont and Texas Instruments have patiently won a large sales volume in the sophisticated Japanese market, for example, which supports their efforts elsewhere. Winning a share of a market that consistently supports product innovation ahead of other markets—like the United States in long-haul jet aircraft—is another leverage point. The competitor with a high share of such a market can always justify new product investment. Or a market can contribute leverage if it supports an efficient scale manufacturing facility for a region—like Brazil for Siemens. Finally, a market can contribute leverage if a position in it can be used to affect a competitor's cash flow.

Organization: The Achilles Heel

Organizational structure and reporting relationships present subtle problems for a global strategy. Effective strategic control argues for a central product-line organization; effective local responsiveness, for a geographic organization with local autonomy. A global strategy demands that the product-line organization have the *ultimate* authority, because without it the company cannot gain systemwide benefits. Nevertheless, the company still must balance product and area needs. In short, there is no simple solution. But there are some guidelines to help.

No one organization structure applies to all of a company's international businesses. It may be unnecessarily cumbersome, for example, to impose a matrix structure on all business. Organizational reporting lines should probably differ by country market depending on that market's role. An important market that offers high leverage, as in the foregoing examples, must work closely with the global business-unit managers at headquarters. Coordination is crucial to success. But the manager of a market outside the global system will require only sets of objectives under a regional reporting system.

Another guideline is that organizational reporting lines and structures should change as the nature of the international business changes. When a business becomes global, the emphasis should shift toward centralization. As countries increase in importance, they must be brought within the global manager's reach. Over time, if the business becomes less global, the company's organization may emphasize local autonomy.

The common tendency to apply one organizational structure to all operations is bound to be a disadvantage to some of them. In some U.S. companies, this approach inhibited development of the global strategy their industries required.

Match Financial Policies to Competitive Realities

If top management is not careful, adherence to conventional financial management and practices may constrain a good competitive response in global businesses. While capital budgeters use such standard financial tools as DCF return analysis or risk profiles to judge investments and creditors and stock analysts prefer stable debt and dividend policies, a global company must chart a different course.

ALLOCATING CAPITAL

In a global strategy, investments are usually a long-term, interdependent series of capital commitments, which are not easily associated with returns or risks. The company has to be aware of the size and timing of the total expenditures because they will greatly influence competitors' new investment response. Most troublesome, however, is that revenues from investments in several countries may have to build up to a certain point before the company earns *any* return on investment.

A global strategy goes against the traditional tests for capital allocation: project-oriented DCF risk-return analysis and the country manager's record of credibility. Global competition requires a less mechanical approach to project evaluation. The successful global competitor develops at least two levels of financial control. One level is a profit and cost center for self-contained projects; the other is a strategy center for tracking interdependent efforts and competitors' performance and reactions. Global competitors operate with a short time frame when monitoring the execution of global strategy investments and a long time frame when evaluating such investments and their expected returns.

DEBT AND DIVIDENDS

Debt and dividend policies should vary with the requirements of the integrated investment program of the whole company. In the initial stages, a company with a strong competitive position should retain earnings to build and defend its global position. When the industry has become global and growth slows or the returns exceed the reinvestment needed to retain position, the company should distribute earnings to the rest of the corporation and use debt capacity elsewhere, perhaps in funding another nascent global strategy.

Honda's use of debt over the last 25 years illustrates this logic (see Exhibit IV). In the mid-1950s, when Honda held a distant second place

Exhibit IV. Honda Motor Company's Financial Policy from 1954 to 1980

Period	Interest-bearing debt-to-equity ratio	Strategic phase
1954-55	3.5 times	Rapid growth in domestic motorcycle market; Honda is low-margin, number two producer
1959-60	0.5	Domestic motorcycle market matured; Honda is dominant, high-margin producer
1964-65	0.7	Honda makes major penetration of U.S. motorcycle market
1969-70	1.6	Honda begins major move in domestic auto market
1974-75	1.3	Investment pause due to worldwide recession; motorcycle is major cash generator
1978-80	1.0	Auto exports are highly profitable, as are motorcycles

Source:
Annual reports.

in a rapidly growing Japanese motorcycle industry, the company had to leverage its equity 3.5 times to finance growth. By 1960, the Japanese market had matured and Honda emerged dominant. The debt-equity ratio receded to 0.5 times but rose again with the company's international expansion in motorcycles. In the late 1960s, Honda made a major move to the automobile market, requiring heavy debt. At that time, motorcycle cash flows funded the move.

Which Strategic Road to Take?

There is no safe formula for success in international business. Industry structures continuously evolve. The Caterpillar, Ericsson, and Honda approaches will probably not work forever. Competitors will try to push industrial trends away from the strengths of the industry leaders, and technological or political changes may force the leading companies to operate in a multidomestic fashion once again.

Strategy is a powerful force in determining competitive outcomes, whether in international or domestic business. And although adopting a global strategy is risky, many companies can dramatically improve their positions by fundamentally changing the way they plan, control, and operate their businesses. But a global strategy requires that managers think in new ways. Otherwise the company will not be able to recognize the nature of competition, justify the required investments, or sustain the change in everyday behavior needed.

If the company can successfully execute a global strategy, it may find itself joining the ranks of the truly successful international companies. Whether they be Japanese, American, European, or otherwise, the strategic thread that ties together companies like IBM, Matsushita, K. Hattori (Seiko), DuPont, and Michelin clearly shows that the rules of the international competitive game have changed.

Notes

1. For a more detailed look at globalization, see Michael E. Porter, *Competitive Strategy* (New York: Free Press, 1980).
2. For more on this subject, see Craig M. Watson, "Counter-Competition Abroad to Protect Home Markets," *Harvard Business Review*, January–February 1982, p. 40.

3
The Globalization of Europe:
An Interview with Wisse Dekker

Nan Stone

Wisse Dekker, chairman of the Supervisory Board of N.V. Philips' Gloeilampenfabrieken, is one of the foremost advocates of a true European common market. During the course of a long and distinguished career, many years of which were devoted to Philips' operations in the Far East, he has spoken forcefully about how global competition and technological development are transforming business and society, in Europe and throughout the world. While Dr. Dekker was president and chairman of Philips' Board of Management, he set the company on a course that has led, under his successor, to the most radical changes in the company's nearly 100-year history.

Dr. Dekker's vision has also led him to take a prominent position among those industrialists who see the need to subordinate national interests to the economic imperatives imposed by globalization. One aspect of this is his involvement first as a founding member and now as chairman of the Roundtable of European Industrialists, a group of business leaders who are chairmen, chief executive officers, or managing directors of large corporations with important manufacturing and technological commitments in Europe. The Roundtable's principal aim is to help strengthen and develop Europe's competitive capabilities by encouraging the creation of a single European market, improving the European business climate, and promoting entrepreneurial drive through such initiatives as Euroventures B.V., a venture-capital company that invests in high-potential service and advanced technology companies throughout Europe.

HBR: *As you look at companies in Europe, what stands out? Is there any particular development that seems to sum up the impact of global competition?*

Wisse Dekker: The conditions of competition have created a new manager, one who is very different from the average European manager of yesterday. Europeans have always been exporters, of course. But either we have exported to one another's countries, or we have exported across the ocean. Now we have to compete globally, which means actually introducing products at the same time in markets around the globe. That's a new phenomenon. So are the product-development challenges that confront managers in information industries like electronics: the fact that the product life cycle is so short; the fact that the investments you have to make are so large and the time you have to recover your costs and make money is so very short. Those are all factors that were unknown to the manager of yesterday. Today they have redefined the way competition is waged.

Competition is also changing who the top managers are in large, multinational companies like Philips. When I was chief executive, most of our subsidiaries were headed by Dutchmen, even though our business core was quite international. At a certain moment, we came to the conclusion that this would be the wrong way to continue. We didn't say that we wouldn't have any Dutch managers any more, but we did say that if it became a tradition that the people on top would be only Dutch, then that would not encourage skilled and talented local people to make a career in Philips. They would feel that they could get only so far and no farther. So we have gradually been changing this state of affairs. In Italy, our top manager is Italian. In Canada, our top man is German. There has been a Norwegian in Brazil, and the top manager in France is Swiss.

We have also set an example by changing the composition of the management board, which runs the company on a day-to-day basis, and the supervisory board, which oversees the work of the management board. Not so long ago, the membership of both of these boards was completely Dutch. Now the supervisory board has Americans, a German, a Frenchman, a Belgian, an Englishman, as well as some Dutchmen, while the management board includes a German and a Belgian.

These developments, like the events we read about in the U.S. press—joint ventures, mergers, hostile takeovers, and takeover attempts—indicate that the pace of change within companies has quickened. Has the pace of change in the Community picked up appreciably too?

Yes. The most important thing happening today is that we are seeing very clearly that we shall have a single European market, an internal market that will be the biggest in the world—some 320 million people compared with 220 million in the United States and 120 million in Japan. It will give European industry an opportunity to organize on a scale big enough to compete with its main rivals in Japan and in the United States. And it will come more quickly than we would have thought possible just two years ago.

What are some of the signs that make this so clear?

The opening up of government procurement is one example. So far, it has been the case that the German government gives priority and preference to German suppliers, the French government to French suppliers, the British to the British, and so on. Now, however, we have the example of British Telecom, which was privatized in 1984 and now routinely awards big orders to non-British companies such as Ericsson. The European Community has also devised and published a directive that, when it is accepted—and it will be accepted—will open up government procurement in all EC countries for European and non-European companies alike. The European telecommunications industry is already restructuring in anticipation of this change, as may be clear from the combination of ITT and CGE (now Alcatel N.V.), the takeover bid GEC and Siemens made for Plessey, and the recent decision in Italy to create a joint venture between Italtel and AT&T.

Another example is the so-called single document, which illustrates how the internal market will make commerce easier and allow companies to save on costs. Since the first of January 1988, truckers have needed only a single document to cross borders within the EC. That may sound like a small thing, but then consider that truck drivers used to have to carry some 35 documents for import-export declarations and community transit forms. And they generally needed several copies of each. Simply dealing with the paperwork made the journey three to five times longer than it needed to be, while the costs of this mass of paperwork were more than 3% of the value of the sales involved.

Provisions for harmonizing regulations and technical standards give us still another sign of progress. One should never forget that for centuries, Europe has been a Europe of different countries. And each of them has had its own standards to protect local producers and to satisfy local customs and tastes. Even today, if you travel to Britain and take an electrical appliance, you will need a different plug than you would need in Holland. That's why they've developed a "Europlug." And there are thousands of these little inconsistencies that make it more costly and difficult for European manufacturers. Think about how different the situation is in Japan and the United States, where for most things there is one standard, so suppliers have access to the whole market and can gain economies of scale.

Just about 30 years ago, there was a similar movement toward European unification. What is different this time? What forces are behind the current drive toward a single European market?

Things never happen in a vacuum. Some of the factors at work here are Europe's own economic performance, competitive pressure from our rivals, especially the Japanese, and the imperatives of technology and technology development.

You may have heard that the Japanese talk about a scenario in which the United States will be the granary of the world, or as they put it, the world's supplier of foodware; the Far East will be the world's supplier of hardware; and Europe will be the world's cultural museum and playground. If you look at Europe's economic performance during the past 15 years or so, you can see why they might say that.

The European economy and European competitiveness passed through a deep trough in the years just before and after 1980. To suggest how deep that trough was, in 1980, the combined results of the largest 100 companies in Europe, excluding the oil companies, showed a profit level of 0%. Unemployment was—and still is—very high, especially among the young. The Community's relative competitive position deteriorated because growth in productivity lagged behind wage increases, while the situation was reversed in Japan and the United States. None of this was very pleasant, but one result was that about five years ago, a widespread attitude of "Europessimism" began slowly to give way. People no longer asked whether something had to be done but rather what had to be done and how and when. Those are the questions we are answering now.

Related to this is the fact that Europe has been fighting for its very survival. Economically powerful competitors from Japan and the United States have been attacking the global market from continent-sized home markets. In response, we have been trying to counterattack from 12 different narrow markets. Strategically, this compartmentalization makes no sense—particularly in industries like electronics, where you must have a real European common market to survive.

Information technology is the fastest growing area of business and industrial activity in the Western world. Without question, it will be the engine of economic growth for at least the rest of the century. But information technology imposes certain requirements on companies because it changes the nature of competition in fundamental ways. Both the cost and the pace of innovation in high technology have increased tremendously. You must win a share of the world market very quickly simply to break even and to earn the funds you need to invest in the next round of innovation. Companies that fail to do this will scarcely get a second chance; they will be forced to quit the race permanently. That is why we need a single European market with common technical standards. Without it, we cannot achieve the optimum scale and the lower unit costs we need to be competitive worldwide. Nor will we have a launching pad for entering the world market, as our Japanese and American competitors have in their home markets.

Besides scale and standards, are there other things that have tended to make European companies less competitive?

The social costs of Europe are one big factor—health care, allowances for unemployment, disability, education, and so forth. If you compare Europe with the other two big blocks of countries—the United States and Canada on the one hand, Japan, Korea, Taiwan, Hong Kong, Singapore, and even China on the other—it is very clear that Europe has the most costly social structure of the three. As a percentage of wages and salary, our social charges are about two times those of our competitors. I'm not saying who is right or wrong or criticizing any other country for what it does or does not have. But that difference alone would make our products less competitive, especially if we're talking about mass-produced goods. So we have to find ways and means to make European industry competitive, both as individual managers and through political changes.

In the United States, companies and industries that have become more competitive did so only after a great deal of internal change and industry restructuring. Is this the pattern you see taking shape in Europe now?

Yes. That is why one should be careful not to be carried away by "Europhoria," the idea that everything is rosy and here we go. The internal market is absolutely necessary. But the internal market will also mean big shakeouts in many industries, and that, of course, hurts. We have already seen this in the consumer electronics industry, and I think we will now see it mainly and most dramatically in the telecommunications industry. There is simply no room in Europe for six or seven telecommunications factories.

On the other hand, one of the blessings of competition is that it makes you go through this sort of experience. In consumer electronics, the bigger companies have been under so much attack by the Japanese that they have had to look very hard at themselves and what they were doing and ask whether it was the right thing. In a situation like that, one of three things can happen. Either you don't ask yourself that question and you try to muddle through, which only gives you a lackluster performance. Or you disappear, as many companies in this industry have in the last few years. Or you take a serious look at yourself and do something about it. And that, of course, also creates the spirit of the entrepreneur. You see this spirit in companies like Philips and Thomson, which both have had a period of mergers, shakeouts, and new ventures. And you see it in newcomers like Nokia of Finland, which is taking over ailing consumer electronics companies in the EC and trying to revive them.

Until now, telecommunications, along with energy, water, and other utilities, has been protected by each national government. But now we understand that it is companies, not countries, that must compete in telecommunications. National monopolies cannot keep charging their customers forever for the inefficiencies their nationalistic policies create. Look at what happened in Britain. The telecommunications network in Britain was so outmoded, so outdated that Mrs. Thatcher had to do something. That kind of change will happen elsewhere too. The shakeout is necessary and inevitable to come to a healthy European industry.

Many commentators have predicted that the effects of 1992's competitive battles will be disproportionately felt by small- and medium-sized companies, which are likely to be squeezed out by pan-European or global competitors. Does the internal market have any advantages for smaller companies?

Most multinationals have already anticipated 1992, whereas for many smaller and medium-sized companies, this is a new game. I talk with quite a few young, up-and-coming entrepreneurs (of whom, fortunately, we still have our share), and they are looking forward to the opportunities 1992 presents. It is the older, locally well-established companies that tend to take a wait-and-see attitude.

The first thing most entrepreneurs will do after they have had some initial success is start looking across the border. The Dutch may look into Germany, which is always a big market for them, or they may do something with Belgium or, if they are more ambitious, with France. Obviously, 1992 will make it easier for this kind of development to take place. So we will see more small companies penetrating other European markets than we have seen so far. Competition will be a little stiffer too, of course, because other European companies will invade your territory. But that's healthy.

Speaking of penetrating markets, how open will the European Community be to non-European companies? Should U.S. and Asian managers be preparing themselves and their companies for "fortress Europe"?

This is a question that comes up regularly, and from one perspective, it is easy to answer. The biggest part of European industry, the companies combined in the European Roundtable, for instance, is absolutely against protectionist behavior. The same is true for individual companies, like Philips. We know that if we were to put up a European fortress, it would backfire on us immediately. It is a matter of well-understood self-interest not to do that.

On the other hand, it is also true that Europe will speak with a stronger voice than it has before. Twelve countries speaking with one voice is much better than twelve countries speaking with twelve voices. Which means that we really will have to thrash out the whole matter of reciprocity. As I see it, reciprocity means that foreign companies wanting to develop their activities in another country will not be discriminated against; they will be able to compete with locally established companies on an equal basis. So, for example, a U.S. bank in Europe would operate under the same conditions as European banks in Europe; and European banks in the United States would operate under the same conditions as U.S. banks in the United States. The same would apply to other business activities.

I think there is a lot of self-projection going on by both Americans and Japanese who think that Europeans will now do to them what they have been doing to European industry. I've been in the United States enough and worked with enough American companies to know that there is a lot of protectionism there too. I don't blame the Americans. It's all part of the game. But it's silly to immediately start shouting and anticipating things that most likely will never happen.

One of the things that has upset many Americans deeply during the last year or so has been the high level of foreign investment in the United States. Do you anticipate similar concerns in Europe as more and more companies that aren't part of the EC move onto the continent?

Any foreign company, be it Japanese, American, Korean, or any other nationality, should be given a full opportunity to invest in Europe. At the same time, however, it is essential to look at the quality of the investment. By that I mean it should be a genuine investment: there should be sufficient added value in the country where the investor is establishing itself, and there should be a transfer of technology.

We have been doing that all our life at Philips. The American mentality is such that they do it too. Look at IBM in Europe. Look at Ford Motor Company. People know that Ford is American, but the Ford factories in Europe are considered European. The same is true of Opel. Opel is GM, but it is considered absolutely European. All these companies develop their own technology; what they do has a huge value added. They may fall back on their American parents from time to time, but it's a two-way street.

The Japanese are not playing the same game. They are afraid to give away or sell their know-how. They think they are killing themselves if they do. So what you get instead is no involvement in real manufacturing but mainly export of ready-made products. When you analyze the investments the Japanese have made, particularly those that have been subsidized—mistakenly, in my opinion—by European governments, you come to some peculiar conclusions. For example, if you see a typewriter factory set up in Scotland with help and subsidies from the Scottish government, and then you discover that every single part is imported from Japan—including the little plate that says "Made in Scotland"—then I think you're right to start protesting.

We've talked about changes for companies and industries. Are there comparable changes occurring in the work force at large? Does Europe have the work force it will need to fight the competitive battles that lie ahead?

It is already absolutely evident that a lot of time and a lot of money have to be spent on educational issues. One aspect of this is to foster more cooperation between universities and industry. Last September, the European Roundtable and the Council of European Rectors signed an agreement in Bologna, Italy to establish a forum between European industry and European universities. Its purpose is to work out practical recommendations for bringing the two spheres closer together.

The main thing, however, is that companies themselves start developing ongoing programs so that employees will have the skills they need to be doing the right things. The European Roundtable has already developed one such program called EuroJob, in which people go from one company to another for a certain period and then come back to their home company. The Roundtable also organizes two-week seminars on future developments in Europe, to which it invites younger people who are already involved in trade and industry.

Another important problem is unemployment. We will have to deal with the fact that the unemployment rate here in Europe is very, very high and that it does not show much sign of coming down. In the United States, you have done a marvelous job of creating new employment, especially in the service industries. I know some people think that is a problem, but I don't agree. Quite a large number of the new jobs Europe needs will have to be created in areas such as financial services and software. This is a sector where Europe, in my opinion, is still lagging compared with the United States. But it will come also.

You've suggested that the European Community could learn about job creation from the United States. Turning the tables, what could the United States best learn from Europe?

One thing U.S. managers could learn is not to be so driven by short-term, bottom-line considerations. Americans almost always live by their quarterly results. The European manager, on the other hand, looks a little bit longer term. Maybe too much so, at times. The European situation isn't ideal. But if it is a good thing to maximize your profits, it is also a good thing to optimize them—to balance profit performance and continuity, which means sticking with an activity once you've started. The United States has given up industries that they should not have given up—particularly consumer electronics.

Are there other lessons U.S. managers could learn from Europeans?

One more. American managers should really understand, not just say they understand, that there are other parts of the world besides the United States. They know about Japan, because they have been attacked by the Japanese so much. So they look at Japan a little, though most U.S. companies—like most European companies—aren't very successful there. But there is also a vast market here in Europe that they tend to ignore.

I understand why American managers think about the U.S. market first. For most products, the United States makes up about 50% of the world market. That's one reason European industry has been very aware of the United States. We know we need a proper share of the U.S. market if we are to compete in the world market. Also, American consumers are usually a little more aggressive, a little more advanced, a little more willing to take on new ideas. So, again, we need to be present in the United States to pick up new ideas and experiment with them.

But that huge U.S. market is also a problem for American managers because so few of them look outside it. We in Europe are still surprised, I must say, that even with the lower dollar, we haven't noticed very much increase in American competition. That's very different from the way the Japanese behave. Even when the dollar/yen ratio changed and the yen rose against the European currencies too, the Japanese didn't let up. We thought that maybe their prices would go up and the competition would get a little less severe. But nothing changed. They just kept attacking the European market as they always have. Americans could learn from that.

There is another consideration. If Americans started doing business with other countries, they would develop greater understanding as well as more trade. And that is the most important thing, after all— that societies be open to each other. To close yourself off is the worst thing that can happen.

4

The Right Way to Go Global: An Interview with Whirlpool CEO David Whitwam

Regina Fazio Maruca

Everybody is talking about going global, but hardly anyone understands what that means, says David R. Whitwam, the 51-year-old chairman and CEO of the Whirlpool Corporation. According to Whitwam, too many managers are still running their businesses with the same old regional fiefdoms and inadequate ways of satisfying customers. As a result, few would-be global companies have escaped the deadly war of attrition in which cost and quality are the only weapons and ever-declining margins the only prize.

When Whitwam became CEO in 1987, Whirlpool was mired in just such an unwinnable war in the North American major-appliances market. Whitwam, who joined Whirlpool in 1968 and rose through the sales and marketing ranks, was determined to make whatever changes necessary to secure real growth for the future. Whitwam's vision of global opportunity led to Whirlpool's daring $1 billion purchase of N.V. Philips' floundering European appliance business in 1989, a move that catapulted Whirlpool into the number-one position in the worldwide appliance business.

Whitwam could have chosen to "fix" Philips through cost-cutting and operating changes. Instead, he followed a more ambitious path: transforming two parochial, margin-driven companies into a unified, consumer-focused organization capable of using its combined talents to achieve breakthrough performance in markets around the world. As a result, the new Whirlpool set the pace for the global appliance industry and its price structure.

HBR: *In 1987, Whirlpool was primarily a North American company. Today it manufactures in 11 countries with facilities in the United States, Europe, and Latin America and markets products in more than 120 locations as diverse as Thailand, Hungary, and Argentina. What's the most crucial lesson you've learned about how a company builds a global competitive advantage?*

David Whitwam: The only way to gain lasting competitive advantage is to leverage your capabilities around the world so that the company as a whole is greater than the sum of its parts. Being an international company—selling globally, having global brands or operations in different countries—isn't enough.

In fact, most international manufacturers aren't truly global. They're what I call flag planters. They may have acquired or established businesses all over the world, but their regional or national divisions still operate as autonomous entities. In this day and age, you can't run a business that way and expect to gain a long-term competitive advantage.

To me, "competitive advantage" means having the best technologies and processes for designing, manufacturing, selling, and servicing your products at the lowest possible costs. Our vision at Whirlpool is to integrate our geographical businesses wherever possible, so that our most advanced expertise in any given area—whether it's refrigeration technology, financial reporting systems, or distribution strategy—isn't confined to one location or one division. We want to be able to take the best capabilities we have and leverage them in all of our operations worldwide.

In the major-appliances industry, both the size of our products and varying consumer preferences require us to have regional manufacturing centers. But even though the features, dimensions, and configurations of machines like refrigerators, washing machines, and ovens vary from market to market, much of the technology and manufacturing processes involved are similar. In other words, while a company may need plants in Europe, the United States, Latin America, and Asia to make products that meet the special needs of local markets, it's still possible and desirable for those plants to share the best available product technologies and manufacturing processes.

Let me use washing machines as an example. Washing technology is washing technology. But our German products are feature-rich and thus considered to be higher-end. The products that come out of our Italian plants run at lower RPMs and are less costly. Still, the reality is that the insides of the machines don't vary a great deal. Both the German and the Italian washing machines can be standardized and simplified by reducing the number of parts, which is true of any product family. Yet when we bought Philips, the washing machines made in the Italian and German facilities didn't have one screw in common. Today products are being designed to ensure that a wide variety of models can be built on the same basic platform. Our new dryer line has precisely this kind of common platform, and other product categories are currently being designed in the same way.

But before you can develop common techniques and processes, don't you have to define the new organization's goals?

Absolutely. You must create an organization whose people are adept at exchanging ideas, processes, and systems across borders, people who are absolutely free of the "not-invented-here" syndrome, people who are constantly working together to identify the best global opportunities and the biggest global problems facing the organization. If you're going to ask people to work together in pursuing global ends across organizational and geographic boundaries, you have to give them a vision of what they're striving to achieve, as well as a unifying philosophy to guide their efforts.

That's why we've worked so hard at Whirlpool to define and communicate our vision, objectives, and the market philosophy that represents our unifying focus. Our vision is to be one company worldwide. Our overarching objective is to drive this company to world-class performance in terms of delivering shareholder value, which we define as being in the top 25% of publicly held companies in total returns through a given economic cycle. (See Exhibit I.)

Our market philosophy suggests that the only way to deliver this value over the long term is by focusing on the customer. Only prolonged, intensive effort to understand and respond to genuine customer needs can lead to the breakthrough products and services that earn long-term customer loyalty. Too many companies implement one improvement program after another but ignore the larger picture, which has to do with establishing enduring relationships between a company and its customers. Many companies would like to think that if they become "world-class" in cost and quality, they'll win. But it takes more than that.

Exhibit I.

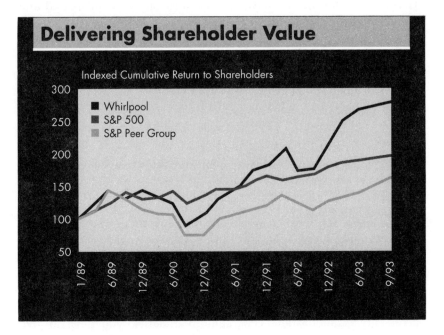

Delivering Shareholder Value

Indexed Cumulative Return to Shareholders

- Whirlpool
- S&P 500
- S&P Peer Group

Why do you think so many international companies aren't managed as global businesses?

Top-level managers often incorrectly assume that since consumers differ from location to location, their businesses can't operate effectively as a unified entity. As a result, they see their industry as a mosaic of specialized businesses, each with its own unique constraints and its own finite opportunities. They look at these "little pictures" when they're creating strategies, and because it's so hard for them to back away from such close-up views, many can't entertain the notion that their industry could evolve into something different over time.

Until the mid-1980s, Whirlpool was not different. When we sat down to plan our future in 1987, it was the first time Whirlpool had ever asked itself what kind of company it wanted to become in the next decade or the next century. This lack of self-scrutiny isn't as surprising as it might sound. Whirlpool was successful, profitable, and reasonably secure in a domestic market that was already eliminating the marginal competitors. The world hadn't broken down our doors the way Japanese automakers had stormed Detroit, for example. If you're a market leader with no imminent catastrophe on the horizon, critical self-examination is more the exception than the rule. But we faced up to that challenge because we could see our future growing more difficult and complicated with each passing year.

How did Whirlpool come to the decision to globalize through this process of self-examination?

We didn't start with the answer that we were going to globalize. We started with the knowledge that if we stuck to the path we were on, the future would be neither pleasant nor profitable. Even though we had dramatically lowered costs and improved product quality, our profit margins in North America had been declining because everyone in the industry was pursuing the same course and the local market was mature. The four main players—Whirlpool, General Electric, Maytag, and White Consolidated, which had been acquired by Electrolux—were beating one another up every day.

So we explored our options. We could have restructured the company financially and paid out a lot to our shareholders. We also looked at diversifying the business. If the major-appliances industry didn't offer growth, were there other industries that did? We looked at other kinds of durable products. We looked at horizontal expansion and vertical expansion. And in the process, it became clear to us that the basics of managing our business and its process and product technologies were the same in Europe, North America, Asia, and Latin America. We were already very good at what we did. What we needed was to enter appliance markets in other parts of the world and learn how to satisfy different kinds of customers.

Before 1987, we didn't see the potential power our existing capabilities could give us in the global market because we had been limiting our definition of the appliance market to the United States. Obviously, this also limited our definition of the industry itself and the opportunity it offered. Our eight months of analysis turned up a great deal of evidence that, over time, our industry would become global, whether *we* chose to become global or not. With that said, we had three choices. We could ignore the inevitable—a decision that would have condemned Whirlpool to a slow death. We could wait for globalization to begin and then try to react, which would have put us in a catch-up mode, technologically and organizationally. Or we could control our own destiny and try to shape the very nature of globalization in our industry. In short, we could force our competitors to respond to us.

Before we began making moves on the global stage, Electrolux was out in front of us. It had bought White Consolidated and had acquired several appliance makers in Europe. But Electrolux appeared to be taking advantage of individual opportunities rather than following a coordinated plan. After our Philips acquisition, we also saw General Electric take some opportunistic steps.

Today, however, Whirlpool is the front-runner when it comes to implementing a pan-European strategy and leveraging global resources. By expanding our strategic horizon, not just our geographic reach, we've been able to build a global management capability that provides us with what we feel is a distinct competitive advantage. Clearly, this should enable us to improve returns to our shareholders significantly. (See Exhibit II.)

The notion that managers should think "global but act local" isn't a new thought. But it seems to have proven to be a lot easier said than done.

The key is getting your organization—and not just top management—to think globally. Most companies never get to that stage because their leaders haven't understood what they can and cannot do. A CEO can forcibly position his or her organization at the beginning of the path to globalization and help employees take the first step or two. But ultimately, employees must cover the miles with their own feet. CEOs have to create the processes and structures to get the organization going and keep people aimed in the right direction, but they cannot achieve anything requiring sustained effort by edict alone. Organizations have changed radically in recent years. When the chairman walked down the halls in my early years with Whirlpool, you found an office to duck into. According to the old paradigm of hierarchy and discipline, it wasn't his subordinates' place to question his decisions.

Employees today question and challenge all the time. They don't accept things at face value. As a result, a contemporary CEO has to convince employees why transformation is necessary. Then there's the critical step of persuading them that they can perform at what seem to be impossibly high levels. For a company to become a truly global enterprise, employees have to change the way they think and act, taking on progressively more responsibility and initiative until the company behaves globally in all of its parts—without the CEO cracking a whip.

Exhibit II.

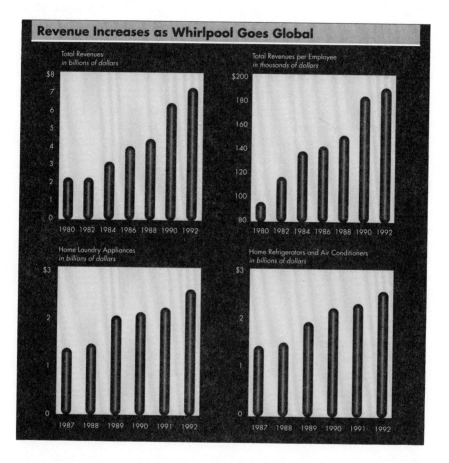

So change at the global level requires more patience than many senior executives seem to have.

In our society, there seems to be an expectation that CEOs should be able to fix things in a flash, even if that entails engineering an organizational transformation overnight. When we acquired Philips, for example, Wall Street analysts expected us to ship 500 people over to Europe, plug them into the plants and distribution systems, and give them six months or a year to turn the business around. They expected us to impose the "superior American way" of operating on the European organization.

But you have to remember that we were planning to build a global enterprise, not a U.S. army of occupation. If you try to gain control of an organization by simply subjugating it to your preconceptions, you can expect to pay for your short-term profits with long-term resistance and resentment. That's why we chose another course. During that first year, I think we had two people from the United States working in Europe, and neither was a senior manager. By the end of the second year, we had maybe half a dozen U.S. managers there—again, none at senior levels. We listened and observed. We worked hard to communicate the company's vision, objectives, and philosophy to the European workforce. Building a shared base of understanding takes time, and we had to learn how to do that in a multilingual, multinational environment. Today we have 15,000 employees in Europe with only 10 from U.S. operations. They all report to European bosses, with the exception of Hank Bowman, executive vice president of Whirlpool Europe.

The hardest part of globalization is avoiding the temptation of trying to build Rome in a day. The purchase contract might state that you own the land. But you don't own the builders; they have to enter into the work contract of their own free will.

It's one thing to get senior managers to buy into globalization. How do you persuade employees throughout the organization?

Very slowly. You can't expect it to happen overnight. Bear in mind that we have many, many employees in our manufacturing plants and offices who have been with us for 25 or 30 years. They didn't sign up to be part of a global experience. Most of our North American employees joined Whirlpool to live in places like Benton Harbor, Michigan, or Clyde, Ohio—not Cassinetta, Italy. And a lot of our Italian colleagues didn't join Philips to work in the United States. In addition, we have a fairly large group of managers around the world, including me, who have acquired all of their experience in very traditional, hierarchical organizations. Suddenly we give them new things to think about and new people to work with. We tell people at all levels that the old way of doing business is too cumbersome.

Changing a company's approach to doing business is a difficult thing to accomplish in the United States, let alone globally. In the beginning, our North American Appliance Group didn't want any part of this new one-company vision. They saw it as a threat. They thought, "Whitwam's running off and spending a billion dollars in Europe, and that's going to take away resources that we need to succeed." In addition, when we first took engineers and manufacturing people from the United States to Europe to go through the plants, they would spend all their time walking around and saying to themselves, "We do all of these things better at home." The Europeans who toured the U.S. facilities had the same parochial attitude. Neither group spent any time looking at what it could learn from the other.

During the first two years after we acquired the Philips business, we didn't concentrate on immediately improving performance. Instead, we spent a lot of time building trust and creating a common vision of our future. We deliberately encouraged our employees to think like owners so that they would come to believe that it was in their best interest to create a global organization. When we started the process, I told the organization that the only reason we existed as a large publicly held company was to create value for the shareholders. Now, the employee who works on a production line or in an office down the hall doesn't necessarily feel very good about that. Think about all the negative stereotypes of fickle shareholders. I explained that creating value for shareholders was the only way we could hope to create value for all our other stakeholders—employees, the communities we live in, our suppliers, and so on. Seeing the connections among interests is a key part of acquiring the global, one-company mentality we need. People don't see that vision just because you say it.

One of the approaches we're using to help employees feel like owners is to give them more responsibility. We need their heads thinking as well as their hands working. In some of our factories today, there is no supervisor on the floor. Teams made up of hourly workers hire new employees, create production line layouts, decide on production levels, and even make employee termination recommendations. They drive the quality process. That's a real change from how industrial companies have traditionally been managed.

Another approach is our compensation system. Its driving principle is "pay for performance." For example, essentially all of our U.S. employees received stock options in 1991. Some operations have gainsharing programs, which allow employees to benefit directly from their own productivity and quality improvements. Other programs, including our 401K program, pay people—from top management to those on the factory floor—on the basis of whether or not we achieve corporate return-on-equity (ROE) or return-on-net-asset (RONA) goals. Employees at Whirlpool all understand what ROE and RONA mean, what drives those measurements, and how they're linked to shareholder value.

It's one thing to empower employees and communicate to them the importance of a common vision. But how did you translate that vision into the fabric of the organization—the day-to-day operations?

By helping employees throughout the organization do it for themselves. Six months after we acquired Whirlpool Europe, we brought 150 of our senior managers to Montreux, Switzerland, and we spent a week developing our global vision. What did it mean? What were the implications? The benefits of a week of "feel good" discussion didn't end when the meeting adjourned, because everyone who attended took away an assignment.

We made those 150 people accountable for educating all of our 38,000 people around the world. When going global, you have to communicate to everyone what the company vision is and what the long-term goals are. And then you have to follow through and design processes that force the interaction to continue. Every single employee must believe that there is great value in managing the company in an integrated way. To do that, you have to bring people together on real projects that tackle real problems or that explore opportunities on a cross-border basis.

To that end, managers at Montreux commissioned 15 projects—what we call One-Company Challenges. They ranged from creating a global product-strategy review process to developing a product-creation process worldwide to establishing a talent-pool system for human resources. Each of these challenges had to have a major impact on the realization of the vision. Each person who attended the meeting at Montreux went back home and gathered a team of employees from all levels of the company to work on a given project.

One of the One-Company Challenges was creating a companywide total-quality-management system, which we now call the Whirlpool Excellence System (WES). When we acquired Philips, we suddenly had one organization that focused on ISO-9000, the European total quality system, and another that focused on the U.S. Baldrige approach to quality.

Instead of imposing one approach on the entire organization, we created a cross-cultural team with members from Europe and North America and asked them to examine the best quality programs in the world, including ISO-9000 and Baldrige. The team then developed a global quality system that was appropriate for the new Whirlpool. The result was WES. It was this Euro-American group that then designed all the details of WES, including the training, communications, and deployment programs needed to create a common approach—a common language of quality—for all our operations.

A company needs to have one management process, one understanding of performance requirements. But it takes more than one person to design that management process if it is to be accepted, used, and turned into a competitive advantage. One of the best ways to change an inflexible mind-set is to expose people to both challenges and the new ideas that can meet those challenges. When they've completed the work at hand, they've also gained a new sense of what is possible and desirable.

Was setting the process of globalization in motion at Montreux all that was required?

No. First, I should stress that we are not "there" yet. Although we've made a lot of progress, we are not yet a truly global organization. It will take more time to become one. Second, I want to make it clear that the art of management is not confined to orchestrating the creation of a bold vision, a great plan, or even one set of actions that causes the organization to face up to the need for change. It must also encompass relentless follow-through, meticulous attention to detail, and the establishment of personal accountability throughout the organization. These are not glamorous functions, perhaps, but like conscience and memory in a human being, they are all that protect good intentions from the distractions of the moment. Without them, the organization cannot maintain interest or momentum, and the initiative—no matter how spectacular the fireworks of the start-up—will fizzle out.

An initiative like globalization doesn't acquire momentum just because it is enormous. You have to push hard to overcome the initial inertia, and then you have to keep pushing so that friction—in the form of fear, uncertainty, and confusion—doesn't stop it in its tracks. We made a good start with the Montreux conference, then brought the same delegates together again the following year, this time in Washington, D.C. There, we studied the implications of WES and developed a whole new set of projects to continue to change company behavior. The Washington delegates were assigned the job of establishing 15 or 20 One-Company Teams to carry out the new projects.

You have to remind everyone over and over again that the new organization and its tenets aren't going to disappear. In addition to annual meetings of our top 150 managers, we have been bringing all development, marketing, and manufacturing leaders together twice a year for global product and technology reviews. We examine our product designs and how consumer needs affect them. Nothing came of it the first year in terms of actual global product creation. But you must expect that. Even if nothing concrete comes out of it, a preliminary session is still creating awareness that building a washing machine in Clyde, Ohio, isn't different from building one in Schorndorf, Germany.

You've made it sound as if an organization can globalize without outside help. Can a collection of regional organizations transform themselves in such short order without an injection of new skills or perspectives?

Absolutely not. When you change a company as rapidly as we did, you wake up one morning and suddenly realize that you don't have the skills and experience you need, and that includes the CEO. I had never run a multinational company until January 1, 1989, when we bought Philips. I've often said that there's only one thing that wakes me up in the middle of the night. It's not our financial performance or economic issues in general. It's worrying about whether or not we have the right skills and capabilities to pull the strategy off.

Traditionally, Whirlpool executives were homegrown. They came up through the ranks, and their knowledge and experience were limited to North America. Needless to say, we experienced some pain as we tried to match existing skills with emerging global management requirements. There were shortfalls at every level, including my own. In some cases, they could be remedied by education and training programs. But some could only be remedied by recruiting from the outside.

It is a simple and inescapable fact that the skills and capabilities required to manage a global company are different from those required for a domestic company. But that's a leap we wanted to make, one that we chose in the interest of the company and its shareholders. And that tends to be a helpful factor when you're negotiating the hard parts: you know you're making these tough changes because you're dramatically increasing the overall opportunity for the company and its employees.

We've moved into a different realm, and there is no turning back. For example, there is no question in my mind that the person who replaces me as CEO and chairman will need experience managing in a foreign environment.

But isn't Whirlpool still planting flags too? For example, you have sales and distribution subsidiaries in Hong Kong, Thailand, and Taiwan, but you have no Asian manufacturing operations.

It may indeed look like flag planting, but that is not our intention. When you enter a new market, your sales organization, your knowledge of the local consumer, and your overall capabilities have to develop to a certain level before your business can hope to become a full-fledged, participating member of the global organization. That is the goal for our Asian business.

In 1988, we began in Asia with what I called the learning phase of the strategy, which resembled flag planting. But the purpose was to build a distribution system in Southeast Asia and to gain an understanding of the consumer. Within the past year, we have opened three regional offices in Asia: an office in Singapore to serve Southeast Asia, an office in Hong Kong to serve Greater China, and an office in Tokyo to serve Japan. We also currently have a design, engineering, and product development center in Singapore for all of Asia, which will help us reach the point at which we can manufacture in our own facilities in Asia. We know when and where these facilities will be established.

Our interim plan is to have a cadre of 80 to 100 people in the Singapore center who can call on Whirlpool resources around the world to shape and direct the plants and the products we produce in Asia. So when we start manufacturing in Asia, it will be as a global company. The beauty of starting a new operation like this one is that you don't have to overcome decades of managing habits that are ineffective when creating a global organization.

You seem to believe that truly global companies can leave their competitors in the dust by scoring breakthroughs in satisfying customers. Given that none of the major players in your industry has been able to pull away from the pack by dramatically slashing costs and improving quality, is this goal a fantasy?

No, it's not a fantasy. Whirlpool, its biggest competitors, and many companies in other industries have been too obsessed with cost and quality at the expense of other variables. You can't achieve a competitive advantage by focusing exclusively on cost and quality. Everybody in this industry is driving down the same cost and quality curve. And let's assume we're all going to become world-class performers. When that occurs, you'll have a handful of companies building great products that will last for 80 years, but no one will make any margins on them. And what then gives one product the edge over another?

Our strategy is based on the premise that world-class cost and quality are merely the ante—the price of being in the game at all. We have to provide a compelling reason other than price for consumers to buy Whirlpool-built products. We can do that only by understanding the consumer better than anyone else does and then translating our understanding into clearly superior product designs, features, and after-sales support. Our goal is for consumers to prefer the Whirlpool brand because it offers greater overall value than competing products. Achieving that goal requires taking a giant step back from our business and rethinking who our customers are and what their needs are. This may not sound earth-shattering, but it is. It means rethinking the very nature of the business.

All of us in this industry have been telling ourselves that we're in "the refrigerator business," "the washing-machine business," or "the range business." None of us saw a great deal of room for product innovation, which is undoubtedly why there hasn't been radical innovation in 30 years, apart from the microwave oven and the trash compactor. If you want to open the door to imagination and innovation, isn't it more useful to think of "the fabric-care business," "the food-preparation business," and "the food-preservation business"?

The starting point isn't the existing product; it's the function consumers buy products to accomplish. When you return to first principles, the design issues dramatically change. The microwave couldn't have been invented by someone who assumed he or she was in the business of designing a range. Such a design breakthrough required seeing that the opportunity is "easier, quicker food preparation," not "a better range."

We are applying these broader definitions in very direct ways. Organizationally, we have created what we call an advanced product development capability to serve markets around the world. Its charter is to look beyond traditional product definitions to the consumer processes for which products of the future will have to provide clear benefits.

Take "the fabric-care business," which we used to call "washing-machine business." We're now studying consumer behavior from the time people take off their dirty clothes at night until they've been cleaned and ironed and hung in the closet. What are we looking for? The worst part of the process is not the washing and drying. The hard part is when you take your clothes out of the dryer and you have to do something with them—iron, fold, hang them up. Whoever comes up with a product to make this part of the process easier, simpler, or quicker is going to create an incredible market.

In other words, you're redefining what it means to satisfy the customer?

Our purpose at Whirlpool is to build a perfect product. With that as the point of departure, you can indeed take the notion of satisfying the customer to a completely different plane, and that's where break-throughs become possible. Reaching such a plane means studying consumers' lifestyles to decipher what they might want even if they cannot articulate that desire in terms of a product request. Ten years ago, what consumer would have said he needed a CD player? Yet today records have virtually ceased to exist. Note that a company could have missed this breakthrough by asking the wrong questions of consumers or by narrowly interpreting consumer answers to good questions. In fact, consumers often speak in code. For example, our market research showed that customers wanted "clean refrigerators." Did this mean refrigerators that were easy to clean? No. We figured out that it meant refrigerators should look clean and hide finger marks, which helped us come up with a textured finish.

In rapidly segmenting consumer markets, you have to understand not only the lifestyles that people have today but also the kinds of lifestyles they are going to have five years from now and beyond. Can you tell me what you want your refrigerator to look like in the year 2010? Of course not. So we have to move away from the traditional approach of reacting to what customers say they want.

How do you do that?

One was is to develop close relationships with organizations in related businesses. For example, we have had a close, well-defined contractual relationship with Procter & Gamble in the United States. We have a long-standing relationship with them, exchanging basic information, ideas, and so forth. But now we have a more intense involvement at the development, engineering, and technology levels. We've established a formal partnership, in which one party is not worried about sharing proprietary information with the other.

We also work with Unilever in Brazil. Our engineers work together on product development, because both companies need to understand where the other is going over the long term. Unilever is working with other manufacturers too, because they can't be designing detergents ten years out for washing machines that can't use them.

Finally, we're moving toward a significant consolidation of our suppliers. Instead of working with five steel suppliers, for example, we want to have an important partnership with one or two. We want to have agreements that give us access to supplier technologies so that we can work together on process improvements in all of our plants. That's difficult to do with a broad supplier base.

As well as redefining customer satisfaction, are you redefining who your customers are?

Yes. There are numerous companies and many improvement experts who talk about satisfying internal customers. At Whirlpool, we once did the same, but we currently believe that internal customers do not exist. In fact, the only customer is the final consumer.

Companies that believe they have internal customers—that manufacturing is marketing's customer, for example—lose sight of what they're trying to accomplish as an organization. Today we're organized around multifunctional processes that are focused on serving the end user. Take, for instance, the product business teams we've established. They behave completely differently than functions at Whirlpool behaved in the past. We used to make a lot of dumb decisions in manufacturing for the sake of manufacturing. We don't do that nearly as much today. The product business teams are meant to divert the focus from the function to the consumer.

Of course, we have to be careful to prevent any weakening of functional excellence. The job of our vice president of manufacturing for the North American Appliance Group is to drive functional excellence. You have to keep benchmarking single functions even as you're working multifunctionally. It's a tough balance. But it's an ongoing effort.

How does this approach change the relationship between the manufacturer and the retailer?

Until you stop thinking about retailers as customers and start thinking about them as part of the process, you're going to be delivering the wrong kinds of products. For too long, we viewed the retailer as a customer.

Sears, Roebuck & Company is a great example. Until 1947 or so,

Sears was our only retailer, and we still do in excess of a billion dollars of business with them. But for too much of our relationship, we treated Sears as a customer. We developed products to sit on their floors in competition with other products that were sitting on their floors. If they said, "I want this washing machine with three whistles and two bells, and I want it to be pink," we gave it to them. Little did we know that the consumer didn't want machines with whistles. Today we don't treat each other as customer/supplier. We see ourselves as partners trying to solve a consumer need.

What is the end of the road? When will you know that Whirlpool has become global?

Strictly speaking, there is no end of the road. Continuous change is the essence of the global market. But there are some milestones I look forward to. For example, I'll know we've arrived as a global company when we have cross-border product business teams—one for washing machines, one for refrigerators, one for ovens, and so on—running all of our operations throughout the world. These teams, which will have functional and brand objectives, will identify the best opportunities and the most important problems to solve and then assess the related trade-offs.

There will also come a day when we'll identify a location where the best skills in a certain product area should be concentrated, and that place will become the development center for that type of product. But here's an important distinction: while we may have only one major design center for a given product, not everyone associated with that product will have to be located there. For example, the development center for refrigeration products may be in Benton Harbor, but we may also have people working for that center in China or Italy. Think about the communication technologies that exist today. People don't need to sit next to each other anymore to work together on the same project. In fact, it's no longer appropriate or effective to design organizations that way. Instead, global competitors will increasingly make use of "virtual teams," as we—and others—are already doing.

Admittedly, we're not an "old hand" at virtual teams yet. But we have used them effectively. For example, we recently developed a super-efficient, chlorofluorocarbon-free refrigerator that won a contest sponsored by a group of U.S. utilities. We used insulation technology from our European business, compressor technology from our Brazilian affiliates, and manufacturing and design expertise from our

U.S. operation. If we had still been the kind of company we were in 1987, we couldn't have pulled off this kind of cross-border teamwork.

As we look to the future, perhaps the greatest trap will be our own successes. Success has a way of drawing attention away from the present and future and onto the past. The history of business is littered with companies that were short-term successes. Complacency should have no part in any organization. It is the responsibility of leaders to manage against it.

PART

II

Developing a Global Strategy

1
What Is a Global Manager?

Christopher A. Bartlett and Sumantra Ghoshal

In the early stages of its drive overseas, Corning Glass hired an American ex-ambassador to head up its international division. He had excellent contacts in the governments of many nations and could converse in several languages, but he was less familiar with Corning and its businesses. In contrast, ITT decided to set up a massive educational program to "globalize" all managers responsible for its worldwide telecommunications business—in essence, to replace its national specialists with global generalists.

Corning and ITT eventually realized they had taken wrong turns. Like many other companies organizing for worldwide operations in recent years, they found that an elite of jet-setters was often difficult to integrate into the corporate mainstream; nor did they need an international team of big-picture overseers to the exclusion of focused experts.

Success in today's international climate—a far cry from only a decade ago—demands highly specialized yet closely linked groups of global business managers, country or regional managers, and worldwide functional managers. This kind of organization characterizes a *transnational* rather than an old-line multinational, international, or global company. Transnationals integrate assets, resources, and diverse people in operating units around the world. Through a flexible management process, in which business, country, and functional managers form a triad of different perspectives that balance one another, transnational companies can build three strategic capabilities:

- global-scale efficiency and competitiveness;
- national-level responsiveness and flexibility; and
- cross-market capacity to leverage learning on a worldwide basis.

While traditional organizations, structured along product or geographic lines, can hone one or another of these capabilities, they cannot cope with the challenge of all three at once. But an emerging group of transnational companies has begun to transform the classic hierarchy of headquarters-subsidiary relationships into an integrated network of specialized yet interdependent units. For many, the greatest constraint in creating such an organization is a severe shortage of executives with the skills, knowledge, and sophistication to operate in a more tightly linked and less classically hierarchical network.

In fact, in the volatile world of transnational corporations, there is no such thing as a universal global manager. Rather, there are three groups of specialists: business managers, country managers, and functional managers. And there are the top executives at corporate headquarters, the leaders who manage the complex interactions between the three—and can identify and develop the talented executives a successful transnational requires.

To build such talent, top management must understand the strategic importance of each specialist. The careers of Leif Johansson of Electrolux, Howard Gottlieb of NEC, and Wahib Zaki of Procter & Gamble vividly exemplify the specialized yet interdependent roles the three types of global managers play.

The Business Manager: Strategist + Architect + Coordinator

Global business or product-division managers have one overriding responsibility: to further the company's global-scale efficiency and competitiveness. This task requires not only the perspective to recognize opportunities and risks across national and functional boundaries but also the skill to coordinate activities and link capabilities across those barriers. The global business manager's overall goal is to capture the full benefit of integrated worldwide operations.

To be effective, the three roles at the core of a business manager's job are to serve as the strategist for his or her organization, the architect of its worldwide asset and resource configuration, and the coordinator of transactions across national borders. Leif Johansson, now president of Electrolux, the Swedish-based company, played all three roles successfully in his earlier position as head of the household appliance division.

In 1983, when 32-year-old Johansson assumed responsibility for the division, he took over a business that had been built up through more than 100 acquisitions over the previous eight years. By the late 1980s, Electrolux's portfolio included more than 20 brands sold in some 40 countries, with acquisitions continuing throughout the decade. Zanussi, for example, the big Italian manufacturer acquired by Electrolux in 1984, had built a strong market presence based on its reputation for innovation in household and commercial appliances. In addition, Arthur Martin in France and Zoppas in Norway had strong local brand positions but limited innovative capability.

As a result of these acquisitions, Electrolux had accumulated a patchwork quilt of companies, each with a different product portfolio, market position, and competitive situation. Johansson soon recognized the need for an overall strategy to coordinate and integrate his dispersed operations.

Talks with national marketing managers quickly convinced him that dropping local brands and standardizing around a few high-volume regional and global products would be unwise. He agreed with the local managers that their national brands were vital to maintaining consumer loyalty, distribution leverage, and competitive flexibility in markets that they saw fragmenting into more and more segments. But Johansson also understood the views of his division staffmembers, who pointed to the many similarities in product characteristics and consumer needs in the various markets. The division staff was certain Electrolux could use this advantage to cut across markets and increase competitiveness.

Johansson led a strategy review with a task force of product-division staff and national marketing managers. While the task force confirmed the marketing managers' notion of growing segmentation, its broader perspective enabled Johansson to see a convergence of segments across national markets. Their closer analysis also refined management's understanding of local market needs, concluding that consumers perceived "localness" mainly in terms of how a product was sold (distribution through local channels, promotion in local media, use of local brand names) instead of how it was designed or what features it offered.

From this analysis, Johansson fashioned a product-market strategy that identified two full-line regional brands to be promoted and supported in all European markets. He positioned the Electrolux brand to respond to the cross-market segment for high prestige (customers characterized as "conservatives"), while the Zanussi brand would fill the segment where innovative products were key (for "trendsetters").

The local brands were clustered in the other two market segments pinpointed in the analysis: "yuppies" ("young and aggressive" urban professionals) and "environmentalists" ("warm and friendly" people interested in basic-value products). The new strategy provided Electrolux with localized brands that responded to the needs of these consumer groups. At the same time, the company captured the efficiencies possible by standardizing the basic chassis and components of these local-brand products, turning them out in high volume in specialized regional plants.

So, by tracking product and market trends across borders, Leif Johansson captured valuable global-scale efficiencies while reaping the benefits of a flexible response to national market fragmentation. What's more, though he took on the leadership role as a strategist, Johansson never assumed he alone had the understanding or the ability to form a global appliance strategy; he relied heavily on both corporate and local managers. Indeed, Johansson continued to solicit guidance on strategy through a council of country managers called the 1992 Group and through a set of product councils made up of functional managers.

In fact, the global business manager's responsibility for the distribution of crucial assets and resources is closely tied to shaping an integrated strategy. While he or she often relies on the input of regional and functional heads, the business manager is still the architect who usually initiates and leads the debate on where major plants, technical centers, and sales offices should be located—and which facilities should be closed.

The obvious political delicacy of such debates is not the only factor that makes simple economic analysis inadequate. Within every operating unit there exists a pool of skills and capabilities that may have taken a lot of time and investment to build up. The global business manager has to achieve the most efficient distribution of assets and resources while protecting and leveraging the competence at hand. Electrolux's household appliance division had more than 200 plants and a bewildering array of technical centers and development groups in many countries. It was clear to Johansson that he had to rationalize this infrastructure.

He began by setting a policy for the household appliance division that would avoid concentration of facilities in one country or region, even in its Scandinavian home base. At the same time, Johansson wanted to specialize the division's development and manufacturing infrastructure on a "one product, one facility" basis. He was determined to allocate important development and manufacturing tasks to each of the company's major markets. In trying to optimize robustness and flexibility in the long term rather than minimize short-term costs, Johansson recognized that a specialized yet dispersed system would be less vulnerable to exchange-rate fluctuations and political uncertainties. This setup also tapped local managerial and technical resources, thereby reducing dependence on the small pool of skilled labor and management in Sweden.

Instead of closing old plants, Johansson insisted on upgrading and tailoring existing facilities, whenever possible. In addition to averting political fallout and organizational trauma, Electrolux would then retain valuable know-how and bypass the startup problems of building from scratch. An outstanding example of this approach is Zanussi's Porcia plant in Italy, which Electrolux turned into the world's largest washing machine plant. After a massive $150-million investment, the Porcia plant now produces 1.5 million units a year.

Although acquisition-fueled growth often leads to redundancy and overcapacity, it can also bring new resources and strengths. Instead of wiping out the division's diversity through homogenization or centralization, Johansson decided to leverage it by matching each unit's responsibilities with its particular competence. Because of the Scandinavian flair for modular design, he assigned the integrated kitchen-system business to Electrolux's Swedish and Finnish units. He acknowledged Porcia's experience in component production by consolidating design and production of compressors there. Johansson's reshaping of assets and resources not only enhanced scale economies and operational flexibility but also boosted morale by giving operating units the opportunity to leverage their distinctive competences beyond their local markets.

Newly developed business strategies obviously need coordination. In practice, the specialization of assets and resources swells the flow of products and components among national units, requiring a firm hand to synchronize and control that flow. For organizations whose operations have become more dispersed and specialized at the same time that their strategies have become more connected and integrated, coordination across borders is a tough challenge. Business managers must fashion a repertoire of approaches and tools, from simple centralized control to management of exceptions identified through formal policies to indirect management via informal communication channels.

Leif Johansson coordinated product flow—across his 35 national sales units and 29 regional sourcing facilities—by establishing broad sourcing policies and transfer-pricing ranges that set limits but left negotiations to internal suppliers and customers. For instance, each sales unit could negotiate a transfer price with its internal source for a certain product in a set range that was usually valid for a year. If the negotiations moved outside that range, the companies had to check with headquarters. As a coordinator, Johansson led the deliberations that defined the logic and philosophy of the parameters; but he stepped back and let individual unit managers run their own organizations, except when a matter went beyond policy limits.

In contrast, coordination of business strategy in Johansson's division was managed through teams that cut across the formal hierarchy. Instead of centralizing, he relied on managers to share the responsibility for monitoring implementation and resolving problems through teams. To protect the image and positioning of his regional brands— Electrolux and Zanussi—he set up a brand-coordination group for each. Group members came from the sales companies in key countries, and the chairperson was a corporate marketing executive. Both groups were responsible for building a coherent, pan-European strategy for the brand they represented.

To rationalize the various product strategies across Europe, Johansson created product-line boards to oversee these strategies and to exploit any synergies. Each product line had its own board made up of the corporate product-line manager, who was chair, and his or her product managers. The Quattro 500 refrigerator-freezer, which was designed in Italy, built in Finland, and marketed in Sweden, was one example of how these boards could successfully integrate product strategy.

In addition, the 1992 Group periodically reviewed the division's overall results, kept an eye on its manufacturing and marketing infrastructure, and supervised major development programs and investment projects. Capturing the symbolic value of 1992 in its name, the group was chaired by Johansson himself and included business managers from Italy, the United Kingdom, Spain, the United States, France, Switzerland, and Sweden.

Indeed, coordination probably takes up more of the global business manager's time than any other aspect of the job. This role requires that a manager have great administrative and interpersonal skills to ensure that coordination and integration don't deteriorate into heavy-handed control.

Many traditional multinational companies have made the mistake of automatically anointing their home country product-division managers with the title of global business manager. Sophisticated transnational companies, however, have long since separated the notions of coordination and centralization, looking for business leadership from their best units, wherever they may be located. For example, Asea Brown Boveri, the Swiss-headquartered electrical engineering corporation, has tried to leverage the strengths of its operating companies and exploit their location in critical markets by putting its business managers wherever strategic and organizational dimensions coincide. In Asea Brown Boveri's power-transmission business, the manager for switchgear is located in Sweden, the manager for power transformers is in Germany, the manager for distribution transformers is in Norway, and the manager for electric metering is in the United States.

Even well-established multinationals with a tradition of tight central control are changing their tack. The head of IBM's telecommunications business recently moved her division headquarters to London, not only to situate the command center closer to the booming European market for computer networking but also "to give us a different perspective on all our markets."

The Country Manager: Sensor + Builder + Contributor

The building blocks for most worldwide companies are their national subsidiaries. If the global business manager's main objective is to achieve global-scale efficiency and competitiveness, the national subsidiary manager's is to be sensitive and responsive to the local market. Country managers play the pivotal role not only in meeting local customer needs but also in satisfying the host government's requirements and defending their company's market positions against local and external competitors.

The need for local flexibility often puts the country manager in conflict with the global business manager. But in a successful transnational like Electrolux, negotiation can resolve these differences. In this era of intense competition around the world, companies cannot afford to permit a subsidiary manager to defend parochial interests as "king of the country."

Nor should headquarters allow national subsidiaries to become the battleground for corporate holy wars fought in the name of globalization. In many companies, their national subsidiaries are hothouses of entrepreneurship and innovation—homes for valuable resources and capabilities that must be nurtured, not constrained or cut off. The subsidiaries of Philips, for one, have consistently led product development: in television, the company's first color TV was developed in Canada, the first stereo model in Australia, and the first teletext in the United Kingdom. Unilever's national subsidiaries have also been innovative in product-marketing strategy: Germany created the campaign for Snuggle (a fabric softener); Finland developed Timotei (an herbal shampoo); and South Africa launched Impulse (a body perfume).

In fact, effective country managers play three vital roles: the sensor and interpreter of local opportunities and threats, the builder of local resources and capabilities, and the contributor to and active participant in global strategy. Howard Gottlieb's experience as general manager of NEC's switching-systems subsidiary in the United States illustrates the importance of all three tasks.

As a sensor, the country manager must be good at gathering and sifting information, interpreting the implications, and predicting a range of feasible outcomes. More important, this manager has the difficult task of conveying the importance of such intelligence to people higher up, especially those whose perceptions may be dimmed by distance or even ethnocentric bias. Today, when information gathered locally increasingly applies to other regions or even globally, communicating effectively is crucial. Consumer trends in one country often spread to another; technologies developed in a leading-edge environment can have global significance; a competitor's local market testing may signal a wider strategy; and national legislative initiatives in areas like deregulation and environmental protection tend to spill across borders.

Gottlieb's contribution to NEC's understanding of changes in the telecommunications market demonstrates how a good sensor can connect local intelligence with global strategy. In the late 1980s, Gottlieb was assigned to build the U.S. market for NEAX 61, a widely acclaimed digital telecom switch designed by the parent company in Japan. Although it was technologically sophisticated, early sales didn't meet expectations.

His local-market background and contacts led Gottlieb to a quick diagnosis of the problem. NEC had designed the switch to meet the needs of NTT, the Japanese telephone monopoly, and it lacked many features U.S. customers wanted. For one thing, its software didn't incorporate the protocol conversions necessary for distributing revenues among the many U.S. companies that might handle a single long-distance phone call. Nor could the switch handle revenue-enhancing features like "call waiting" and "call forwarding," which were vital high-margin items in the competitive, deregulated American market.

In translating the needs of his U.S. division to the parent company NEC, Gottlieb had a formidable task. To convince his superiors in Japan that redesigning NEAX 61 was necessary, he had to bridge two cultures and penetrate the subtleties of the parent company's Japanese-dominated management processes. And he had to instill a sense of urgency in several corporate management groups, varying his pitches to appeal to the interests of each. For instance, Gottlieb convinced the engineering department that the NEAX 61 switch had been underdesigned for the U.S. market and the marketing department that time was short because the Bell operating companies were calling for quotes.

A transnational's greater access to the scarcest of all corporate resources, human capability, is a definite advantage when compared with strictly local companies—or old-line multinationals, for that matter. Scores of companies like IBM, Merck, and Procter & Gamble have recognized the value of harvesting advanced (and often less expensive) scientific expertise by upgrading local development labs into global centers of technical excellence.

Other companies have built up and leveraged their overseas human resources in different ways. Cummins Engine, for example, has set up its highly skilled but surprisingly low-cost Indian engineering group as a worldwide drafting resource; American Airlines's Barbados operation does much of the corporate clerical work; and Becton Dickinson, a large hospital supply company, has given its Belgian subsidiary pan-European responsibility for managing distribution and logistics.

Indeed, the burden of identifying, developing, and leveraging such national resources and capabilities falls on country managers. Howard Gottlieb, after convincing Tokyo that the United States would be an important market for NEC's global digital-switch design, persuaded headquarters to permit his new engineering group to take part early on in the product development of the next generation switch—the NEAX 61 E. He sent teams of engineers to Japan to work with the original designers; and, to verify his engineers' judgments, Gottlieb invited the designers to visit his customers in the United States. These exchanges not only raised the sensitivity of NEC's Japan-based engineers to U.S. market needs but also significantly increased their respect for their American colleagues. Equally important, the U.S. unit's morale rose.

As a builder, Gottlieb used this mutual confidence as the foundation for creating a software-development capability that would become a big corporate asset. Skilled software engineers, very scarce in Japan, were widely available in the United States. Gottlieb's first move was to put together a small software team to support local projects. Though its resources were limited, the group turned out a number of innovations, including a remote software-patching capability that later became part of the 61 E switch design. The credibility he won at headquarters allowed Gottlieb to expand his design engineering group from 10 to more than 50 people within two years, supporting developments not only in North America but also eventually in Asia.

In many transnationals, access to strategically important information—and control over strategically important assets—has catapulted country managers into a much more central role. As links to local markets, they are no longer mere implementers of programs and policies shaped at headquarters; many have gained some influence over the way their organizations make important strategic and operational decisions. In most of today's truly transnational companies, country managers and their chief local subordinates often participate in new product-development committees, product-marketing task forces, and global-strategy conferences. Even at the once impenetrable annual top management meetings, national subsidiary managers may present their views and defend their interests before senior corporate and domestic executives—a scenario that would have been unthinkable even a decade ago.

Of course, the historic position of most national units of worldwide companies has been that of the implementer of strategy from headquarters. Because the parent company's accepted objectives are the outcome of discussion and negotiation involving numerous units, divisions, and national subsidiaries, sometimes a country manager must carry out a strategy that directly conflicts with what he or she has lobbied for in vain.

But a diverse and dispersed worldwide organization, with subsidiaries that control many of the vital development, production, and marketing resources, can no longer allow the time-honored "king of the country" to decide how, when, and even whether his or her national unit will implement a particular strategic initiative. The decision made by the North American subsidiary of Philips to outsource its VCRs from a Japanese competitor rather than the parent company is one of the most notorious instances of how a local "king" can undermine global strategy.

At NEC, Howard Gottlieb spent about 60% of his time on customer relations and probing the market and about 30% managing the Tokyo interface. His ability to understand and interpret the global strategic implications of U.S. market needs—and the software-development group he built from scratch—allowed him to take part in NEC's ongoing strategy debate. As a result, Gottlieb changed his division's role from implementer of corporate strategy to active contributor in designing that strategy.

The Functional Manager: Scanner + Cross-Pollinator + Champion

While global business managers and country managers have come into their own, functional specialists have yet to gain the recognition due them in many traditional multinational companies. Relegated to support-staff roles, excluded from important meetings, and even dismissed as unnecessary overhead, functional managers are often given little chance to participate in, let alone contribute to, the corporate mainstream's global activity. In some cases, top management has allowed staff functions to become a warehouse for corporate misfits or a graveyard for managerial has-beens. Yet at a time when information, knowledge, and expertise have become more specialized, an organization can gain huge benefits by linking its technical, manufacturing, marketing, human resources, and financial experts worldwide.

Given that today's transnationals face the strategic challenge of resolving the conflicts implicit in achieving global competitiveness, national responsiveness, and worldwide learning, business and country managers must take primary responsibility for the first two capabilities. But the third is the functional manager's province.

Building an organization that can use learning to create and spread innovations requires the skill to transfer specialized knowledge while also connecting scarce resources and capabilities across national borders. To achieve this important objective, functional managers must scan for specialized information worldwide, "cross-pollinate" leading-edge knowledge and best practice, and champion innovations that may offer transnational opportunities and applications.

Most innovation starts, of course, when managers perceive a particular opportunity or market threat, such as an emerging consumer trend, a revolutionary technological development, a bold competitive move, or a pending government regulation. When any of these flags pops up around the world, it may seem unimportant to corporate headquarters if viewed in isolation. But when a functional manager acts as a scanner, with the expertise and perspective to detect trends and move knowledge across boundaries, he or she can transform piecemeal information into strategic intelligence.

In sophisticated transnationals, senior functional executives serve as linchpins, connecting their areas of specialization throughout the organization. Using informal networks, they create channels for communicating specialized information and repositories for proprietary knowledge. Through such links, Electrolux marketing managers first identified the emergence of cross-market segments and NEC's technical managers were alerted to the shift from analog to digital switching technology.

In the same manner, Wahib Zaki of Procter & Gamble's European operations disapproved of P&G's high-walled organizational structures, which isolated and insulated the technical development carried out in each subsidiary's lab. When Zaki became head of R&D in Europe, he decided to break down some walls. In his new job, he was ideally placed to become a scanner and cross-pollinator. He formed European technical teams and ran a series of conferences in which like-minded experts from various countries could exchange information and build informal communication networks.

Still, Zaki needed more ammunition to combat the isolation, defensiveness, and "not invented here" attitude in each research center. He distributed staff among the European technical center in Brussels and the development groups of P&G's subsidiaries. He used his staff teams to help clarify the particular role of each national technical manager and to specialize activities that had been duplicated on a country-by-country basis with little transfer of accumulated knowledge.

In response to competitive threats from rivals Unilever, Henkel, and Colgate-Palmolive—and to a perceived consumer trend—P&G's European headquarters asked the Brussels-based research center to develop a new liquid laundry detergent. By that time, Zaki had on hand a technical team that had built up relationships among its members so that it formed a close-knit network of intelligence and product expertise.

The team drew the product profile necessary for healthy sales in multiple markets with diverse needs. In several European markets, powdered detergents contained enzymes to break down protein-based stains, and the new liquid detergent would have to accomplish the same thing. In some markets, a bleach substitute was important; in others, hard water presented the toughest challenge; while in several countries, environmental concerns limited the use of phosphates. Moreover, the new detergent had to be effective in large-capacity, top-loading machines, as well as in the small front-loading machines common in Europe.

Zaki's team developed a method that made enzymes stable in liquid form (a new technique that was later patented), a bleach substitute effective at low temperatures, a fatty acid that yielded good water-softening performance without phosphates, and a suds-suppressant that worked in front-loading machines (so bubbles wouldn't ooze out the door). By integrating resources and expertise, Zaki cross-pollinated best practice for a new product.

The R&D group was so successful that the European headquarters adopted the use of teams for its management of the new brand launch. P&G's first European brand team pooled the knowledge and expertise of brand managers from seven subsidiaries to draft a launch program and marketing strategy for the new liquid detergent Vizir, which ensured its triumphant rollout in seven countries in six months. P&G's homework enabled it to come up with a product that responded to European needs, while Colgate-Palmolive was forced to withdraw its liquid detergent brand, Axion—which had been designed in the United States and wasn't tailored for Europe—after an 18-month market test.

As a reward for his performance in Europe, Wahib Zaki was transferred to Procter & Gamble's Cincinnati corporate headquarters as a senior vice president of R&D. He found that researchers there were working on improved builders (the ingredients that break down dirt) for a new liquid laundry detergent to be launched in the United States. In addition, the international technology-coordination group was working with P&G's Japanese subsidiary to formulate a liquid detergent surfactant (the ingredient that removes greasy stains) that would be effective in the cold-water washes common in Japanese households, where laundry is often done in used bath water. Neither group had shared its findings or new ideas with the other, and neither had incorporated the numerous breakthroughs represented by Vizir—despite the evidence that consumer needs, market trends, competitive challenges, and regulatory requirements were all spreading across national borders.

Playing the role of champion, Zaki decided to use this development process to demonstrate the benefits of coordinating P&G's sensitivity and responsiveness to diverse consumer needs around the world. He formed a team drawn from three technical groups (one in Brussels and two in the United States) to turn out a world liquid laundry detergent. The team analyzed the trends, generated product specifications, and brought together dispersed technical knowledge and expertise, which culminated in one of Procter & Gamble's most successful product launches ever. Sold as Liquid Tide in the United States, Liquid Cheer in Japan, and Liquid Ariel in Europe, the product was P&G's first rollout on such a global scale.

As Zaki continued to strengthen cross-border technology links through other projects, Procter & Gamble gradually converted its far-flung sensing and response resources into an integrated learning organization. By scanning for new developments, cross-pollinating best practice, and championing innovations with transnational applications, Wahib Zaki, a superlative functional manager, helped create an organization that could both develop demonstrably better new products and roll them out at a rapid pace around the world.

The Corporate Manager: Leader + Talent Scout + Developer

Clearly, there is no single model for the global manager. Neither the old-line international specialist nor the more recent global generalist can cope with the complexities of cross-border strategies. Indeed, the dynamism of today's marketplace calls for managers with diverse skills. Responsibility for worldwide operations belongs to senior business, country, and functional executives who focus on the intense interchanges and subtle negotiations required. In contrast, those in middle management and front-line jobs need well-defined responsibilities, a clear understanding of their organization's transnational mission, and a sense of accountability—but few of the distractions senior negotiators must shoulder.

Meanwhile, corporate managers integrate these many levels of responsibility, playing perhaps the most vital role in transnational management. The corporate manager not only leads in the broadest sense; he or she also identifies and develops talented business, country, and functional managers—and balances the negotiations among the three. It's up to corporate managers to promote strong managerial specialists like Johansson, Gottlieb, and Zaki, those individuals who can translate company strategy into effective operations around the world.

Successful corporate managers like Floris Maljers, co-chairman of Unilever, have made the recruitment, training, and development of promising executives a top priority. By the 1980s, with Maljers as chairman, Unilever had a clear policy of rotating managers through various jobs and moving them around the world, especially early in their careers. Unilever was one of the first transnationals to have a strong pool of specialized yet interdependent senior managers, drawn from throughout its diverse organization.

But while most companies require only a few truly transnational managers to implement cross-border strategies, the particular qualities necessary for such positions remain in short supply. According to Maljers, it is this limitation in human resources—*not* unreliable or inadequate sources of capital—that has become the biggest constraint in most globalization efforts.

Locating such individuals is difficult under any circumstances, but corporate managers greatly improve the odds when their search broadens from a focus on home-country managers to incorporate the worldwide pool of executives in their organization. Because transnationals operate in many countries, they have access to a wide range of managerial talent. Yet such access—like information on local market trends or consumer needs that should cross organizational boundaries—is often an underexploited asset.

As a first step, senior executives can identify those in the organization with the potential for developing the skills and perspectives demanded of global managers. Such individuals must have a broad, nonparochial view of the company and its operations yet a deep understanding of their own business, country, or functional tasks. Obviously, even many otherwise talented managers in an organization aren't capable of such a combination of flexibility and commitment to specific interests, especially when it comes to cross-border coordination and integration. Top management may have to track the careers of promising executives over a number of years before deciding whether to give them senior responsibilities. At Unilever, for example, the company maintains four development lists that indicate both the level of each manager and his or her potential. The progress of managers on the top "A1" list is tracked by Unilever's Special Committee, which includes the two chairmen.

Once corporate managers identify the talent, they have the duty to develop it. They must provide opportunities for achievement that allow business, country, and functional managers to handle negotiations in a worldwide context. A company's ability to identify individuals with potential, legitimize their diversity, and integrate them into the organization's corporate decisions is the single clearest indicator that the corporate leader is a true global manager—and that the company itself is a true transnational.

2
Manufacturing's New Economies of Scale

Michael E. McGrath and Richard W. Hoole

In the 1990s, manufacturing companies face the challenge of globally integrating their operations. Just as companies were forced to rationalize operations within individual plants in the 1980s, they must now do the same for their entire system of manufacturing facilities around the world. Multinationals that can no longer rely on sheer size and geographic reach can still integrate far-flung plants into tightly connected, distributed production systems—and seize the opportunity for a new manufacturing scale advantage.

For years, the diverse operations of many multinationals made good business sense. At one extreme, companies manufactured products close to their customers, tailoring regional operations at scattered plants to meet local needs. Other companies chose to centralize manufacturing, offering a selection of standard, lower priced products to all of the markets they served. Yet given the current competition, which includes smaller, more focused companies as well as other multinationals, leading manufacturers must step beyond what has succeeded in the past. As our work with Xerox Corporation, Digital Equipment Corporation, Coulter Electronics, and other companies indicates, moving toward global integration is a long, involved process that begins at the top, filters down through the organization, and includes innovations across all functions.

Of course, there are no easy solutions to the need for change on such a large scale. All multinationals must grapple with their own unique problems; each must come up with its own innovations. Still, while the focus varies from company to company, many manufacturers have tried similar approaches. Some have created international teams for different functions: international design teams or commodity management teams, for example. Others have emphasized doing a critical activity only once, such as designing a core product or entering a customer order.

Regardless of the ways in which companies initiate change, one fact remains the same: multinationals *must* integrate their operations if they expect to compete in the volatile global arena. They cannot go backward to complete centralization of manufacturing, or they will lose access to essential markets. Nor can they remain a disconnected system of geographically scattered operations. With a tightly coordinated network of plants in high-cost end markets and low-cost manufacturing centers, multinationals can achieve new economies of scale and cut costs by eliminating redundant processes. But in becoming globally integrated, these same companies must balance the tension between a monolithic central authority and the need to integrate independent units. And they must focus specific changes in functions and at individual sites by articulating a vision shared by the entire organization.

First Steps: Globalizing Xerox

No multinational manufacturer can claim complete global integration, perfectly implemented, with no hitches or complaints, or provide an exact blueprint for others. However, Xerox Corporation, with its complex web of international operations, embarked on a general strategy of global integration—and affirmed it publicly—at the right time.

At the end of the 1970s, Xerox was a typical multinational. The parent company, Xerox Corporation, designed and produced products in the United States for the U.S. market; Rank Xerox, a 51%-owned Xerox company, developed products for the European market; Fuji Xerox, an equal partnership between Rank Xerox and Fuji, created products for the Japanese market; and a number of other Xerox operating companies manufactured and sold a variety of peripherals and subassemblies throughout the world.

Each Xerox company controlled its own suppliers, assembly plants, and distribution channels. Plants in Mexico, the United States, Canada, Asia, Europe, and Brazil produced according to independently set schedules, based on forecasts from each individual operating company. The managers of these scattered plants gave little thought to how each one fit into the overall production plans of Xerox Corporation and rarely communicated with each other. And since Xerox had a near monopoly on the worldwide copier market, no one, including top management at parent headquarters, felt pressured to do so.

Nevertheless, in 1981, senior managers at Xerox began to rethink the company's structure, focusing on ways to cut costs, reduce excessive inventory, and speed up product delivery. Global integration was far from a well-defined strategy at the time, and managers did not pursue it with any urgency. But they accumulated information on the benefits of moving from a collection of independent regional units to a more integrated company.

Then, as the 1980s progressed, the competitive landscape started to shift. Xerox competitors such as Canon and Ricoh penetrated the U.S. and European markets with low-cost copiers. In 1983, Xerox dominated the top ten copier companies in the world with a 57% share of revenue; just two short years later, Xerox's share had fallen to 52%. More tellingly, in 1985, Canon announced it was globalizing production of its copiers. Until that time, Canon had manufactured primarily in Japan and sold through a worldwide distribution network; it was, in effect, a typical centralized, export-oriented company. But with new design and manufacturing facilities planned for the United States and Europe, Canon transformed itself into a decentralized multinational.

As competitive pressures bore down, Xerox picked up its own pace, pursuing an explicit strategy of global integration. Exhibit I illustrates changes in operating income and revenue that reflect the company's growth. During the critical period between 1982 and 1991, Xerox made rapid innovations in many functions, which are highlighted in the time line that follows.

1982: Senior managers at Xerox realized the potential for cutting costs if the company consolidated raw material sources. They created a central purchasing group that included representatives from over a dozen of Xerox's multinational operating companies. This group of commodity managers identified and cultivated suppliers that could provide Xerox with high-quality, low-cost components on a worldwide basis. In the process, Xerox trimmed its global supply base from about 5,000 suppliers to just over 400, which now accounts for more than 90% of raw material purchases. For instance, Xerox now buys many of the lamps for its copiers from a single supplier with plants in Asia, Europe, and the United States. Because the consolidation of raw materials simplified purchasing, overhead rates have fallen from 9% of total costs for materials in 1982 to about 3% today. The result: Xerox now saves over $100 million annually on raw materials.

Exhibit I.

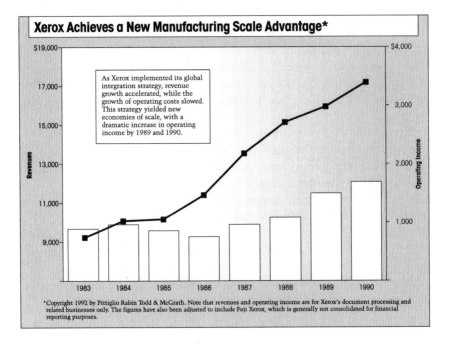

Xerox Achieves a New Manufacturing Scale Advantage*

As Xerox implemented its global integration strategy, revenue growth accelerated, while the growth of operating costs slowed. This strategy yielded new economies of scale, with a dramatic increase in operating income by 1989 and 1990.

*Copyright 1992 by Pittiglio Rabin Todd & McGrath. Note that revenues and operating income are for Xerox's document processing and related businesses only. The figures have also been adjusted to include Fuji Xerox, which is generally not consolidated for financial reporting purposes.

1983: Xerox Corporation introduced its Leadership Through Quality program to improve product quality, streamline and standardize manufacturing processes, cut costs, and increase return on assets. Senior managers recognized the power of such a program to improve communication of new management principles throughout its entire system of multinational operating companies and within the ranks of each company. Leadership Through Quality provided a common language of quality and a standard set of management practices that all of Xerox's companies now share.

1985 to 1986: Xerox instituted a new product-delivery process designed to standardize procedures. Functionally and geographically integrated teams took responsibility for introducing a new product in all major markets. Each product team managed the design, component sources, manufacturing, distribution, and follow-up customer service on a worldwide basis. One team designed a new product with universal power supplies and dual-language displays—for example, in both English and French—to eliminate the cost of reengineering for new markets at a later date. In general, using integrated teams has cut as much as one year from the overall product development cycle and saved millions of dollars.

1988: Xerox created a multinational task force to gather more specific and focused data on global integration. This task force identified three levels of integration and used them as a basis for restructuring various operations at all facilities. Xerox plants were required to (1) adopt global standards for basic processes that apply to all operations (for example, databases for managing materials); (2) maintain common business processes but, where necessary, tailor them to local needs (for example, just-in-time programs); and (3) set site-specific processes for only those systems that must conform to local needs (for example, government reporting requirements).

Information from this task force allowed top managers at Xerox to compare product cost and inventory data at different plants so they could balance production levels and improve utilization of excess inventory. Over a two-year period, these activities saved Xerox $20 million. And when Xerox initiated a common just-in-time system, it also created a worldwide council that developed a set of metrics and goals for all plants to follow. At some plants, 90% of products are now delivered on a just-in-time basis, a quantum improvement, given that less than 50% were delivered in this way in 1988.

1989: Top managers at Xerox Corporation calculated that they could eliminate $1 billion in inventory and $200 million in inventory-related costs by linking customer orders more closely with production. They formed a multinational organization called Central Logistics and Asset Management (CLAM) and four multifunctional, product-focused teams to integrate the supply chain across geographic boundaries. The aim of CLAM is to base individual plant production levels on customer orders and to reduce excess inventory. One team developed a new process that took more than a month out of the production forecasting cycle. And Xerox has now reduced its worldwide inventories by $500 million.

1990: Xerox introduced its 5100 copier, the first product jointly designed for a worldwide market by Fuji Xerox and Xerox Corporation engineers. The 5100, manufactured in U.S. plants, was launched in Japan in November 1990 and in the United States the following February. Before that time, Xerox had never introduced a major product in two distinct markets so quickly.

In the past, the unique needs of the Japanese market, such as lighter weight paper, common use of blue pencils, and difficulties in copying *kanji* characters, meant separate product development programs for

Western and Asian markets. That, in turn, meant products developed in this fashion required reengineering for other markets. However, Xerox assembled a team of Japanese and American engineers to design the 5100 copier from concept to finished drawings. The design team also received feedback from customer groups in the United States, Europe, and Japan. The 5100's global design process reduced overall time-to-market and saved the company more than $10 million in development costs.

1991: Xerox began integrating its product delivery activities. A CLAM team and several operating groups created a Western Hemisphere distribution center for spare parts, consolidating safety stocks previously held independently for the U.S., Canadian, and Latin American markets. Once again, such integration of operations saved Xerox several million dollars annually.

The Five Basics: Focusing Change

Xerox Corporation evolved its global-integration strategies over time and, to some extent, by trial and error. Realistically, changes at most multinationals do not happen neatly or in a fixed sequence. Similar small innovations may spark at the same time in several operating companies: automating certain parts of the manufacturing process, for example, or processing customer orders in a new way.

While there is no fixed starting point for globally integrating an organization, managers, both at the top and in individual operations, should begin with focused projects that address specific problems. It makes sense to focus first on a part of the organization where immediate and substantive improvement is possible. Xerox began its global-integration process in purchasing raw materials because management decided that was where it could make the most immediate and greatest gains.

The starting point might be in any of what we call the "five basics": product development, purchasing, production, demand management, or order fulfillment. The following sections provide suggestions for integrating each function and, while not definitive, show the range of possibilities.

PRODUCT DEVELOPMENT. Designing products once and only once for the global market benefits companies in a number of important ways. Such a design process can eliminate costly, after-the-fact redesigns every time a company wants to enter a new market with a particular product. And combining this new process with international design teams can turn a multinational's scattered operations into a competitive advantage.

Each development project should revolve around the design of a core product, including the capacity for design variations and derivatives tailored to meet the needs of local markets. In some cases, companies have included derivative designs in software or a "country kit" that contains items such as preprogrammed memory chips, labels, documentation, and special power cords. In other cases, extra elements must be included in the core product so it can pass the regulatory requirements of specific countries. Often the cost of overdesigning a product to begin with is lower than that of redesigning the product later to meet idiosyncratic specifications in different countries. For example, one electronics company designs all of its products with additional shielding to prevent damage from liquid spills, even though only the United Kingdom and a few other European countries require such protection.

Creating international design teams is another crucial part of globalizing product development. If members of a product design team are located all over the world rather than clustered at a central site, each designer can monitor local tastes, technical standards, and changing government regulations. Designers in the field can also stay abreast of local technology developments and gain quicker access to competitors' products.

Of course, the global distribution of a design team introduces communication problems. But a good communications system, a necessary component of any world-class global enterprise, makes these problems manageable. For example, Digital Equipment Corporation, a pioneer in computer networking, created an electronic-mail network that links 100,000 employees worldwide. That means an engineer in Shrewsbury, Massachusetts can ask for help on a technical problem relating to disk-drive technology by typing a quick e-mail message. Within 24 hours, she may receive responses from fellow designers around the world that detail possible solutions. DEC estimates that the use of this application has contributed to a twofold reduction in product development time since 1988.

PURCHASING. Economies of scale in purchasing come from consolidating raw material sources and paring down a company's supplier base. By purchasing on a global instead of a local basis, companies have the freedom to choose the best suppliers in the world, no matter where their operations are located. And because global contracts are often significantly larger than local ones, suppliers can offer buyers more favorable unit costs and delivery schedules. Some suppliers may even agree to set up local operations for a buyer if the contract is big enough.

To integrate purchasing, companies can create commodity management teams for all important materials. Commodity management teams select suppliers around the world and monitor their performance. Local plant-materials managers can execute the purchase orders and oversee daily supply flow. As for low-volume, low-cost commodities (particularly those with high transportation costs), individual plant staff can manage them based on local needs.

Each commodity management team is responsible for setting the cost, quality, and lead-time performance of the appropriate worldwide suppliers. Team members can be located anywhere in the world, although they must operate as a single group and make decisions for the company as a whole. Teams should include members from purchasing, engineering, finance, and quality assurance so that, as a group, they have the necessary expertise to identify world-class suppliers and ensure that the company gets the best performance for its money.

For example, Coulter Electronics, which produces medical electronics equipment, created commodity management teams that included representatives from all five of its plants. Early on, the semiconductor commodity team found that the company could consolidate half of all semiconductors it purchased into a few large contracts, saving more than $1 million a year. In another instance, the team discovered that the same three-way solenoid valve cost $20.87 in France, $17.50 in the United Kingdom, and $10.54 in the United States. By consolidating the purchasing of this valve, Coulter saved over $100,000 annually.

PRODUCTION. To take advantage of their larger capacity and geographic diversity, multinational manufacturers must streamline the flow of inventory between plants. That means coordinating production of components in low-cost manufacturing centers with final assembly in high-cost locations close to customers. Mass producing component parts in Chinese or Malaysian plants, for example, can clearly cut production costs for a multinational. However, operating final assembly plants in places such as the United States or Germany is also essential for a number of reasons; for example, shipping the assembled product may be prohibitively expensive. In some instances, customers identify more closely with a company that has manufacturing facilities in their own country. In addition, many governments levy lower duties if final assembly is done locally; or they may require local assembly to sell products in that market, as in Brazil.

Of course, many companies are unable to coordinate existing production facilities after years of rapid and often haphazard expansion. While new ventures, acquisitions, or mergers may lead to new markets, they may also leave a manufacturer with too much uncoordinated worldwide capacity in locations that make little strategic sense. And because the age and type of capital equipment varies from plant to plant, the quality and cost of each plant's global production also varies.

Managers can begin restructuring production by analyzing how materials flow from plant to plant. Coordinating and simplifying materials flow requires two things: (1) balancing production *vertically* within the production pipeline, from component manufacturing to final assembly; and (2) balancing production *horizontally* between plants that manufacture the same or similar products.

Balancing production vertically requires tightening the connection between scattered final assembly, subassembly, and component plants. We have found that creating a global system analogous to single-plant, just-in-time inventory management ensures the tightest connection. To do this, companies should first take their end-product forecasts and communicate general requirements to all plants at all levels in the production process. Each plant can use these forecasts for capacity and materials planning. Then, operating in parallel, real customer orders become the "pull signals" for the upstream plant in the system to produce necessary components. But while a pull signal in a single plant is often a physical signal (an empty kanban bin, for instance), in a global system with multiple production facilities the signal probably would be an electronic message sent over a computer network.

Horizontal balancing, on the other hand, requires central coordination of plants that handle the same step in the manufacturing process, such as production of a particular component or final assembly. Because the same products are often manufactured by different plants in an organization, horizontal balancing involves assigning production based on cost, plant capacity, technical capabilities, availability of materials, and closeness to the customer.

For example, one company operates final assembly plants in two countries, each with dedicated metal-fabrication facilities that in the past manufactured many identical parts. One fabrication shop's outdated equipment produced complex turned parts very inefficiently.

The other shop produced them quite efficiently, but because its skilled laborers received higher wages, its costs for manufacturing simple sheet-metal parts were far above the first shop's. By reallocating production—such as assigning more complex turned parts to the plant with highly paid, skilled workers—the company capitalized on the strengths of both shops and saved almost $1 million annually.

DEMAND MANAGEMENT. Managers use marketing and sales forecasts—the core of demand management—to set sales quotas, plan production schedules and inventory requirements, negotiate supplier contracts, and establish corporate revenue plans. If for no other reason than demand management, a sophisticated global forecasting system is necessary. Companies must gather information on the local level, integrate it into a central system, and then distribute the consolidated data back to all local operations.

However, before investing in a technical solution, management should first understand how the company uses current demand forecasts to set production. The biggest problem many multinationals face is that demand forecasting is a politically charged process. From central headquarters, which may be halfway around the world from the company's manufacturing facilities, senior managers set the annual forecast at the beginning of each fiscal year. This is then handed down to manufacturing operations to use for scheduling production. But because the forecast is also used by Wall Street analysts as a baseline for evaluating the company's performance, senior managers frown on any deviations from the plan. So if customer orders begin to fall, but production levels remain the same to meet corporate expectations, inventory accumulates and manufacturing managers are blamed. In fact, official adjustments to production forecasts often take months to make.

To address the problem, manufacturing managers should have the authority to adjust production levels to reflect actual orders. Over the last few years, Xerox has reengineered its global demand management process with this change in mind. Today teams of production planners and demand analysts at each operating company meet weekly to review production of each product family and adjust production and inventory levels. Each team uses an interactive modeling system that graphically displays historical and projected customer demand, production output, and inventory levels, including relevant data from other related Xerox companies.

These demand management teams have the experience to make informed decisions on production changes and the authority to implement them, which has shaved weeks and even months off production planning times. In one case, a quick change in a plant's production schedule of copiers saved $100,000 in inventory and freight costs.

ORDER FULFILLMENT. To gain a new scale advantage in order fulfillment, companies must focus on coordinating customer orders with distribution at the global level. The result is more efficient order management, a decrease in total finished goods inventories, and quicker, more direct delivery. Companies should strive to cut all unnecessary warehousing and transportation of finished products on their way to customers. Ideally, orders are linked to the most appropriate factory, which then ships the product directly to the customer.

Companies can move toward this goal by first creating a globally networked order management system that keeps track of where different products are made, how they can be configured, where the customer is located, and how products are priced in different markets. In addition, the system assigns product automatically to a plant close to the customer. And by electronically transmitting, validating, pricing, and scheduling an order, the company can cut significant time out of the entire fulfillment cycle.

Take, for example, the complex order fulfillment problems of Digital Equipment Corporation, which must bundle a unique set of components—computer platforms, displays, printers, storage units, and communications equipment—that are manufactured by a variety of plants around the world and then ship a single, complete package to the customer. Just a few years ago, DEC's unwieldy fulfillment system involved endless negotiations between individual plants and distribution centers that added time and expense to each delivery.

Now DEC has simplified the process: the goal is to enter an order only once. Order processors use an expert system to configure each product, then coordinate production and shipment of each part to one of DEC's new consolidation centers. Even before the component parts arrive, employees at the consolidation center prepare the shipping documents and schedule a carrier for final delivery. The new process reduces the number of transactions, streamlines the distribution flow, considerably improves delivery time, and increases the accuracy of orders—and customer satisfaction.

Setting the Stage for Global Integration

Specific functional changes each contribute to a new scale advantage: flexible products, reduced costs, simplified manufacturing processes, realistic planning based on demand, or better customer service. But once a multinational acknowledges the need for global integration, the ultimate goal should be to make changes in all five basics.

Obviously, this is not a simple task. Rationalizing every scattered facility and operation as part of a coherent whole and establishing new systems may take years to accomplish, especially for a large multinational. While Xerox, DEC, and other innovative companies have integrated some systems, even they are still in the early stages. We recognize that change often happens by fits and starts and doesn't always spring from an overarching vision. Still, companies can use three general guidelines to set the stage for global integration and drive the first changes in the right direction.

1. Affirm a global manufacturing mission. The manufacturing strategy must support the company's global business strategy and be consistent across all facilities. However tautological this statement sounds, it rarely holds. At some companies, regional operations often set their own manufacturing priorities, and corporate management has little power to coordinate their strategies. At other companies, there is no formal manufacturing strategy at all, only a series of manufacturing decisions made at different times and under different conditions in the company's history. In both cases, the end result is a poor match between manufacturing strategy and business strategy.

To align the two strategies, top management should analyze existing plants, including their location, capacity, the range of products they produce, and the ability and willingness of their managers to communicate with each other. Studying the manufacturing infrastructure in the context of a worldwide business strategy can point up glaring weaknesses and provide a foundation for a meaningful manufacturing mission.

But creating the manufacturing mission is only the first step. Senior management must *publicly* declare its commitment to global integration, outlining to employees, customers, and suppliers the vision it holds for the company. In this way, everyone understands the context for any and all changes that follow.

In 1990, Gaynor Kelley, chairman of Perkin-Elmer Corporation, issued a call to become "one company, global yet compact, coordinated, efficient." His company plan, which was distributed to all employees, is an outline for shifting Perkin-Elmer's focus away from optimizing each plant's manufacturing assets toward the coordination of all plants.

Similarly, in early 1991, NEC Corporation's president Tadahiro Sekimoto publicly announced plans for globally integrating the company. "Until a few years ago," he said, "we expanded through linear globalization, with control flowing from Tokyo to overseas units. Now we are pursuing *mesh globalism*, which means decentralized but still connected." Companies such as NEC have not only recognized the need for "mesh globalism" but also the fact that integration cannot happen without the knowledge and support of everyone involved.

2. Develop a profile of capabilities. Senior managers must first understand the strengths and weaknesses of the existing manufacturing structure. They must have a realistic idea of what capabilities the company still needs and where to focus attention first before they can draft a specific plan of action.

Any inventory of requisite capabilities should begin with an effective communications and information processing system. Teleconferencing equipment, electronic mail, electronic data interchange, distributed computing, and multivendor connectivity are all essential to tie facilities together. In fact, since achieving a new scale advantage depends on quick and accurate communication between far-flung plants, top managers should make compatibility of computer and communications equipment a corporate priority.

Of course, well-connected facilities are useless if employees don't understand each other. Creating a common management "language"—a universal set of management practices and measurement systems—is also crucial. At Xerox, for example, the Leadership Through Quality program set the stage for the company's global networking efforts.

As a company evolves its information network and improves its global communication skills, it should also evaluate how to rationalize operations, but on a global rather than single-plant basis. For instance, by benchmarking its capabilities against the competition, a company can identify performance gaps. Managers then use this information to set aggressive goals for improving capabilities.

More important, benchmarking not only provides information on the product or plant level but also illuminates strengths and weaknesses at the corporate level. One international electronics company benchmarked its plants by function (purchasing, logistics, manufacturing) along a number of critical dimensions (customer satisfaction, product and process quality, cost) and uncovered several performance gaps. But in the process, management found that several plants had extremely efficient manufacturing processes. At the time, there was no mechanism for transferring such expertise to other plants. However, by identifying successes, the company could then focus on transforming the manufacturing process throughout the organization rather than just addressing specific performance gaps.

This company has now set up a database that includes information on all plants, organized by 250 separate performance measures. Top management actively encourages individual plant managers to use the database to compare their facility's performance with others in the organization and share knowledge of the most successful practices.

3. Identify options, pick a plan of action, and target specific results. The most immediate, nuts-and-bolts issues senior managers will address are redeployment of plants and equipment and the reengineering of critical processes. Managers must decide which plants to close immediately and which ones to target for expansion. They must determine which manufacturing processes require reengineering and which ones can continue as they are.

One large capital equipment manufacturer, for example, considered the entire range of choices for restructuring its five plants, from total centralization to total decentralization. It developed a model for all options, which included the impact of each location on local sales volume and the company's cost structure over time. The company also included the effects of varying 11 critical functions in each scenario it studied. For instance, management looked at what product development process would work best in a system of four manufacturing plants as compared with a system of two, weighing the costs and the benefits of each scenario. While time consuming, this company's analysis produced a final plan that was widely supported across the organization.

Of course, once a company has selected a plan of action, it must also get quick, highly visible results. Even though change is a long-term process, management needs to demonstrate progress in the short term. Otherwise, its larger mission may fail, given the competitive marketplace. Coulter Electronics started coordinating its worldwide purchasing by setting up a simple, PC-driven database. The system was up and running within a few months at minimal expense and paved the way for other fundamental organizational improvements in purchasing.

In fact, a company can target specific results in any of the five basic functions to establish early victories, set the stage, and build momentum for the ultimate goal: a fully integrated global manufacturing system. Taken one step further, a multinational's new scale advantage will come from increased interaction *across* functions. When companies globalize the design process, for example, they may also create products that are easier to manufacture. And when companies globalize purchasing, manufacturing is no longer tied to a specific plant, and designers are not limited by local suppliers.

A multinational of the future, fully integrated yet still flexible, may supply its component plants with raw materials from a single source; standardize the manufacturing process in its British, German, and American final assembly plants; enter customer orders into a worldwide order fulfillment system so that products are assembled in and distributed from the most convenient site; and install a sophisticated electronic network that links product designers, demand analysts, and production planners at all facilities. Companies like this will rationalize operations from a global perspective, even if it means making hard and initially costly decisions, such as laying off workers at one plant in Tennessee to expand another in Brazil.

Those multinational manufacturers that successfully coordinate and balance their global resources will evolve into stronger, more responsive companies, better able to cut costs and serve their customers around the world. And multinationals of all sizes that integrate their operations—and achieve a new manufacturing scale advantage—will control the competition today and in the future.

3
The Global Logic of Strategic Alliances

Kenichi Ohmae

Companies are just beginning to learn what nations have always known: in a complex, uncertain world filled with dangerous opponents, it is best not to go it alone. Great powers operating across broad theaters of engagement have traditionally made common cause with others whose interests ran parallel with their own. No shame in that. Entente—the striking of an alliance—is a responsible part of every good strategist's repertoire. In today's competitive environment, this is also true for corporate managers.

But managers have been slow to experiment with genuinely strategic alliances. A joint venture here and there, yes, of course. A long-term contractual relationship, certainly. But the forging of entente, rarely. A real alliance compromises the fundamental independence of economic actors, and managers don't like that. After all, for them, management has come to mean total control. Alliances mean sharing control. The one precludes the other.

In stable competitive environments, this allergy to loss of control exacts little penalty. Not so, however, in a changeable world of rapidly globalizing markets and industries—a world of converging consumer tastes, rapidly spreading technology, escalating fixed costs, and growing protectionism. I'd go further. Globalization mandates alliances, makes them absolutely essential to strategy. Uncomfortable, perhaps—but that's the way it is. Like it or not, the simultaneous developments that go under the name of globalization make alliances—entente—necessary.

Why, then, the reluctance of so many companies either to experiment with alliances or to stick with them long enough to learn how to make them work? To some extent, both foot dragging and early exit are born of fear—fear that the alliance will turn out to be a Trojan horse that affords potential competitors easy access to home markets. But there is also an impression that alliances represent, at best, a convenience, a quick-and-dirty means of entry into foreign markets. These attitudes make managers skittish and impatient.

Unless you understand the long-run strategic value of entente, you will grow frustrated when it proves—as it must—not to be a cheap and easy way of responding to the uncertainties of globalization. If you expect more of your partners than is reasonable, you will blame them too quickly when things do not go as planned. Chances are your impatience will make you much less tolerant of them than you would be of your own subsidiary overseas.

When you expect convenience, you rarely have much patience for the messy and demanding work of building a strong competitive position. Nor do you remember all the up-front overseas investments that you did *not* have to make. And without memory or patience, you risk precipitating exactly what you fear most: an unhappy or unsatisfied partner that decides to bow out of the alliance and try to tackle your markets on its own.

Alliances are not tools of convenience. They are important, even critical, instruments of serving customers in a global environment. Glaxo, the British pharmaceutical company, for example, did not want to establish a full business system in each country where it did business. Especially given its costly commitment to topflight R&D, it did not see how it could—or why it should—build an extensive sales and service network to cover all the hospitals in Japan and the United States. So it decided to link up with first-class partners in Japan, swap its best drugs with them, and focus its own resources on generating greater sales from its established network in Europe. *That* kind of value creation and delivery is what alliances make possible.

Few companies operating in the Triad of Japan, the United States, and Europe can offer such topflight levels of value to all their customers all the time all by themselves. They need partners. They need entente. They might wish things were otherwise. But deep down they know better. Or they should.

The Californiazation of Need

To understand why alliances are a necessity and not just a fad or a fashion, you first have to understand *why* globalization makes them essential as vehicles for customer-oriented value.

The explanation begins with a central, demonstrable fact: the convergence of consumer needs and preferences. Whatever their nationality, consumers in the Triad increasingly receive the same information, seek the same kinds of life-styles, and desire the same kinds of products. They all want the best products available, at the lowest prices possible. Everyone, in a sense, wants to live—and shop—in California.

Economic nationalism flourishes during election campaigns and infects what legislatures do and what particular interest groups ask for. But when individuals vote with their pocketbooks—when they walk into a store or showroom anywhere in the Triad—they leave behind the rhetoric and the mudslinging and the trappings of nationalism.

Do you write with a Waterman or a Mont Blanc pen or travel with a Vuitton suitcase because of national sentiments? Of course not. It does not matter if you live in Europe or Japan or the United States. You buy these pens or pieces of luggage because they represent the kind of value that you're looking for.

At the cash register, you don't care about country of origin or country of residence. You don't think about employment figures or trade deficits. You don't worry about where the product was made. It does not matter to you that a "British" sneaker by Reebok (now an American-owned company) was made in Korea, a German sneaker by Adidas in Taiwan, or a French ski by Rossignol in Spain. All you care about is the product's quality, price, design, value, and appeal to you as a consumer.

This is just as true for industrial customers. The market for IBM computers or Toshiba laptops is not defined by geographic borders but by the inherent appeal of the product to users, regardless of where they live. And with the proliferation of trade journals, trade shows, and electronic data bases, users have regular access to the same sources of product information.

Chip makers buy Nikon steppers because they are the best, not because they are made by a Japanese company. Manufacturers buy Tralfa industrial robots for the same reason and not because they happen to be Norwegian. The same goes for robots made by DeVilbiss in the United States. Companies around the world use IBM's MRP and CIM systems to shorten production times and cut work-in-process. Because of the demands of contemporary production modes, they use Fujitsu Fanuc's machine tools made in Japan. In fact, this one company dominates the numerically controlled (NC) machine-tool market worldwide: its market share in Japan is 70%; around the globe, 50%. This is neither accident nor fashion. These NC machines deliver value, and everyone knows it. But the national identity of these products has effectively disappeared.

The Dispersion of Technology

Today's products rely on so many different critical technologies that most companies can no longer maintain cutting-edge sophistication in all of them. The business software that made IBM PCs such an instant hit—1-2-3—was not, of course, an IBM product. It was a creation of Lotus Development Corporation. Most of the components in the popular-priced IBM PC itself were outsourced as well. IBM simply could not have developed the machine in anywhere near the time it did if it had tried to keep it 100% proprietary. In fact, the heart of IBM's accomplishment with the PC lay precisely in its decision—and its ability—to approach the development effort as a process of managing multiple external vendors.

Lotus provided applications software, and Microsoft wrote the operating system on an Intel microprocessor. Of course, Lotus, Microsoft, and Intel don't want to sell only to IBM. Naturally, they want to sell their products to as wide a range of customers as possible. Just as IBM needs to rely on an army of external vendors, so each vendor needs to sell to a broad array of customers. The inevitable result is the rapid dispersion of technology. No one company can do it all, simultaneously. No one company can keep all the relevant technologies in-house, as General Motors did during the 1930s and 1940s. And that means no one can truly keep all critical technologies out of the hands of competitors around the globe.

Even original equipment manufacturers with captive technology are not immune to this dispersion. NEC may develop a state-of-the-art memory chip for its own mainframes, but it can sell five times the volume to other computer makers. This generates cash, lowers unit costs, and builds up the experience needed to push the technology still further. It also gets them better information about its products: external customers provide tougher feedback than do internal divisions. To be a world-class producer, NEC must provide the best new technology to global customers.

In short order, the technology becomes generally available, making time even more of a critical element in global strategy. Nothing stays proprietary for long. And no one player can master everything. Thus, operating globally means operating with partners—and that in turn means a further spread of technology.

The Importance of Fixed Costs

The convergence of customer need, together with this relentless dispersion of technology, has changed the logic by which managers have to steer. In the past, for example, you tried to build sustainable competitive advantage by establishing dominance in all of your business system's critical areas. You created barriers to entry where you could, locked away market share whenever possible, and used every bit of proprietary expertise, every collection of nonreplicable assets to shore up the wall separating you from competitors. The name of the game in most industries was simply beating the competition. If you discovered an ounce of advantage, you strengthened it with a pound of proprietary skill or knowledge. Then you used it to support the defensive wall you were building against competitors.

The forces of globalization turn this logic on its head. You can't meet the value-based needs of customers in the Triad entirely on your own. You can't do without the technology and skills of others. You can't even keep your own technology to yourself for very long. Having a superior technology is important, of course, but it is not sufficient to guarantee success in the market. Meeting customer needs is the key— no matter what the source of the technology. No wall you erect stands tall. No door you slam stays shut. And no road you follow is inexpensive.

To compete in the global arena, you have to incur—and somehow find a way to defray—immense fixed costs. You can't play a variable-cost game any more. You need partners who can help you amortize your fixed costs, and with them you need to define strategies that allow you to maximize the contribution to your fixed costs.

The evidence for this lesson is overwhelming. As automation has driven the labor content out of production, manufacturing has increasingly become a fixed-cost activity. And because the cost of developing breakthrough ideas and turning them into marketable products has skyrocketed, R&D has become a fixed cost too. In pharmaceuticals, for instance, when it takes $50 million or more to come up with an effective new drug, R&D is no longer a variable-cost game. And you can't count on being able to license a new drug—a variable cost—from companies not operating in your primary markets. Not unless you have your own proprietary drug to offer in return. With globalization, all major players in your industry are—or may become—direct competitors. You can't be sure in advance that they (or you) will want to share a particular piece of technology. You need partners, but you need your own people and your own labs too. That's fixed cost.

In much the same way, building and maintaining a brand name is a fixed cost. For many products, a brand name has no value at all if brand recognition falls below certain levels. When a company decides to buy a paper copier, for example, it usually calls up two or three producers in the order of their brand familiarity. If your copier is not among them, you don't even get a chance to try to sell your product. You simply *have* to be there to enjoy a high level of awareness among customers. And that means you have to pay for the privilege.

Trying to save money on brand promotion makes no sense if what you're selling is a consumer "pull" product: you spend a little money but not enough to realize any "pull" benefits. And a half-baked, half-supported brand is worse than no brand at all. With some products, you can better use the same money to enhance commissions so that the sales force will push them. In branded competition, if you want to play, you have to ante up the fixed costs of doing so.

The past decade has seen a comparable movement toward fixed costs in sales and distribution networks. Sure, you can try to play the variable-cost game by going through dealers. You can, at least, to an extent. But your sales force still has to provide the support, the training, and the manuals. And all these are fixed costs.

You can also try to make some of these costs variable on your own. You can chase low-cost labor, for example, by moving production to developing countries, but that won't get you very far these days. In the past, you could make costs variable with your computers and management information systems by time-sharing. But experience has shown that you can't use time-sharing if you want a system that's dedicated to your own needs, a system capable of providing competitive advantage. So today, information technology is pretty much a fixed cost. Over the long term, of course, all these fixed costs become variable through adjustments in investment (capital expenditure) levels. But for the short term, they remain fixed. And the need to bolster contribution to them points in a single, clear direction: toward the forging of alliances to share fixed costs.

This is a fundamental change from the competitive world of 15 or even 10 years ago. And it demands a new logic for management action. In a variable-cost environment, the primary focus for managers is on boosting profits by reducing the cost of materials, wages, labor hours. In a fixed-cost environment, the focus switches to maximizing marginal contribution to fixed cost—that is, to boosting sales.

This new logic forces managers to amortize their fixed costs over a much larger market base—and this adds yet more fuel to the drive toward globalization. It also forces managers to rethink their strategies as they search for ways to maximize contribution to these fixed costs. Finally, this logic mandates entente—alliances that both enable and facilitate global, contribution-based strategies.

In practice, this means that if you don't have to invest in your own overseas sales force, you don't do it. If you run a pharmaceutical company with a good drug to distribute in Japan but no sales force to do it, find someone in Japan who also has a good product but no sales force in your country. You get double the profit by putting two strong drugs through your fixed-cost sales network, and so does your new ally. Why duplicate such huge expenses all down the line? Why go head-to-head? Why not join forces to maximize contribution to each other's fixed costs?

Maximizing the contribution to fixed costs does not come naturally. Tradition and pride make companies want to be the best at everything, to do everything themselves. But companies can no longer afford this solitary stance. Take the machine-tool market. If a German manufacturer clearly excels in custom-made segments, why should highly automated Japanese producers like Mori Seiki and Yamazaki tackle those segments too? Why not tie up with the Germans and let them dominate those segments worldwide? Why not try to supply them with certain common components that you can make better—or more cheaply—than they do? Why not disaggregate the product and the business system and put together an alliance that delivers the most value to customers while making the greatest contribution to both partners' fixed costs?

Why not do this? Companyism gets in the way. So does a competitor-focused approach to strategy. So does not knowing what it takes to operate globally and how alliances help with fixed costs. Managers must overcome these obstacles. And that will not happen by chance.

Dangers of Equity

Global alliances are not the only valid mechanisms for boosting contribution to fixed costs. A strong brand umbrella can always cover additional products. You can always give heightened attention to, say, an expensive distribution system that you've already built in Japan or Europe. And there is always the possibility of buying a foreign company. Experience shows, however, that you should look hard—and early—at forging alliances. In a world of imperfect options, they are often the fastest, least risky, and most profitable way to go global.

You can expand brands and build up distribution yourself—you can do everything yourself—with enough time, money, and luck. But all three are in short supply. In particular, you simply do not have the time to establish new markets one-by-one throughout the Triad. The "cascade" model of expansion no longer works. Today you have to be in all important markets simultaneously if you are going to keep competitors from establishing their positions. Globalization will not wait. You need alliances and you need them now. But not the traditional kind.

In the past, companies commonly approached international expansion by doing it on their own, acquiring others, or establishing joint ventures. Now, the latter two approaches carry important equity-related concerns. Let equity—the classic instrument of capitalism—into the picture, and you start to worry about control and return on investment. There is pressure to get money back fast for the money you put in and dividends from the paper you hold.

It's a reflex. The analysts expect it of you. So do the business press, colleagues, and stockholders. They'll nod politely when you talk about improved sales or long-term strategic benefits. But what everybody really wants in short order is chart-topping ROI.

No one's going to argue that dividends aren't nice to tuck in your pocket. Of course they are. But the pressure to put them there can wreak havoc with your initial goals, especially if they include competing successfully in global markets by maximizing the contribution to fixed costs.

Managers must also overcome the popular misconception that total control increases chances of success. Companies that have enjoyed successful joint ventures for years can have things quickly go sour when they move to a literal, equity- and contract-based mode of ownership. Naturally, details vary with the particular case, but the slide into disarray and disappointment usually starts with the typical arguments that broke up one transnational chemical joint venture:

(Soon-To-Be) New Owner: You guys never make decisions in time.

(Soon-To-Be) Former Partner: Speedy decisions are not everything. Consensus is more important.

NO: Well, just tell the dealers that our products are the best in the world. Tell them that they sell everywhere except here.

FP: But the dealers complain that your products are just okay, not great. Even worse, they are not really tailored to the needs or aesthetic preferences of local customers.

NO: Nonsense. What customers buy, everywhere in the world, is the physical performance of the product. No one matches us in performance.

FP: Perhaps. Still, the dealers report that your products are not neatly packaged and often have scratches on the surface.

NO: But that has no effect on performance.

FP: Tell that to the dealers. They say they cannot readily see—or sell—the performance difference you're talking about, so they have to fall back on aesthetics, where your products are weak. We'll have to reduce price.

NO: Don't you dare. We succeeded in the United States and in Europe by keeping our prices at least 5% above those of our competitors. If we're having trouble in Japan it's because of you. Your obvious lack of effort, knowledge, even confidence in our products—that's what keeps them from selling. Besides, your parent keeps on sending our joint venture group a bunch of bumbling old incompetents for managers. We rarely get the good people. Maybe the idea is to kill off our relationships entirely so they can start up a unit of their own making imitation products.

FP: Well, if you feel that way, there is not much point in our continuing on together.

NO: Glad you said that. We'll buy up the other 50% of the equity and go it on our own.

FP: Good luck. By the way, how many Japanese-speaking managers do you have in your company—that is, after we pull out all the "bumbling old incompetents" from our joint venture?

NO: None. But don't worry. We'll just hire a bunch of headhunters and get started up in record time.

This is a disaster waiting—no, rushing—to happen. Back when this arrangement was a functioning joint venture, however, both partners, and especially the middle managers, really made an effort to have things work. Under a cloud of 100% control, things are different. You can buy a company's equity, but you cannot buy the mind or the spirit or the initiative or the devotion of its people. Nor can you just go hire replacements. In different environments, the availability of key professional services—managerial, legal, and so on—varies considerably.

The lesson is painful but inescapable: having control does not necessarily mean a better managed company. You cannot manage a global company through control. In fact, control is the last resort. It's what you fall back on when everything else fails and you're willing to risk the demoralization of workers and managers.

This need for control is deeply rooted. The tradition of Western capitalism lies behind it, a tradition that has long taught managers the dangerously incorrect arithmetic that equates 51% with 100% and 49% with 0%. Yes, of course, 51% buys you full legal control. But it is control of activities in a foreign market, about which you may know little as you sit far removed from the needs of customers in your red-carpeted office in Manhattan, Tokyo, or Frankfurt.

When Americans and Europeans come to Japan, they all want 51%. That's the magic number because it ensures majority position and control over personnel, brand decisions, and investment choices. But good partnerships, like good marriages, don't work on the basis of ownership or control. It takes effort and commitment and enthusiasm from both sides if either is to realize the hoped-for benefits. You cannot own a successful partner any more than you can own a husband or a wife.

In time, as the relationship between partners deepens and as mutual trust and confidence build, there may come a point when it no longer makes sense to remain two separate entities. Strategy, values, and culture might all match up so well that both sides want to finish the work of combination. Hewlett-Packard's presence in Japan started out in 1963, for example, as a 51-49 joint venture with Yokogawa Electric. Over two decades, enough confidence had built up that in 1983, Yokogawa Electric gave Hewlett-Packard another 24%.

The point is, it took two decades for Hewlett-Packard to reach a significant ownership position. Control was never the objective. All along, the objective was simply to do things right and serve customers well by learning how to operate as a genuine insider in Japan. As a result, Hewlett-Packard now owns 75% of a $750 million company in Japan that earns 6.6% net profit after tax.

An emphasis on control through equity, however, immediately poisons the relationship. Instead of focusing on contribution to fixed costs, one company imperialistically tells the other, "Look, I've got a big equity stake in you. You don't give me all the dividends I want, so get busy and distribute my product. I'm not going to distribute yours, though. Remember, you work for me."

This kind of attitude problem prevents the development of intercompany management skills, which are critical for success in today's

Exhibit I.

ICL's Do's for Successful Collaboration

1. Treat the collaboration as a personal commitment. It's people that make partnerships work.

2. Anticipate that it will take up management time. If you can't spare the time, don't start it.

3. Mutual respect and trust are essential. If you don't trust the people you are negotiating with, forget it.

4. Remember that both partners must get something out of it (money, eventually). Mutual benefit is vital. This will probably mean you've got to give something up. Recognize this from the outset.

5. Make sure you tie up a tight legal contract. Don't put off resolving unpleasant or contentious issues until "later." Once signed, however, the contract should be put away. If you refer to it, something is wrong with the relationship.

6. Recognize that during the course of a collaboration, circumstances and markets change. Recognize your partner's problems and be flexible.

7. Make sure you and your partner have mutual expectations of the collaboration and its time scale. One happy and one unhappy partner is a formula for failure.

8. Get to know your opposite numbers at all levels socially. Friends take longer to fall out.

9. Appreciate that cultures—both geographic and corporate—are different. Don't expect a partner to act or respond identically to you. Find out the true reason for a particular response.

10. Recognize your partner's interests and independence.

11. Even if the arrangement is tactical in your eyes, make sure you have corporate approval. Your tactical activity may be a key piece in an overall strategic jigsaw puzzle. With corporate commitment to the partnership, you can act with the positive authority needed in these relationships.

12. Celebrate achievement together. It's a shared elation, and you'll have earned it!

Postscript
Two further things to bear in mind:
1. If you're negotiating a product OEM deal, look for a quid pro quo. Remember that another product may offer more in return.

2. Joint development agreements must include joint marketing arrangements. You need the largest market possible to recover development costs and to get volume/margin benefits.

global environment. But these skills must be learned. Peter L. Bonfield, chairman and managing director of International Computers Ltd., has a plastic name-card holder that he distributes to all his people who are in touch with Fujitsu, ICL's mainframe computer partner in Japan. On one side there is a place for the cards; on the other, a proven list of "Do's" for making such collaborative arrangements work. (See Exhibit I.) Nothing here about 51% or establishing control.

Equity by itself is not the problem in building successful alliances. In Japan, we have a lot of "group companies," known as *keiretsu*, where an equity stake of, say, 3% to 5% keeps both partners interested in each other's welfare without threatening either's autonomy. Stopping that far short of a controlling position keeps the equity holder from treating the other company as if it were a subsidiary. Small equity investments like these may be the way to go.

Joint ventures may also work, but there are two obstacles that can trip them up. First, there is a contract, and contracts—even at their best—can only reflect an understanding of costs and markets and technologies at the moment companies sign them. When things change, as they always do, the partners don't really try to compromise and adjust. They look to the contract and start pointing fingers. After all, managers are human. They are sweet on their own companies and tolerant of their own mistakes. Tolerance goes way down when partners cause mistakes.

The second problem with joint ventures is that parent companies behave as parents everywhere often do. They don't give their children the breathing space—or the time—they need to grow. Nor do they react too kindly when their children want to expand, especially if it's into areas the parents want to keep for themselves. "Keep your hands off" is the message they send, and that's not a good way to motivate anyone, let alone their own children.

This is not to say that joint ventures cannot work. Many work quite well. Fuji Xerox, for example, a very successful 50-50 arrangement between Rank Xerox and Fuji Film, earns high profits on its $3 billion annual sales and attracts some of the best people in Japan to work for it. Equally important, it has enough autonomy to get actively involved in new areas like digital-imaging technology, even though both parents have strong interests there themselves. The head of Fuji Xerox, Yotaro Kobayashi, who is the son of the founder of Fuji Film, now sits on the board of Xerox, which has benefited greatly from Fuji Xerox's experience in battling the Japanese companies that have attacked Xerox's position in the medium- to low-end copier segments in the United States.

On balance, however, most parents are not so tolerant of their joint ventures' own ambitions. There have to be better ways to go global than a regular sacrifice of the firstborn. There are.

Going global is what parents should do together—through alliances that address the issue of fixed costs. They work. Nissan distributes Volkswagens in Japan; Volkswagen sells Nissan's four-wheel drive cars in Europe. Mazda and Ford swap cars in the Triad; GM and Toyota both collaborate and compete in the United States and Australia. Continental Tyre, General Tire (now owned by Continental), Yokohama Rubber, and Toyo Tire share R&D and swap production. In the United States, for example, General Tire supplies several Japanese transplants on behalf of Yokohama and Toyo, both of which supply tires on behalf of General and Continental to car companies in Japan. No equity changes hands.

In the pharmaceutical industry, where both ends of the business system (R&D and distribution) represent unusually high fixed costs, companies regularly allow their strong products to be distributed by (potential) competitors with excellent distribution systems in key foreign markets. In the United States, Marion Laboratories distributes Tanabe's Herbesser and Chugai's Ulcerlmin; Merck, Yamanouchi's Gaster; Eli Lilly, Fujisawa's Cefamezin. In Japan, Shionogi distributes Lilly's Ceclor as Kefral (1988 sales: $700 million). Sankyo distributes Squibb's Capoten; Takeda, Bayer's Adalat; Fujisawa, SmithKlines's Tagamet. Sales in Japan of each of these medicines last year were on the order of $300 million.

The distribution of drugs is a labor- and relationship-intensive process. It takes a force of more than 1,000 detail people to have any real effect on Japanese medicine. Thus, unless you are committed to building and sustaining such a fixed cost in Japan, it makes sense to collaborate with someone who has such a force already in place—and who can reciprocate elsewhere in the Triad.

Despite the typical "United States vs. Japan" political rhetoric, the semiconductor industry has given rise to many forms of alliances. Most companies feel shorthanded in their R&D, so they swap licenses aggressively. Different forces prompted cooperative arrangements in the nuclear industry. General Electric, Toshiba, Hitachi, ASEA, AMU, and KWU (Siemens) banded together during the late 1970s to develop an improved nuclear boiling-water reactor. They shared their upstream R&D on a global basis but kept downstream construction and local customer relationships to themselves. During the 1980s, the first three (core) members of the alliance continued their R&D collaboration and, in face, developed an advanced boiling-water reactor concept. This time around, they split the orders from Tokyo Electric Power, among others, one-third each. As confidence builds, the activities open to joint participation can begin to encompass the entire business system.

Hitachi Kenki, a maker of construction equipment, has a loose alliance in hydraulic excavators with Deere & Company in North America and with Fiat Allis in Europe. Because Hitachi's product line was too narrow for it to set up its own distribution networks throughout the Triad, it tied up with partners who have strong networks already in place, as well as good additional products of their own, like bulldozers and wheel loaders, to fill in the gaps in Hitachi's product line. So effective have these arrangements been that the partners are now even committed to the joint development of a new wheel loader.

In the oligopolistic sheet glass industry, there is a noteworthy alliance between PPG and Asahi Glass, which began in 1966 with a joint venture in Japan to produce polyvinyl chloride. In 1985, the same pair formed a joint automotive-glass venture in the United States in hopes of capturing the business of Japanese automakers with U.S. production facilities. They built a second such plant in 1988. That same year they set up a chloride and caustic soda joint venture in Indonesia, along with some local participants and Mitsubishi Trading Company. During all this time, however, they remained fierce global competitors in the sheet glass business.

Another long-term relationship is the one between Brown Shoe and Nippon Shoe, which introduced a new technology back in 1962 to produce Brown's "Regal" shoes. Today the relationship encompasses several other brands of Brown's shoes. For Brown, this has proven a most effective way to participate in a Japanese market for leather goods that would be otherwise closed to them for both social reasons (historically, Japanese tanners have been granted special privileges) and reasons of appropriate skill (Brown's expertise in, for example, managing its own retail chains is not so relevant in an environment where sky-high real estate prices make direct company ownership of retail shops prohibitively expensive).

There are more examples, but the pattern is obvious: a prudent, non-equity-dependent set of arrangements through which globally active companies can maximize the contribution to their fixed costs. No surprise here. These alliances are an important part of the way companies get back to strategy.

The Logic of Entente

One clear change of mind necessary to make alliances work is a shift from a focus on ROI to a focus on ROS (return on sales). An ROS orientation means that managers will concern themselves with the ongoing business benefits of the alliance, not just sit around and wait for a healthy return on their initial investment. Indeed, equity investments almost always have an overtone of one company trying to control another with money. But few businesses succeed because of control. Most make it because of motivation, entrepreneurship, customer relationships, creativity, persistence, and attention to the "softer" aspects of organization, such as values and skills.

An alliance is a lot like a marriage. There may be no formal contract. There is no buying and selling of equity. There are few, if any, rigidly binding provisions. It is a loose, evolving kind of relationship. Sure, there are guidelines and expectations. But no one expects a precise, measured return on the initial commitment. Both partners bring to an alliance a faith that they will be stronger together than either would be separately. Both believe that each has unique skills and functional abilities the other lacks. And both have to work diligently over time to make the union successful.

When one partner is weak or lazy or won't make an effort to explore what the two can do together, things can come apart. One-sidedness and asymmetry of effort and attention doom a relationship. If a wife goes out and becomes the family's breadwinner *and* does all the housework *and* raises the children *and* runs the errands *and* cooks the meals, sooner or later she will rebel. Quite right. If the husband were in the same position, he'd rebel too. As soon as either partner starts to feel that the situation is unfair or uneven, it will begin to come apart. Alliances are like that. They work only when the partners do.

It's hard work. It's all too easy for doubts to start to grow. A British whiskey company used a Japanese distributor until it felt it had gained enough experience to start its own sales operation in Japan. Japanese copier makers and automobile producers have done this to their U.S. partners. It happens. There's always the danger that a partner is not really in it for the long haul.

But the odds run the other way. There is a tremendous cost—and risk—in establishing your own distribution, logistics, manufacturing, sales, and R&D in every key market around the globe. It takes time to build skills in your own people and develop good relations with vendors and customers. Nine times out of ten, you will want to stay in the alliance.

Inchcape, a British trading house with a strong regional base in Asia, distributes Toyota cars in China, Hong Kong, Singapore, elsewhere in the Pacific region, and in several European countries. It also distributes Ricoh copiers in Hong Kong and Thailand. This arrangement benefits the Japanese producers, which get access to important parts of the world without having to set up their own distribution networks. It also benefits Inchcape, which can leverage its traditional British connections in Asia while adding new, globally competitive products to its distribution pipeline to replace the less attractive offerings of declining U.K.-based industries.

In practice, though, companies do start to have doubts. Say you've started up a Japanese alliance, not invested all that much, and been able to boost your production at home because of sales in Japan. Then you look at the actual cash flow from those sales, and it doesn't seem all that great. So you compare it with a competitor's results—a competitor that has gone into Japan entirely on its own. It's likely that you've forgotten how little effort you've put in when compared with the blood, sweat, and tears of your competitor. All you look at are the results.

All of a sudden you start to feel cheated; you remember every little inconvenience and frustration. You yield to the great temptation to compare apples with oranges, to moan about revenues while forgetting fixed costs. You start to question just how much the alliance is really doing for you.

It's a bit like going to a marriage counselor and complaining about the inconveniences of marriage because, had you not married, you could be dating anyone you like. You focus on what you think you're missing, on the inconveniences, and forget entirely about the benefits of being married. It's a psychological process. Alliance partners can easily fall into this kind of destructive pattern of thought, complaining about the annoyances of coordination, of working together, of not having free rein. They forget the benefits.

Actually, they forget to *look* for the benefits. And most accounting and control systems only make this worse. For instance, if you are running your own international sales operation in Japan, you know where to look for accurate measures of performance. You know how to read an income statement, figure out the return on invested capital, consolidate the performance of subsidiaries.

But when you're operating through a partner in Japan and you're asking yourself how that Japanese operation is doing, you forget to look for the benefits at home in the contribution to the fixed costs of R&D, manufacturing, and brand image. The financials don't highlight them; they usually don't even capture them. Most of the time, these contributions—like the extra production volume for OEM export—are simply invisible, below the line of sight.

Companies in the United States, in particular, often have large, dominant home-country operations. As a result, they report the revenues generated by imports from their overseas partners as their own domestic sales. In fact, they think of what they're doing not as importing but as managing procurement. Exports get recorded as overseas sales of the domestic divisions. In either case, the contribution of the foreign partner gets lost in the categories used by the U.S.-based accounting system.

It takes real dedication to track down the domestic benefits of a global alliance. And you're not even going to look for them if you spend all your time complaining. The relationship is never going to last. That's too bad, of course, if the alliance really does contribute something of value. But even when alliances are good, you can outgrow them. Needs change, and today's partner might not be the best or the most suitable tomorrow.

Financial institutions shift about like this all the time. If you're placing a major issue, you may need to tie up with a Swiss bank with deep pockets. If you need help with retail distribution, you may turn to Merrill Lynch or Shearson Lehman Hutton. In Japan, Nomura Securities may be the best partner because of its size and retail strength. You don't need to be good at everything yourself as long as you can find a partner who compensates for your weak points.

Managing multiple partners is more difficult in manufacturing industries but still quite doable. IBM in the United States has a few important allies; in Japan it has teamed up with just about everyone possible. (There has even been a book published in Japanese, entitled *IBM's Alliance Strategy in Japan*.) It has links with Ricoh in distribution and sales of low-end computers, with Nippon Steel in systems integration, with Fuji Bank in financial systems marketing, with OMRON in CIM, and with NTT in value-added networks. IBM is not a jack-of-all-trades. It has not made huge fixed-cost investments. In the eyes of Japanese customers, however, it has become an all-around player. No wonder IBM has achieved a major "insider" position in the fiercely competitive Japanese market, along with handsome sales ($7 billion in 1988) and profits ($1.2 billion).

Sure, individual partners may not last. Every business arrangement has its useful life. But maintaining a presence in Japan by means of alliances *is* a permanent endeavor, an enduring part of IBM's strategy. And acting as if current arrangements are permanent helps them last longer. Just like marriage. If you start cheating on day two, the whole thing gets shaky fast.

Why does the cheating start? You're already pretty far down the slippery slope when you say to yourself, "I've just signed this deal with so-and-so to distribute my products. I don't need to worry about that anymore as long as they send me my check on time." You're not holding up your half of the relationship. You're not working at it. More important, you're not trying to learn from it—or through it. You're not trying to grow, to get better as a partner. You've become a check casher, a coupon clipper. You start to imagine all sorts of grievances. And your eye starts to wander.

One of Japan's most remarkable success stories is 7-Eleven. Its success, however, is not due to the efforts of its U.S. owner, Southland Corporation, but rather to the earnest acquisition of "know-how" by Ito-Yokado, the Japanese licensee. Faced with a takeover threat, Southland management collected something on the order of $5 billion through asset stripping and junk bond issues. The high-interest cost of the LBO caused the company to report a $6 million loss in 1987. Meanwhile, since the Japanese had completely absorbed the know-how for running 7-Eleven, the only thing Southland had left in Japan was its 7-Eleven brand.

When Southland's management asked Ito-Yokado to buy the 7-Eleven brand name for half a billion dollars, Ito-Yokado's counterproposal was to arrange an interest-free loan of ¥41 billion to Southland in exchange for the annual royalty payment of $25 million, with the brand name as collateral. Should something happen to Southland so that it cannot pay back the debt, it will lose the brand and its Japanese affiliation completely. Yes, Southland got as much as half a billion dollars out of Japan in exchange for mundane know-how, so they should be as happy as a Yukon River gold miner. On the other hand, the loss of business connections in Japan means that Southland is permanently out of one of the most lucrative retail markets in the world. That's not a marriage. It's just a one-night stand.

Another company, a U.S. media company, took 10% of the equity of a good ad agency in Japan. When the agency went public, the U.S. investor sold off 3% and made a lot of money over and above its original investment. It still had 7%. Then the stockholders started to complain. At Tokyo's crazy stock market prices, that 7% represented about $40 million that was just sitting in Japan without earning dividends. (The dividend payout ratio of Japanese companies is usually very low.) So the stockholders pushed management to sell off the rest and bring the money back to the United States, where they could get at least a money-market level of return. No growth, of course. No lasting position in the booming Japanese market. Just a onetime killing.

Much the same logic seems to lie behind the sale by several U.S.-based companies of their equity positions in Japanese joint ventures. McGraw-Hill (Nikkei-McGraw-Hill), General Electric (Toshiba), B.F. Goodrich (Yokohama Rubber), CBS (CBS-Sony), and Nabisco (Yamazaki-Nabisco), among others, have all realized handsome capital gains in this fashion. If they had not given up their participation in so lucrative a market as Japan, however, the value of their holdings would now be many times greater still. GE, for example, probably realized more than $400 million from its sale of Toshiba shares during the early 1980s. But those same shares would be worth roughly $1.6 billion today. Similarly, B.F. Goodrich's investments in Yokohama Rubber would now be worth nearly $300 million, compared with an estimated $36 million that it realized from selling its shares during the late 1970s and early 1980s. Of course, such funds have since found other opportunities for profitable investment, but they would have to do very well indeed to offset the loss of so valuable an asset base in Japan.

This kind of equity-based mind-set makes the eye wander. It sends the message that alliances are not a desirable—or effective—means of coping with the urgent and inescapable pressures of globalization or of becoming a genuine insider throughout the Triad market. It reinforces the short-term orientation of managers already hard-pressed by the uncertainties of a new global environment.

When a dispute occurs in a transnational joint venture, it often has overtones of nationalism, sometimes even racism. Stereotypes persist. "Americans just can't understand our market," complain some frustrated partners. "The Germans are too rigid," complain others. "Those mechanical Japanese may be smart at home, but they sure as hell are dumb around here." We've all heard the comments.

It does not take companies with radically different nationalities to have a "clash of cultures" in a joint venture. Most of the cross-border mergers that took place in Europe during the 1970s have resulted in divorce or in a takeover by one of the two partners. In Japan, mergers between Japanese companies—Dai-Ichi Kangyo Bank and Taiyo Kobe Bank, for example—have journalists gossiping about personal conflicts at the top between, say, ex-Kangyo and ex-Dai-Ichi factions lingering on for ten years and more.

Good combinations—Ciba-Geigy and Nippon Steel (a combination of Yawata and Fuji), for example—are the exception, not the rule. Two corporate cultures rarely mesh well or smoothly. In the academic world, there is a discipline devoted to the study of interpersonel relationships. To my knowledge, however, there is not even one scholar who specializes in the study of *intercompany* relationships. This is a serious omission, given the importance of joint ventures and alliances in today's competitive global environment. We need to know much more than we do about what makes effective corporate relationships work.

Having been involved with many multicompany situations, I do not underestimate this task. Still, we must recognize and accept the inescapable subtleties and difficulties of intercompany relationships. That is the essential starting point. Then we must focus not on contractual or equity-related issues but on the quality of the people at the interface between organizations. Finally, we must understand that success requires frequent, rapport-building meetings at at least three organizational levels: top management, staff, and line management at the working level.

This is hard, motivation-testing work. No matter what they say, however, many companies don't really care about extending their global reach. All they want is a harvesting of the global market. They are not interested in the hard work of serving customers around the world. They are interested in next quarter's ROI. They are not concerned with getting back to strategy or delivering long-term value or forging entente. They want a quickie. They want to feel good today and not have to work too hard tomorrow. They are not serious about going global or about the painstaking work of building and maintaining the alliances a global market demands.

Yet the relentless challenges of globalization will not go away. And properly managed alliances are among the best mechanisms that companies have found to bring strategy to bear on these challenges. In today's uncertain world, it is best not to go it alone.

4
Cooperate to Compete Globally

Howard V. Perlmutter and David A. Heenan

Increasingly, to be globally competitive, multinational corporations must be globally cooperative. This necessity is reflected in the acceleration of global strategic partnerships (GSPs) among companies large and small. GSPs have become an important new strategic option that touches every sector of the world economy, from sunrise to sunset industries, from manufacturing to services.

For smaller companies, these global partnerships with both peers and giants represent the most profitable route to future opportunities. Few companies will achieve international leadership and few nations will prosper in the world economy without some set of GSPs in their portfolios. Some examples:

AMC's link with Renault seven years ago both gave the U.S. automaker an infusion of capital and experience with front-wheel-drive cars, and opened up the U.S. market to the French company. Since then, Ford, GM, and Chrysler have consummated production deals with Mazda, Toyota, Suzuki, Isuzu, and Mitsubishi, as well as emerging South Korean automakers.

AT&T signed twin accords with Europe's leaders in information technology, Olivetti and Philips. By combining corporate expertise, AT&T hopes to gain a foothold first in Europe and then around the world.

Through its alliance with France's state-owned SNECMA, General Electric produces a low-pollution engine for high-performance aircraft. In coming together, both sides agreed to share the estimated $800 million development cost, an amount neither company was prepared to commit on its own.

Madison Avenue has seen a wave of international ventures, triggered in 1981 by Young & Rubicam's linkup with Tokyo's Dentsu, the world's largest advertising agency. The American agency further plans to merge its Marsteller Advertising unit with Havas Conseil and the other European affiliates of Eurocom, the French market leader.

The number of East-West ventures is growing. A recent example is the venture between North Korea and two Japanese trade companies, Asahi Corporation and Ryuko Trading Company, to set up a chain of 31 stores in North Korea to sell goods from Japan and the Communist bloc.

American high-tech companies formed two coalitions, the Microelectronics and Computer Cooperative and the Semiconductor Research Cooperative, to buffer the competitive shocks of similar groups from Japan, the "second Japans," and Western Europe.

While these specific examples show giants teaming with giants, GSPs are not the exclusive province of large MNCs. Enormous companies will frequently combine with smaller ones to exploit their entrepreneurial capabilities and market niches. This was the case when IBM teamed up with Microsoft to exploit the latter's growing expertise in software for desktop computers. The smaller companies, like Microsoft, benefit by gaining access to global markets and the resource strength of their bigger partners.

In another case, an American multinational that buys plastic molds from a number of suppliers has changed the nature of its relationship with these smaller companies and now encourages them to go overseas as part of a shared global strategy. The pattern holds in retailing as well, where thousands of small companies supplying everything from corduroy suits to kitchen appliances strike deals with retailers all over the world for global distribution of their products. Other industries are also initiating global partnerships. Some of these industries include: furniture, hand tools, insurance, toys, and apparel.

The idea of GSPs, however, may not be easily accepted. Many U.S. managers still adhere to the traditional competitive model of the corporation, where cooperation is regarded with skepticism and suspicion. These tenets generally act as a barrier against collaboration. So it is important to investigate what GSPs are and why some companies need them.

What Is a GSP?

Not all the efforts to mold international coalitions are either global or strategic; some are mere extensions of traditional joint ventures—localized partnerships with a focus on a single national market. One example of a localized partnership is GM's venture with China to coproduce diesel engines and transmissions in that country. Neither the product nor the market is global. Other partnerships are loose amalgams of companies from different countries with little intention of attacking world markets systematically; these alliances usually want a short-term, tactical edge in manufacturing or marketing. A few partnerships widen their scope in order to focus their energies on a geographic region, such as the European Economic Community.

More important, but still not global, are those ventures aimed at the tricenters of economic power: the United States, Western Europe, and Japan. Even these ventures, however, are not global strategic partnerships by our definition. GSPs are those alliances in which:

1. Two or more companies develop a common, long-term strategy aimed at world leadership as low-cost suppliers, differentiated marketers, or both, in an international arena.
2. The relationship is reciprocal. The partners possess specific strengths that they are prepared to share with their colleagues.
3. The partners' efforts are global, extending beyond a few developed countries to include nations of the newly industrializing, less developed, and socialist world.
4. The relationship is organized along horizontal, not vertical, lines; technology exchanges, resource pooling, and other "soft" forms of combination are the rule.
5. The participating companies retain their national and ideological identities while competing in those markets excluded from the partnership.

Philips' GSP portfolio. The number of new coalitions that meet these five criteria is growing. Holland's Philips is one of several MNCs well on its way to developing a portfolio of GSPs. The Dutch electronic giant is discarding a corporate culture based on 94 years of self-sufficiency for one relying heavily on multiple ventures with outsiders. (See Exhibit I for a partial list of Philips' partnerships.)

Philips' chairman, Wisse Dekker, sees GSPs as serving two aims: blunting the forces of American, Japanese, and, more recently, Taiwanese and Korean competition in high-quality electronics; and re-

Exhibit	**Partial list of Philips's partnerships**	

Industry	Participating companies	Country of incorporation
Advanced telephone systems	AT&T	U.S.A.
Compact discs	Sony	Japan
Electronic credit cards	Compagnie des Machines Bull	France
Lighting and electronic components	Matsushita	Japan
	Electronic Devices	Hong Kong
Minicomputer software	Compagnie des Machines Bull	France
	ICL PLC	Britain
	Siemens	West Germany
	Nixdorf Computer	West Germany
	Olivetti	Italy
Mobile communications	CIT-Alcatel	France
	Thomson	France
	Siemens	West Germany
Personal memory systems	Control Data	U.S.A.
Personal computers	Corona Data Systems	U.S.A.
	Siemens	West Germany
Semiconductors and microchips	Intel	U.S.A.
	Siemens	West Germany
	Advanced Semiconductor Materials International	Holland
Video recorders	Grundig	West Germany
	Victor Company	Japan
Videotex software and systems	Enidata	Italy

ducing the company's dependence on Europe, where one-half of its sales and almost two-thirds of its work force and assets are located. Philips has recharted its world into three "competence centers": Europe, North America, and the Pacific Basin. In the next five to ten years the company plans to reposition itself to do 30% of its business in each of these centers with the balance going to newly industrializing countries.[1]

Philips is teaming up with its neighbor Siemens in West Germany to take on the United States and Japan in advanced microtechnology. This undertaking, which carries $140 million in grants from the Dutch and German governments in addition to the partners' $435 million investment, will pool 500 researchers in an effort to develop superchips that each company will market separately. "These projects are so large," claims one company spokesperson, "you have to take a European approach."

But in keeping with the GSP philosophy, Philips' ambitions go beyond Europe. "We are aware that what we do has to have global dimensions—world products and world systems," says Gerrit Jeelof, the management board member in charge of telecommunications and computers.[2] The Dutch MNC is keen to exploit its current relationship with Matsushita beyond the Japanese market, while continuing to press ahead with other coproduction agreements in Hong Kong, Taiwan, and Singapore. In the developing countries Philips is joining forces with other MNCs. One example is its recent pact with AT&T and France's CIT-Alcatel to improve the Venezuelan telephone system.

Even more important is Philips' partnership with AT&T, an agreement designed to strengthen Philips' hold on the North American market, which generates 27% of its sales, and to gain access to AT&T's vaunted technology in light and electronic components. AT&T, a neophyte to the world of international business, can borrow heavily from Philips' comprehensive overseas network. The Dutch company is trading its geographical expertise for its partner's state-of-the-art technology.

Philips and other MNCs have long recognized that joining forces can lead to large-scale economies, technology and resource pooling, improved access to foreign markets, and avoidance of national regulations. But Philips' more recent ventures have the makings of GSPs— they represent a systematic effort to fuse the principles of competitive advantage with global strategy.

The company's partnership with DuPont in compact laser-disk products, for instance, links Philips' leadership in consumer markets with the U.S. company's expertise in developing high-density optical disks for data storage. Their coming together represents the first attempt to supply the entire range of optical disks on a worldwide basis. Moreover, every Philips alliance has cost leadership and/or differentiated product superiority in at least one national market as its objective. This goal of strategic mutual advantage is prompting Philips and other MNCs to restructure their global portfolios along more cooperative lines.

GSPs also allow multinationals to join together in specific products or markets while retaining autonomy in others. The companies involved, therefore, do not sacrifice their national or ideological identities. In this respect, they are quite different from earlier coventures such as Royal Dutch/Shell, Unilever, and Scandinavian Airline Systems—long-standing multinational corporations that manage global strategy from a single or, occasionally, a dual headquarters. A GSP preserves its national and corporate roots and so prepares the ground for future cooperation and competition.

Obstacles on the Road

GSPs are not achieved without hardship. Companies that want the edge a GSP can provide must cope with a host of constraints—from nationalism to cultural differences to antitrust attitudes.

Since the days of Senator Sherman, U.S. companies have been wary of cooperation. Today America's ideological position shows little sign of changing; even well-structured, "safe" combinations still proceed with caution. Because of the careful drafting of the GM-Toyota venture, both parties were confident that they would not stumble over an antitrust technicality. "But let's face it," admitted one GM official, "the idea of even talking to each other is bound to be a little scary to some people."[3] Those people include the Federal Trade Commission's "trustbusters." Only after extended deliberations and the negotiation of the venture's limited 12-year pact did the FTC bless the proposal. In an era of GSPs, America's antiquated concepts of antitrust will need rethinking if our GSPs are to emerge as a major competitive force.

Inevitable problems from within are as challenging as the outside obstacles. History has shown that companies have a hard time sustaining long-term relationships. Cultural differences, poor communication, and political infighting can lead to the demise of a potential GSP. For example:

> One of the first cross-border mergers, the union of two large European tire makers, Britain's Dunlop Holdings and Italy's Pirelli & Company, broke up in 1981. A combination of nationalism and sick home economies made profitability difficult. Also, top management was unable to shape an Anglo-Italian corporate culture.

> In the early 1970s, Dutch, French, and German computer makers sent off hundreds of their top engineers to a multinational venture called Unidata, Europe's would-be answer to IBM. But Unidata dissolved in 1975 without developing a single global product. The Dutch accused the French of not cooperating and the Germans had great difficulty making machines that were compatible with anyone else's.

> London-based consortium banks also fell apart. In 1982, Den Norske Creditbank of Norway bought out its Swedish, Danish, and Finnish partners in the Nordic Banking Group. Previously, Standard Chartered Bank had followed the same course with London's oldest consortium bank, Midland and International Banks. In March 1981, the Orion Bank, whose members included Chase Manhattan, National Westminster, Credito Italiano, Mitsubishi, and Westdeutsche Landesbank, folded. Conflicts of interest, political infighting, inadequate financial controls, and the inability to develop a global strategy undermined the venture.

Corporate collaboration is difficult to achieve, especially where it involves diverse backgrounds and cultures. Our research on GSPs shows that an atmosphere of mutual distrust and domination by one partner jeopardizes the stability of the alliance.[4] To overcome these obstacles, top executives need to focus on the elements that promote successful GSPs.

Six Signs of Success

The health of GSPs depends on the participating companies learning and sharing their abilities. Joint management seminars and multipartner international task forces can accelerate the learning process. Here are six areas that deserve special attention:

1. Mission. Participants in a potential GSP must be committed to a "win-win" sense of mission—that is, each partner must believe the

other has something it needs. Top executives and divisional managers must convince middle managers and affiliates on both sides to build on strengths and reduce weaknesses. An example of this is the pact between AT&T and Olivetti.

Their collective mission is to capture a major share of the global information processing and communications market. Olivetti gives AT&T access to the lucrative European market. AT&T gives Olivetti a much-needed $260 million cash infusion, technical support in microprocessors and telecommunications, and muscle in the U.S. market. By coming together both AT&T and Olivetti should win.

In contrast, AT&T's other efforts to attract Italian and British partners have failed because the American company could not demonstrate mutual advantage. Its discussions with STET, Italy's state-owned telecommunications company, broke down because AT&T would not allow STET to export its wares to attractive foreign markets. Inmos, the British government's semiconductor manufacturer, rejected an alliance with the American multinational for public policy reasons—thinking that a GSP could destroy the British company's national identity.

2. Strategy. MNCs sometimes rush into a partnership, hoping that a synergistic plan will somehow evolve. But strategy must come first. Partners must avoid "niche collision." It occurs when separate deals produce an untenable overlap between cooperation and competition. For instance, when Philips established its pact with AT&T to market the American multinational's digital telephone-switching systems, the Dutch company hoped that the relationship would extend to other products. AT&T then teamed up with Olivetti, a major Philips competitor in the office machine market, and prospects for wider cooperation vanished.

Prospective partners can avoid colliding by carefully analyzing what each can contribute in various national, regional, and world markets—then they must craft their GSPs with these niches in mind.

Balancing cooperation with competition is critical to achieving strategic synergy. Far too often the accords fall apart as once friendly colleagues revert to hostile competitors. In the Ricoh-Savin, Pentax-Honeywell, and Canon-Bell & Howell alliances, Japanese colleagues took advantage of valuable U.S. technology and marketing know-how only to discard their American partners. Similarly, South Korea's Lucky-Goldstar Group, a $7 billion multinational, ended several ventures with Japanese companies because the Japanese were unwilling to transfer vital technology to a potential competitor.

On the other hand, Rolls-Royce, the state-owned British aircraft engine manufacturer, is staking its future on pacts with two American competitors, Pratt & Whitney and General Electric. The Pratt partnership is an admission that neither company dares to develop a new jet engine without the other. In the GE case, Rolls hopes to exploit the U.S. company's weakness in medium-sized engines while joining forces in the upper end of the market. Despite the risks, Rolls remains convinced that teaming with the enemy is a must.

The tricky balancing of cooperation and competition is especially troublesome in resource allocation decisions. Several sponsoring companies, for example, have balked at surrendering their sharpest minds to a venture that might help the opposition. Some MNCs have gone so far as to offer raises and bonuses to their key people if they promise not to join the partnership.

Some potential GSPs solve this problem by using "nonaligned personnel," individuals not associated with any of the participating companies, to manage the venture. At DMS Laboratories, a diagnostic testing venture linking FCS Industries of New Jersey with France's API Systems Inc., all sales and marketing people as well as top management will be outsiders. Similarly, the Microelectronics and Computer Technology Corporation has chosen to appoint six of its seven major project directors and more than half of its research staff from companies totally removed from the 20-member consortium. Using inside people, however, is usually a better strategy since they are more likely to have the loyalty an alliance needs to survive.

3. Governance. Americans have historically harbored the belief that power, not parity, should govern collaborative ventures. In contrast, the Europeans and Japanese often consider partners as equals, subscribe to management by consensus, and rely on lengthy discussion to secure stronger commitment to shared enterprises.

During the Renault-AMC negotiations, some U.S. executives feared a French takeover. It never materialized. Instead, the French multinational has tried to support, not control, its American partner, and the Americans are doing the same. Only 4 of AMC's top 24 officers and 6 of its 15 board members are from Renault. Also, AMC enjoys equal status in making key model changes. In the Alliance's design, for instance, Americans rejected the allegedly inferior French air-conditioning system and expressed their dissatisfaction with Renault's ideas on rear-wheel openings on the four-door cars. Eventually these disputes were settled by "arm wrestling over a bottle of wine," according to one insider. In our view, any prospective GSP that resorts to dominance is inherently weak. Its chances for success are slim.

4. Culture. The most important factor in the endurance of a global alliance is chemistry. The partners must be willing to mold a common set of values, style, and culture while retaining their national identities. This missing dimension in the Dunlop-Pirelli venture led to its demise.

Cultural incompatibility can produce enormous operational difficulties. Consider the problems confronted by Pittsburgh's Alcoa and Japan's NEC. Because of language differences, Alcoa and NEC each thought the other was responsible for a part called a "feed horn" on their jointly manufactured satellite television receiver. But when they finished the first prototype, they discovered this vital item was missing. Eventually the partners rectified the problem and avoided further misunderstandings.

In contrast, the GSP formed by the advertising giants, Young & Rubicam and Dentsu, seems well on its way to developing corporate themes that combine both cultures. "In the West I say, 'Go out and buy it,'" explains Alexander Brody, president and CEO of DYR, the holding company. "In the East I talk about the sea and the stars. . . . I create a feeling."[5] Simply stated, DYR is telling its clients that it can give them either the American hard-sell technique or Japan's more low-key approach.

This flexible approach may not work in every instance. One Japanese executive we interviewed is doubtful that MNCs from the East and West can fashion a common culture. "The best we can, or should, do," he argues, "is foster a shared appreciation for the cultural strengths and weaknesses of each partner."

5. Organization. The new approach to partnerships mandates new organizational patterns. Mindful of the lessons of the ill-fated Concorde, Airbus Industrie (AI) is shaping its own version of a composite organization in part because of the logistical complexities of multi-country management. Assembly of its A300 and A310 wide-body aircraft takes place in Toulouse, with the Germans responsible for the main fuselage; the British, the wings; the French, the cockpit; and the Spanish, the tailfin.

Accordingly, AI's articles of incorporation include several features enabling the consortium to blend the talents of French Aerospatiale, Deutsche Airbus, British Aerospace, and elements of the Spanish aerospace industry with a minimum of organizational fragmentation. For example:

The alliance was formed under French law as a "groupement d'intêret économique," which permits a group of companies to create a single structure. Under this arrangement, the partners must act as mutual guarantors for all of AI's commitments to third parties.

A supervisory board acts as a buffer between AI's operating management and the respective aircraft manufacturers. It controls all the consortium's strategic decisions.

A "convention cadre" is singularly responsible for generating common solutions to partnership disputes in areas ranging from aircraft design changes to amortization of development costs.

While some conflicts inevitably persist, these and other provisions have reduced tension among the members. To compete effectively with its U.S. rivals, Boeing and McDonnell Douglas, the consortium needs to maintain these new organizational methods within the international partnership.

6. Management. A GSP changes the nature of daily decision making and places new pressures on an enterprise. Before formalizing any coalition, MNCs must identify those operational issues—from transfer pricing to personnel matters—that are most likely to cause friction, and must then set up unitary management processes where one decision point has the authority to commit all the partners. Far too often, however, managers neglect this important step. As a result, the new venture suffers from unclear lines of authority, poor communication, and slow decision making.

Look at TRW and Japan's Fujitsu—a potential GSP that got bogged down in bureaucratic red tape. A "double management system" requiring dual approvals interfered, and the coalition ended with Fujitsu reorganizing the business as a much simpler, wholly owned subsidiary.

Besides adopting unitary management methods, MNCs must develop an ongoing surveillance system to sense potential disputes between the partners. Progress reports on the partnership, which analyze growing or declining mutual trust and respect, should supplement operational progress and performance reports. Invariably, many of the initial expectations of the participating companies prove to be unrealistic. Disillusionment sets in and the partnership eventually dissolves. Building mutual trust and respect is the key to forging a long-term GSP; the partnership depends on both sides sharing their expertise for mutual gain. This requires an in-depth understanding of the strengths and weaknesses of each partner and a commitment to build on the plusses while reducing the minuses.

These are the six main elements in operating a GSP. Both sides must be committed to the alliance: they must share an appreciation for what makes a mutually beneficial partnership. Top executives ready to forge these new values and beliefs will possess a much different perspective on international business than their predecessors ever did.

In the traditional view, competitive advantage is a product of a home-country orientation, proprietary technology, centralized decision making, vertical planning systems, and market dominance. The new global model, on the other hand, is more flexible about ownership and managerial control. It encourages joint decision making, vertical and horizontal planning, and the fusion of competent allies from around the world despite cultural differences. Managers who want to implement GSPs must be ready to make fundamental philosophical changes. Without a new mind-set GSPs are bound to fail.

Looking Ahead

Consider just one recent week's worth of multinational joint venture announcements. In Washington, the Pentagon disclosed its agreement to exchange proprietary radar technology for Japanese expertise in missile-guidance systems, opening the door for further U.S.-Japan cooperation in defense. In Madrid, Telefónica, Spain's semiprivate telephone monopoly with $7.8 billion in sales, announced its plans to go multinational through alliances with prospective competitors: AT&T, Philips, Fujitsu, and the Pacific Telesis Group. In Detroit, Ford was negotiating with a European rival, Fiat, while in New York, IBM announced that it had acquired a major interest in MCI. This hectic partnering is becoming commonplace today as MNCs search frantically for the best set of corporate colleagues.

Negotiating and implementing this slew of new partnerships requires a new, global orientation. MNCs are vying for strategic position in a global chess game. And as GSPs proliferate, strategic issues will become even more complicated, and the boundaries between companies will become blurred. It is unlikely, for instance, that the global planning process can be conducted exclusively from a single corporation. Furthermore, if single companies no longer set strategy, and if groups of companies negotiate common interests with the government—at the government's initiative—the international political arena is bound to change.

GSPs may challenge our traditional concept of national sovereignty. Notions about economic competitiveness, based on the competitive model of the nation, may be rendered obsolete. No country can afford to be excluded from partnering just as no company can avoid the shifting patterns of global supply and demand. Indeed, the nation-states that prosper in the years ahead will be those that nurture a series of GSPs that stress the values of parity and mutual benefit.

We are, of course, a long way from shaping multilateral industrial policies at the national level. But at the corporate level we are already at the stage where such policies are in force. The automobile and advanced electronics industries are two such examples; over time, agriculture, textiles, and other mature, low-growth industries may follow suit.

Building GSPs represents a tremendous challenge for the multinationals of the future. Companies must learn to join forces in some areas, while pursuing independent courses in others. These trade-offs require managers to think of their companies almost as if they were living entities, seeking to compete and to survive.

The noted biologist Lewis Thomas expressed it best when he argued that survival of the fittest does not mean that nature is red in the tooth and claw—as nineteenth century evolutionary theory argued. Nor does it mean that only the strongest, shrewdest, and most dominating will win. The fittest—those who survive—Thomas suggested, are those who cooperate best with other living things.

Notes

1. "Philips in a New Light," *Economist*, January 5, 1985, p. 60.
2. John Tagliabue, "The New Philips Strategy in Electronics," *New York Times*, January 15, 1984.
3. John Koten, "GM-Toyota Venture Stirs Antitrust and Labor Problems," *The Wall Street Journal*, June 10, 1983.
4. See David A. Heenan and Howard V. Perlmutter, *Multinational Organization Development: A Social Architectural Perspective* (Reading, Mass.: Addison-Wesley, 1979), chapter 5.
5. Steven P. Galante, "Japan-U.S. Ad Agency Attempts to Go Global," *The Wall Street Journal*, April 20, 1984.

5
Inside Unilever:
The Evolving Transnational Company

Floris A. Maljers

These days, Unilever is often described as one of the foremost transnational companies. Yet our organization of diverse operations around the world is not the outcome of a conscious effort to become what is now known among academics as a transnational. When Unilever was founded in 1930 as a Dutch-British company, it produced soap, processed foods, and a wide array of other consumer goods in many countries. Ever since then, the company has evolved mainly through a Darwinian system of retaining what was useful and rejecting what no longer worked—in other words, through actual practice as a business responding to the marketplace.

But regardless of the process, Unilever has become a transnational company in the most basic sense: we think globally as well as act locally. The very nature of our products requires proximity to local markets; economies of scale in certain functions justify a number of head-office departments; and the need to benefit from everybody's creativity and experience makes a sophisticated means of transferring information across our organization highly desirable. All of these factors led to our present structure: a matrix of individual managers around the world who nonetheless share a common vision and understanding of corporate strategy.

At Unilever, major product groups are responsible for profits in Europe and North America, and regional groups are responsible elsewhere. Some of our brands, like Lipton Tea and Lux Soap, are known even in Albania and Cambodia—that is, even in countries where Unilever does not have its own industrial operations. In each of some 75 countries, we do business through one or more operating companies, with a total of about 500 companies in the Unilever group. In our case, "thinking transnationally" means an informal type of worldwide cooperation among self-sufficient units.

Of course, there has to be a formal structure of some sort that encourages managers to think and act in the way corporate policy dictates. But everyone must also share the values that lead to flexibility on every level. In a worldwide company incorporating both unity and diversity, business strategy and structure are inextricably linked—and always evolving.

While Unilever's organizational structure has developed, at least to some extent, through trial and error, we still have a consistent and long-standing policy when it comes to one thing: the importance of managing people rather than simply analyzing problems. The two companies that formed Unilever, Margarine Unie of the Netherlands and Lever Brothers of the United Kingdom, had a long tradition of expanding their businesses through both export and local production. Initially, local operations were almost exclusively managed by Dutch and British expatriates; however, even in the early days of Unilever, the new company started developing local managers and decentralizing the organization. Yet the head office also recognized the need for a common culture among its many scattered units and set up formal training programs aimed at the "Unileverization" of all its managers.

In essence, Unilever's story, idiosyncratic though it may be, is one example of how a single company has come to manage far-flung units that share a common culture. Over the course of its particular lifetime, the company has successfully weathered numerous changes. Within just the last 30 years, for example, Unilever's most important product group, the foods business, has gone through two major reorganizations. The details of how the foods business has reshaped itself in response to new market trends illustrate Unilever's overall combination of structural formality and managerial flexibility.

From Margarine to Global Fast Food

Until the mid-1960s, the national management in every country where Unilever operated was fully responsible for the profits of all units in its territory. Product groups worked only in an advisory capacity, and their ability to affect how certain products were marketed or distributed basically depended on the attitude of the local manager.

Up to that time, especially during World War II, the foods industry was driven by raw materials. At Unilever, the two most important raw materials were tea and edible oils, the latter being necessary for the company's large business in margarines and table oils. But when raw-material sourcing became less important, our focus of attention shifted to preservation technology and distribution systems. Because of the competitive advantages we developed in the logistics of handling frozen products, Unilever became the world's largest ice cream company and achieved strong market positions in many other frozen foods.

In 1966, the company drastically reorganized responsibilities for all products, including those handled by the foods business, in its main European countries. Product groups became responsible for profits, while national managements worked in an advisory role—although in areas like industrial negotiations, local finance, and government relations, their advice usually determined decisions. While this switch of responsibilities may sound simple, it took many years of patience, persuasion, and even some early retirements before the last remnants of the old structure disappeared.

In setting up the new profit-responsible groups, the head office created three separate foods units. They were based partially on raw-materials considerations and partially on the new distribution requirements. The company established an edible fats group, a frozen food and ice cream group, and a food and drinks group that took care of everything else—mainly soup, tea, and salad dressings.

This setup worked well enough for some time; indeed, it enabled Unilever's foods business to grow overall, especially in Europe and North America. With the benefit of hindsight, we could have grown even more rapidly, for example, in eastern Asia. But on the whole, Unilever kept its strong market position in the key foods products.

Since the mid-1970s, however, the foods industry has become increasingly consumer-driven. Effective marketing is now a company's prime competitive advantage, and marketing efforts have led to concepts like low-calorie products, health foods, convenience foods, and the use of natural ingredients. In addition, manufacturers now face a new challenge in the ongoing concentration of power in food retailing, particularly in northwestern Europe and North America.

Therefore, as time passed, the allocation of products to the three foods units started to hinder rather than help Unilever's progress. The market for low-calorie products, for example, has grown steadily since the 1970s. Yet, until 1988, our low-calorie spreads were the responsibility of the edible fats group, low-calorie soups belonged to food and drinks, and low-calorie frozen meals were part of the frozen food and ice cream group.

Clearly, shared use of well-known brand names, new food-processing technologies, and consumer research can benefit a company with worldwide operations. But it takes time and energy to forge a coordinated policy, assuming that's even possible. By the late 1980s, despite the good will of all who participated in the old foods-unit system, it was clear we had to reconsider our organization of the business again. In this, as in all of Unilever's reorganizations historically, top management has tried to combine a decentralized structure (which has the advantage of providing deep understanding of local markets) with a degree of centralized control. In other words, we strive for unity in diversity.

The first step in our new reorganization was to create the necessary unity by forming a committee of three board directors, which we called the "Foods Executive." (All 16 members of our board have executive responsibilities.) Located at our head office in Rotterdam, these three directors are now responsible collectively for all of Unilever's foods interests. They no longer have specific responsibilities for a group of products, as they did in the past; instead, working together as an executive triad, the three directors are in charge of our full range of present and future foods. In addition, control of the foods companies is now based on geography rather than the products they sell, with each of the directors responsible for profits in a group of countries.

In theory, we could have appointed one director with worldwide responsibility for foods. But at Unilever, the span of control would have been too broad for one person. It would have led to a second and perhaps a third layer of management, which we considered undesirable. By creating a group of three directors, we maintained the flat organizational structure and diversity we value so highly; and by letting these directors work as one group on product strategy, we achieved the unity that had been missing in our previous organization.

Foods products at Unilever are now concentrated in five strategic groups: edible fats, ice cream, beverages, meals and meal components, and professional markets. (The last group includes catering, bakery items, and other nondomestic food industries.) These groups are not responsible for profits but remain important centers of product expertise. They advise the profit-responsible directors of the Foods Executive and the relevant operating companies. And their advice carries much more weight than that of Unilever's product groups in the early 1960s.

In product terms, the company has improved its position because the new strategic groups are more in line with identified consumer needs. In geographic terms, we continue to rely on the knowledge of our operating companies to judge what product expertise to use in their local markets. In short, we now have more unity and can also make better use of the many and various opportunities offered by diversity.

However, the foods industry is still in considerable flux. The balance shifts continuously between centralized requirements (like research, finance, and packaging) and the need to stay close to local markets. The latest market trends are moving in three directions, and each will require a different approach of some sort in the future.

First, there is what one might call "global fast food"—the hamburger, fried chicken, and certain soft drinks, for example. How far or how fast globalization of such popular Western products will go is not yet clear. The much-publicized launch of the hamburger in Moscow and the record-breaking popularity of fried chicken in Tokyo may or may not be the beginning of a trend. In this particular instance, perhaps Andy Warhol was right when he said that progress is not always good for food.

Second, there is international food. Such food is common in one country but also transferrable to others. In the United Kingdom, Indian, Chinese, French, and Italian foods are good current examples. In addition, the popularity of Lebanese, Mexican, and other types of meals seems to be on the rise.

Third, there is national food. Again, in the United Kingdom, steak and kidney pie, Yorkshire pudding, and the banger for breakfast all represent typically British food.

The picture becomes even more complicated when one considers that the same word can cover a range of foods products. Take a seemingly simple product like tea. The British drink it hot and highly diluted with milk, people of the Middle East take it hot and strongly sugared, and Americans usually like it iced. While a global idea may exist for the type of compact disc player customers want, there is no uniform concept for tea or frozen pizza, even in Europe.

Given that the market for foods—and all of Unilever's products, for that matter—may change in unpredictable ways, it's likely we will reorganize again, adapting to a whole new set of trends or consumer needs in the future. Up to now, we've been fortunate enough not to face major discontinuities in our technology or markets during crucial reorganizations. Still, a transnational's structure and strategy must constantly adapt, regardless of the difficulties, in order to keep pace with the changing marketplace.

Although Unilever's most recent reorganization was based on our strategic intention to concentrate on the foods business in the broadest sense, one of our marketing directors in Switzerland or a factory manager in Italy might not have shared that perspective at first. While change is one of the few inevitabilities in transnational companies, any major reorganization requires flexible, responsive employees—and time. To get the support of company boards, we don't rush to implement necessary changes. At Unilever, we see organizational change as a long march forward rather than one big jump. And we are too cautious to risk breaking a leg.

A Matrix of Managers

In the early 1940s, Unilever began actively recruiting local managers to replace the Dutch and British executives from the head office who had been running most of its local units. Starting with the Indian subsidiary in 1942, Unilever put into place a management process that company insiders referred to as "ization." In other words, filling local executive and technical positions with Indian managers led to the "Indianization" of that subsidiary—along with "Australianization," "Brazilianization," and other examples of localization of management in various countries with Unilever operations.

The company's "ization" policy, as well as an increasing number of local competitors and the isolation of many of Unilever's operating companies during World War II, created a decentralized organization of self-sufficient subsidiaries. Yet the head office also recognized the danger of becoming too decentralized. Without the Unileverization of those Indian, Australian, Brazilian, and other local managers, the company's many scattered units would not have shared any common corporate culture or vision.

By 1955, Unilever had opened Four Acres, its international management training college near London. Now every year, the head office sends 300 to 400 managers from all over the world to this international training ground. In addition, training courses are organized on a local basis in many countries, sometimes in our own centers (for example, in the city of Megamendung on Java), sometimes in hired facilities.

Once the proper formal organization is in place—such as, in Unilever's case, a matrix that combines local initiative with some centralized control—its managers must still be encouraged to think transnationally. While we continue to develop local talent in our subsidiaries, we also expect managers to gain experience in more than one country or product line. A matrix, however well designed, cannot work if the people across the organization aren't prepared to accept its flexibility. At Unilever, the recruitment and training policies that reinforce the matrix are not only held in high esteem, they are also a matter of long-standing practice.

Since the 1950s, we have pioneered new managerial selection systems in western Europe. And in many developing countries, we use advanced methods to recruit the best university graduates. For instance, teams of Unilever managers are charged with spotting talent in local universities at an early stage; or prizes are given for work done by young scientists to make contact with them. The company also sponsors an extensive program of business courses for university students in many countries, from Turkey to the United Kingdom. Through these courses, Unilever instructors and students get to know each other, determining what they have in common. Every candidate who survives this initial screening is then reviewed by a panel of senior managers, which often includes boardmembers from the parent company.

The greatest challenge of recruiting, of course, is to find the best and brightest who will fit into the company. We certainly do not want a *homo unileverensis*; but for international careers in our current operating companies, we look for people who can work in teams and understand the value of cooperation and consensus.

For managerial trainees, preparation includes both on-the-job experience and courses at Four Acres. In fact, many have joked that Unilever is really a management education institute financed by soap and margarine. Our courses go beyond teaching specific subjects like "Edible Oil Refining" or "Developments in the Retail Trade." We also offer the "International Management Seminar" and the "Senior Management Course." These general courses are often taught by visiting professors from well-known business schools, with Unilever instructors participating occasionally.

Every trainee becomes part of a group of 25 to 30 people recruited for similar managerial positions. This shared experience creates an informal network of equals who know one another well and usually continue to meet and exchange experiences. Such an exchange is particularly important in an organization that has an extremely diverse group of international managers. Unilever's board includes members from six different countries, and virtually every operating company contains expatriates. We have an Italian managing our large company in Brazil, a Dutchman in Taiwan, an Englishman in Malaysia, and an American in Mexico.

Another element that lends coherence to Unilever's management is our extensive system of attachments. A manager can be placed for a short or long period in a head-office department or a subsidiary. In the early 1980s, when I was responsible for profits for a large group of companies, we had a staff of about 20 people. Of these, there were usually two bright young managers on temporary assignment from several of our far-flung operating companies. After a period of 6 to 12 months, they would move on to new positions—as marketing director in Brazil, for instance, or development manager in Turkey.

When these managers return home, they are still part of the Unilever network. They know whom to call in case of need and what to expect. They also realize that their own ideas can make an important contribution to Unilever's overall progress. Exposure to another environment not only gives them more know-how but also improves their "know-who."

In addition, cross-postings between companies are very important for establishing unity, a common sense of purpose, and an understanding of different national cultures and attitudes. Such postings may be to other countries or across product lines. My own career took me to Colombia and Turkey, where I learned that using logic to solve problems, based on my studies at Amsterdam University, often didn't match the approach of local citizens. For example, while setting up preventive maintenance systems in factories seemed obvious to me, the local attitude was to wait until a machine broke down before deciding what to do.

In a company with a product portfolio of fast-moving consumer goods, it's also useful for young managers to work in more than one product group. Clearly, not all of the creative ideas used to market skin cream are applicable to instant soups, but a surprising number of good ideas result from cross-fertilization between product groups.

Of course, we did not design our extensive system of recruitment, training, and attachments with the idea of forming a "transnational network." However, in practice, this network—as represented by both the company's formal structure and the informal exchanges between managers—may well be one of the ingredients in the glue that holds Unilever together.

First, the network is fundamental to the transfer of ideas among companies. Transfer can take place either through one of our head offices, which then acts as a clearing house for ideas, or through direct contact between two operating companies. While our network may seem disorderly, it does work. Formal systems of information transfer certainly exist, but sometimes it's simply much faster for a product manager in Brazil, for example, to fax a rough sketch of a new innovation to her opposite number in Italy.

Second, through the network, international working parties, committees, and similar groups form either ad hoc to solve a problem or to follow a subject on a more permanent basis. This procedure works effectively because the network exists; but it can also play an important part in extending and strengthening the network itself.

For instance, a group has been charged with the strategic planning and monitoring of what we call "ice cream snacks." In this rapidly growing market, which requires equally rapid innovation, Unilever sells a number of extremely successful products, like Magnum, Europe's most popular chocolate ice cream bar. The strategy team is chaired by a marketing director from Birds Eye Wall's in the United Kingdom and has five additional members, most of whom are marketers, from other operating companies in Italy, Germany, and the Netherlands. This team cooperates closely with the relevant strategic group at the head office but also has the authority to implement strategy on its own.

The use of major conferences is one more important element in creating and maintaining Unilever's large network of managers. Once a year, each of the two chairmen addresses a meeting of 350 to 500 senior managers from all over the world. One conference takes place in Rotterdam, and the other is in London. At these conferences, over good food and drink, our most senior people meet, exchange views, and reconfirm old friendships.

The chairmen can also make major announcements to a large group of senior managers on these occasions. When we wanted to change our strategic direction some six years ago, we chose such a meeting as the place to explain why. When we needed to pursue a more active acquisitions program, we disclosed our intentions at a conference. When we wanted to explain the new foods structure and other major changes in the organization, we did so at the chairman's review meeting.

After such meetings, every chairman of an operating unit and every manager of a department gets a copy of the main points and presents a similar review to the middle management in his or her own unit. In this way, we reach most managers in the Unilever matrix effectively. In fact, shifting toward a concentration on the foods industry, our largest core business, would not have been possible if we hadn't been able to convince senior and middle managers that this move was logical and necessary for future growth.

Of course, in order to maintain a flexible organization with well-trained, dedicated managers, we must constantly reassess the balance between our centralized and decentralized activities. The relations among Unilever's head offices in Rotterdam and London, regional groups (such as those that cover the European Community and eastern Asia), and national operating companies must be monitored on an ongoing basis.

We are currently experimenting with involving members from operating company boards in head-office decision making. For example, our strategy for detergents in Europe is determined by a board that includes a few members from Lever Europe in Brussels and the CEOs of the main European operating companies. We call this new organizational arrangement the "Extended Head Office." This structure is certainly not yet cast in stone but, if successful, it will require an additional and perhaps even a different type of training program for our managers.

Learning the Quadrille

Whether we like it or not, those of us who work for transnational companies can no longer rely on only a formal organizational structure to get things done. A number of recent developments require that we adopt and maintain flexible organizations. The European market after 1992, the rise of eastern Asia as an economic region, the increasing importance of the developing world, to name just the main examples, will all demand a new mixture of global technology and local know-how. Building a company that continually evolves, in which the emphasis shifts depending on circumstances and the people concerned, is the only way forward.

While Unilever has certainly evolved into what is now called a transnational in academic and business policy circles, our actual progress was not made by the application of theory but through a much messier evolution of trial and error. Yet the company has focused on two consistent and related practices to underpin all structural changes: recruitment and training of high-quality managers; and the importance of linking decentralized units through a common corporate culture.

At Unilever, we have realized over time that the transnational way of working helps to maintain common standards of behavior in our far-flung units. Formulating and defining such standards with any precision is almost impossible, except in obvious cases like prohibiting bribery. Nevertheless, there are generally accepted standards in labor relations, communications with governments, care for the environment, and other social issues. Maintaining these standards depends as much on everybody in the organization understanding and accepting them as on formal instruction manuals.

Still, there are also risks in the informal transnational network. For instance, management can lose its sense of urgency. Everybody may be so busy with friends elsewhere—with the interesting training program, the well-organized course, the next major conference—that complacency sets in. Unfortunately, we have seen this happen in some of our units, especially the more successful ones. It may be necessary to shake up the system from time to time, either entirely (as Unilever did with a shift in its core strategy) or partially (as we did with the changes in our foods business). And major shake-ups are tasks for the chief executive, tasks that can be delegated only to a limited degree.

But complacency is not a real problem if everyone takes his or her sometimes shifting roles and responsibilities seriously. I like to use an analogy with a dance called the quadrille. This is an old-fashioned dance, in which four people change places regularly. This is also how a good matrix should work, with sometimes the regional partner, sometimes the product partner, sometimes the functional partner, and sometimes the labor-relations partner taking the lead. Flexibility rather than hierarchy should always be a transnational's motto—today and in the future.

PART

III

Winning in Foreign Markets

1
Beware the Pitfalls of Global Marketing

Kamran Kashani

It's fashionable today to enthuse over globalized markets and cite glowing examples of standardized marketing winners around the world. True, some markets *are* globalizing, and more companies are taking advantage of them with signal success. But the rosy reports of these triumphs usually neglect to mention the complexities and risks involved; for every victory in globalization there are probably several failures that aren't broadcast. It's not fashionable to talk about failure.

To get an idea of the complexity and the risks in global marketing, examine the case of Henkel, West Germany's leading industrial and consumer adhesives producer. In 1982, Henkel decided to pump new life into its internationally accepted but stagnating consumer contact-adhesive brand, Pattex. The strategy called for expanding the Pattex brand to include newly introduced products in fast-growing segments of the market. The idea of using Pattex as an umbrella faced heavy opposition, however, from among Henkel's country subsidiaries worldwide. "People were shaking their heads and saying it can't be done and shouldn't be done," recalls the product manager responsible for the decision.

The subsidiaries' doubts led to a consumer test of the umbrella branding concept in West Germany, Austria, and Benelux. According to the test results, Pattex could be repositioned without hurting sales, and it could enhance the prospects of a broader product range. The highly positive survey responses helped soften local managements' opposition. The global branding of Pattex as "strong universal bonding" took effect soon after.

Almost from the beginning, the relaunched brand showed good

results. Today Pattex is Henkel's top brand in consumer adhesives in Europe and in 20 other countries. Surpassing all management expectations, the new products account for close to one-half of the brand's total sales of approximately 100 million deutsche marks.

Thus encouraged, Henkel's management took a similar step a few months after the relaunch of Pattex. This time the subject of umbrella treatment was Pritt, the company's number one brand around the world in glue sticks. Previously, Henkel had repositioned Pritt from "stick gluing" to "simple all-purpose gluing," but with little success. Nevertheless, the experience with Pattex gave top management reason to hope that a coordinated, standardized package design and communication strategy might do the trick this time.

Besides, the major subsidiaries had changed their tune: they endorsed an internationally harmonized Pritt line. In fact, the champion of the concept was the Benelux unit, one of Henkel's largest. Many executives in headquarters in Düsseldorf also viewed the Pritt decision as the next logical step after Pattex.

What more could central product management possibly ask for?

There was one potential problem, however, with the Pritt plan. A quickly arranged consumer survey in West Germany and Benelux had shown that the harmonized line might still be insufficient to turn the broader Pritt umbrella brand around. While comparative test results indicated some improvement over the current package design, they still put UHU, Pritt's global archrival, ahead along many consumer-perceived dimensions. But Pattex's encouraging performance and the unusually strong support from the leading subsidiaries persuaded the head office to proceed with the harmonized line anyway.

In the months that followed, while Pattex maintained its sales climb, the new strategy failed to improve Pritt's ho-hum performance, to everybody's surprise. The brand did not lend support to the lesser products under its umbrella, and their sales continued to stall. Today worldwide sales still hover far below expectations, and Pritt remains a one-product brand standing for stick gluing and not much more.

What explains the success of one program in the face of heavy subsidiary opposition and the failure of the other in spite of warm local support? Henkel management has discovered two reasons. Headquarters let forceful subsidiary officers drown out early warnings based on research about Pritt, and they hastened the decision. It was a case of enthusiasm substituting for hard data. Moreover, when the early results disappointed hopes, the subsidiaries diverted Pritt's promotion funds to other products in a search for immediate payoff. With no central follow-up, the local units did nothing to make up the lost promotion support.

Accordingly, the Pritt plan got neither the initial scrutiny nor the later subsidiary backup that Pattex had enjoyed. Combined, the two handicaps proved fatal to Pritt's global branding.

Winners and Losers

To ascertain why certain global marketing decisions succeed while others fail, I recently studied 17 cases of marketing standardization at 9 American and European multinationals. Nine of the ventures were successes, but in eight, the companies failed to meet their objectives. This article reports on the findings of the study.

A systematic comparison of the "winners" and "losers" reveals that the differences in outcome often depend on the processes underlying the decision making. In other words, my study shows that the ways global decisions are conceptualized, refined, internally communicated, and, finally, implemented in the company's international network have a great deal to do with their performance.

I have identified five pitfalls that handicap global marketing programs and contribute to their suboptimal performance or even demise. The pitfalls include insufficient use of formal research, tendency to overstandardize, poor follow-up, narrow vision in program coordination, and inflexibility in implementation. I'll take these up in turn.

INSUFFICIENT RESEARCH

Formal research is of course not alien to marketing decision making, yet many a global program has been kicked off without the benefit of a reality test. Nearly half of the programs examined included no formal research before startup. And most of the companies paid for this omission afterwards.

A case in point was Lego A/S, the Danish toy marketer, which undertook American-style consumer promotions in Japan a few years ago. Earlier, the company had measurably improved its penetration of U.S. households by employing "bonus" packs and gift promotions. Encouraged by that success, it decided to transfer these tactics unaltered to other markets, including Japan, where penetration had stalled. But these lures left Japanese consumers unmoved. Subsequent investigation showed that consumers considered the promotions to be wasteful, expensive, and not very appealing. Similar reactions were recorded in several other countries. Lego's marketers thus got their first lesson on the limitations of the global transferability of sales promotions.

Lego management examined consumer perceptions of promotions only *after* the program had failed. In the words of one headquarters executive close to the decision concerning Japan, "People at the head office in Billund and locally believed so much in the U.S. experience and its transferability that they didn't see any need to test the promotions."

This case typifies managerial complacency toward use of market information. At the extreme, it exhibits itself as "we know what we need to know," an attitude that discounts the necessity of research in the early phases of a program. This blinkered outlook often accompanies an assumption that one market's experience is transferable to others—as though the world has finally converged and market idiosyncrasies have disappeared. Even managers' enthusiasm can get in the way of research. Henkel learned this point in its almost casual dismissal of Pritt's consumer survey results.

Shortcutting the early step of research in a decision process is likely to be costly. Of the cases in the sample, nearly two-thirds of the global programs that did not benefit from formal research before launch failed in their mission, while the same proportion of those that relied on research succeeded.

OVERSTANDARDIZATION

Paradoxically, without some diversity of practice in the organization, marketing standardization will not work. When a program is burdened with too many standards, local inventiveness and experimentation close to the markets dry up. Local innovation is exactly what a global program needs to keep itself updated and responsive to evolving market conditions.

In the mid-1970s, when Polaroid introduced its pathbreaking SX-70 camera in Europe, the company employed the same advertising strategy—including TV commercials and print ads—it had used in the triumphant launch of the product in the United States. To headquarters in Cambridge, Massachusetts, the camera was a universal product with a universal consumer benefit: the pleasure of instant photography. Therefore, the communication approach should be standard around the world. Well, the product was surely universal, but the television commercials, featuring testimonials from personalities well known in the United States, like Sir Laurence Olivier, were not necessarily transferable to Europe. At least, that's what Polaroid's executives there thought.

Unperturbed by subsidiaries' concerns, Cambridge set strict guidelines to discourage deviation from the global plan. Even local translations of the English spoken in the commercials had to get approval from the head office. As one senior European executive recalls, "We were treated like kids who have to be controlled every step along the way."

The Europeans were proved to be right. The testimonials by "unknown" personalities left consumers cold. The commercials never achieved much impact in either raising awareness of Polaroid for instant photography or pulling consumers into the stores for a closer look at the camera. Even though the SX-70 later became a winner in Europe, local management believes that the misguided introductory campaign in no way helped its performance.

Fortunately, the lesson was not forgotten a decade later, when Polaroid's European management launched a program of pan-European advertising to reposition Polaroid's instant photography from a "party camera" platform, which had eroded the brand's image and undermined camera prices, to a serious, utilitarian platform. But this time, headquarters didn't assume it had the answer. Instead, it looked for inspiration in the various advertising practices of the European subsidiaries. And it found the answer in the strategy of one of the smallest subsidiaries, Switzerland's. With considerable profit, the Swiss unit had promoted the functional uses of instant photography as a way to communicate with family and friends. A pan-European task force charged with setting the advertising strategy tested the concept in major markets. These tests proved that the Swiss strategy was transferable and indeed produced the desired impact.

Thus was born the "Learn to Speak Polaroid" campaign. The two-year European project is considered one of the company's most successful advertising efforts. Subsidiaries outside Europe, including those in Australia and Japan, liked the strategy so much that they adopted it too. The experience is a source of pride for European management and a reaffirmation that "Europe can take care of itself."

What made the SX-70 and "Learn to Speak Polaroid" campaigns decidedly different was the decision-making processes involved. Promoting the SX-70 was a top-down process. But in "Learn to Speak Polaroid," the subsidiaries were offered the opportunity to influence the outcome, and they took it. Furthermore, "Learn . . ." was a product of the diversity found in the subsidiaries' communication strategies. The task force had the luxury of choosing among several solutions to the problem. It also had the wisdom to test the chosen strategy for confirmation of its impact around Europe.

Finally, and perhaps most important, even after adopting the pan-European program, local management retained the freedom to adapt the campaign to domestic tastes and needs. For example, where tests showed that the "Learn . . ." tag didn't convey the intended meaning in the local language, the subsidiary was free to change it. The message was more important than the words. Moreover, while the copy and layout for print ads remained fixed throughout Europe, local units could choose their preferred illustrations from a large set of alternatives prepared by the ad agency.

The contrasting outcomes of these two campaigns underscore a point clear to experienced marketers that, for a global program to achieve its aims, the scope of standardization need not be total. Any such program usually can attain its objectives through standardization of a few elements in the marketing mix of a product or service. Never too many elements, however, these are the leverage points around which the rationale for standardization is built.

With Pattex, for instance, the global branding strategy depended on the use of a successful brand for new products, uniform positioning of the entire range, and harmonized package designs. Local units, on the other hand, had authority over a set of decisions including communication strategy, pricing, and distribution channels. They could even decide on the package illustrations pertaining to the uses of adhesives. These matters, though important to the marketing success of Pattex in each country, did not impinge on the rationale or the crucial elements of standardization.

Nor did the flexibility allowed in the execution of "Learn to Speak Polaroid" advertising weaken the campaign. Deviations in execution didn't distract from the common mission; rather, they helped strengthen the effort by bringing local expertise to bear on the details. Overstandardization would have destroyed the incentive for local contribution, a price no global marketing program can afford to pay.

POOR FOLLOW-UP

Impressive kickoff meetings, splashy presentations to country heads, and the like are important attention-getters at the start of a campaign. But the momentum will be lost, as in the case of Pritt's promotional support, if these are not followed by lower key yet concrete steps to monitor progress and solve problems as they come along. These post-launch activities can determine whether a program survives the domestic organization's other priorities.

The differing experiences of Digital Equipment Corporation and another U.S.-based computer company, which I will call Business Electronic Systems (BES), are instructive. Not long ago, DEC's European operation installed a standardized sales management program in its 17 regional subsidiaries. Aimed to improve sales force productivity and customer service, the program touched on many aspects of overseeing the region's 2,500-strong sales force. But as sales operations were traditionally considered a local matter, sales managers were at first predictably unenthusiastic about using the system. It was considered an infringement on their authority.

What gradually sold them on it was the continuity of attention the program got in the two years after its highly visible launch. Through watchful monitoring of progress toward full implementation, coordinating sessions among local sales managers, and periodic messages of reinforcement from top management, sponsors at regional headquarters made sure that the program received priority from subsidiary officials. The coordinating sessions for subsidiary sales managers were particularly helpful, highlighting the payoffs from use of the system and furnishing a forum for dealing with common problems. These sessions proved to be invaluable for taking a creative solution produced in one market and spreading it to the other 16.

At BES, which installed a standardized software-house cooperation program in Europe, the picture was much different. Regional headquarters conceived the program to help penetrate a market segment where BES was weak—small and medium-sized accounts. The program required a big change in sales force operation: no longer in control of the hardware and software package, the sales force had to determine its content jointly with a software house that had access to the smaller accounts. The success of the standardized program depended on how well the sales force carried out its new assignments in BES's eight country and subregional European operations.

Like DEC, BES gave the project a highly visible launch. Top management left no doubt that the software-house cooperation strategy enjoyed its wholehearted support. But the program never got the follow-up attention it needed. The responsibility for overseeing the project kept changing hands in the head office. Partly as a result of these switches in management, efforts to monitor progress in the subsidiaries dwindled.

The main problem, however, was the absence of a communication channel for sharing and building on subsidiary experiences. Each unit was obliged to find its own solutions to problems common to many. Hence the wheel was reinvented every time. Moreover, many country sales managers resented having to implement an unpopular program. Some gave up; others reluctantly carried on to the end, which came in three years. The reason: poor performance.

The quality of follow-up is of paramount importance when a global program introduces abrupt changes in local practice. As DEC's example shows, timely follow-up measures can go a long way to ensure subsidiary involvement and compliance. Without such measures, as BES learned, the program can easily succumb to local management's lukewarm interest.

NARROW VISION

A coordinating organization is needed to look after the health of a global marketing program because, as we have seen, a program's success depends so much on what happens after its launch—whether problems in implementation are resolved, and how the program's content is adapted to evolving internal and market conditions.

Two common mechanisms employed to manage a global program through its launch and beyond are those based, respectively, in the headquarters and a "lead market." Under a headquarters mechanism, the formal authority for a program rests with a central line or staff function like worldwide product management, regional management, or international marketing coordination. Under a lead market mechanism, a subsidiary is assigned the responsibility to define and manage a given program for all the participating "follower" countries. The choice of a lead market is usually a function of its expertise or experience with a particular product or service.

Though popular, both approaches have serious weaknesses. Headquarters, by definition removed from the firing line, nevertheless makes decisions that are supposed to keep the program fine-tuned to changing subsidiary market conditions. Similarly, the lead-market structure lacks the global perspective and information sources to coordinate international activities well. That is especially true when the lead market is also the home base for successful products that are globalization candidates. In these cases, management isn't always willing to adopt its "tried and proven" marketing ideas to different conditions prevailing elsewhere in the international organization.

But the main problem with both mechanisms is narrow vision; in each, only a single perspective is represented. As such they are not open to a continuous stream of inputs from local markets. Nor do they provide a forum for debating alternatives or sharing solutions to common problems. As a result, local management often justifiably regards headquarters or lead-market decisions as narrow, insular, top-down, and even dictatorial.

Unilever's experience with its household cleaner Domestos shows how a decision-making structure representing a single view can hamper global marketing. In the 1970s, the Anglo-Dutch company targeted Domestos for international expansion and assigned development of a global "reference mix" to the brand's lead market in the United Kingdom, where Domestos had been well established for a long time. But years and several market entries later, top management was still waiting for a repeat elsewhere of the UK's success story. Later analysis identified a key contributor to the problem: the lead market's insistence on a home-brewed recipe of positioning Domestos as a "lavatory germ killer" in markets already crowded with specialized and lower priced competition.

Where the product had won penetration, it had done so largely by deviating from the lead market's guidelines and staking out a whole new product category. In West Germany, Domestos was positioned as an all-purpose sanitary cleaner, and in Australia as a "bathroom plaque remover"—an innovative platform with potential for universal application, as consumers in many markets now show a growing concern with the appearance of their bathrooms.

To avoid the problems inherent in center-based or lead-market mechanisms, Unilever's detergent unit recently opted for a multisubsidiary structure to coordinate brands in Europe. The European Brand Group (EBG) is a decision-making body that includes executives from headquarters and a number of large subsidiaries.

So far, the company's experience with this mixed organization has been encouraging. As an example, EBG was instrumental in developing and launching a lemon-scented version of Vif, Unilever's successful abrasive liquid cleaner, across Europe in record time of a few months. Most important, the introduction outfoxed Procter & Gamble, which was known to be planning a similar move with its Mr. Clean; Vif Lemon won the race to market in every single country. Unilever management hopes that such gains in coordination will reinforce EBG's mandate to "view Europe as one business" and help speed up harmonization of marketing practices around the continent.

RIGID IMPLEMENTATION

Standardized marketing is a means of reaching an end, never an end in itself. When global marketers forget that obvious truth, standardization risks becoming rigid and ultimately self-defeating. Two common manifestations of rigidity are forced adoption and automatic piloting.

Forced adoption is the outcome of a tendency to ignore local units' reservations about implementing a standardized marketing program. Higher level management's typical reaction is to close the exit door on this ground: "After all, what's left of global marketing if the implementation isn't universal?" Theoretically, this is right. And ardent globalizers would argue that local resistance can be expected in any standardized effort and that without some central direction, a program would never get off the ground. But forced compliance rarely delivers the anticipated rewards. Among the programs I studied, every case of forced adoption had eventually flopped.

It is true that a subsidiary's objection may stem from resistance to ideas originating from outside. But local management's reservations may also be based on a sound understanding of its domestic market. When Nestlé launched its innovative cakelike Yes chocolate bar in Europe, the UK organization refused to take the product because a soft bar assertedly would not appeal to British tastes. Subsequent market tests validated this local opinion. Forced adoption would have led to failure on a large scale.

Whatever the reasons for local opposition, forced compliance destroys any commitment to program implementation. And no global program, no matter how sound, can survive such absence of commitment.

Automatic piloting is symptomatic of inflexible program management in the face of changing market conditions. Lego's costly difficulties in the United States illustrate this problem. The company, whose motto has been "kids are kids and alike around the world," pioneered standardized marketing in its industry and became a truly global enterprise by marketing its educational toys in the same fashion in more than 100 countries.

Recently, however, Lego has encountered stiff competition from look-alike and lower priced rival products from Japan, the United States, and other countries. In the United States, where the competition has been the fiercest, Tyco, a leading competitor, began putting its toys in plastic buckets that could be used for storage after each play. This utilitarian approach contrasted with Lego's elegant see-through cartons standardized worldwide. But American parents seemed to prefer the functional toys-in-a-bucket idea over the cartons. Seeing a potential for serious damage, Lego's alarmed U.S. management sought permission from Denmark to package Lego toys in buckets. The head office flatly refused the request.

The denial was based on seemingly sound arguments. The bucket idea could cheapen Lego's reputation for high quality. Moreover, the Lego bucket would rightly be seen as a "me too" defensive reaction from a renowned innovator. Finally, and perhaps most important, buckets would be a radical deviation from the company's policy of standardized marketing everywhere. Even U.S. consumer survey results comparing buckets favorably with cartons weren't considered a good enough reason for a change from the global concept.

Two years later, however, headquarters in Billund reversed itself. The impetus was a massive loss of U.S. market share to competitive goods sold in buckets. Soon after, the American subsidiary began marketing some of its toys in a newly designed bucket of its own. Now, to the delight of many in Billund, the buckets are outselling the cartons, and the share erosion has reassuringly halted. (Last Christmas the bucket was introduced worldwide and was a smashing success.) An observer of Lego's about-face in the United States attributed the two-years-late response to automatic piloting on the part of its global marketers.

The Lego story highlights the principle adhered to by some, but ignored by many others, that international conformity to global standards may have to be sacrificed to respond to shifting conditions in particular markets. As one Lego executive put it ruefully, "While kids will always be alike around the world, parents who buy the toys may change their behavior."

Improving the Process

The pitfalls I have examined can all be traced to shortcomings in a global program's decision-making process. But the winners in my sample show that such traps can be avoided. Analysis of them leads to the following observations on ways of upgrading the process and the decisions that result from it.

Market research helps a global marketing program in two ways: by influencing decisions to more accurately reflect the commonalities as well as the differences among subsidiary markets; and by winning support for the program in local organizations when research results are especially encouraging.

Useful research is multisite in geographic coverage and uniform in methodology. The multisite criterion ensures enough local diversity to make the findings valid for the program's international scope. Needless to say, a global marketing program doesn't have to be tested everywhere. Some companies find the inclusion of at least one major subsidiary market and a few others considered representative of the rest sufficient not only for geographic diversity purposes but also for building internal credibility for the results. Uniform methodology, on the other hand, ensures comparability of international research data, which is so often a problem for global marketers. "Without similar methods," one experienced executive noted, "the local organizations can kill a good global program with their own research."

Local initiative and decision making are often the keys to a program's long-term success. To avoid sterile uniformity at one extreme and a free-for-all at the other, global marketers have to delineate early on the few standards that are essential to attaining a program's objectives and the many that are not. They must insist on compliance with the essential standards. But at the same time, local experimentation with the less critical elements should be allowed and even encouraged. Astute marketers will keep an eye on the local experiments and in due course incorporate the successful innovations into an evolving and dynamic set of global standards.

Effective follow-up—as important as any prelaunch measure—means identifying common problems hampering implementation, spreading creative solutions found by local units, and winning support for the program over parochial priorities. But these tasks don't get performed automatically; they need to be recognized and assigned.

The responsibility for initiating and directing post-launch activities must therefore be focused by a central program manager or a management team. The chosen individual(s) should possess not only the international overview necessary to administer the program but also negotiating skills for bypassing organizational barriers and building consensus and support for the project. These skills become particularly useful in cases where globalization demands radical departures in local practices.

While the *process* for formulating a program, starting it, and following it through may be driven centrally by, say, program management, decisions on its *content* are best left to the subsidiaries or country organizations. So an ad hoc decision-making mechanism incorporating a number of subsidiaries offers more openness to local input than one centered at headquarters or in a lead market.

To prevent this process from becoming cumbersome, headquarters should limit the group's membership to a few of the larger and more influential subsidiaries and confine its participants to those local marketing managers with deep knowledge of the issues and the organizational weight to see decisions through to implementation. The experience of a growing number of companies employing such ad hoc mechanisms suggests, not surprisingly, that their effectiveness improves as the participants get practice working together on issues of concern to most member countries. That experience also suggests that thorny problems are best left for resolution after the group has established a track record of successful decisions.

Flexibility should be built into a global program's implementation. That means a willingness on its sponsors' part selectively to sacrifice global standards when local conditions so dictate or to leave open an exit door when local management argues against adoption of a program. In the absence of flexibility, standardized marketing risks becoming an obstacle to competitive advantage.

But what to do in those frequent cases when global marketers and their subsidiary colleagues differ on the standards appropriate in a certain market? A number of companies in my study have a "facts-over-opinions" policy to get around this potentially volatile problem. A subsidiary gains exemption from having to conform in part or altogether if, and only if, careful research confirms its doubts. By letting facts decide each case, the policy helps focus the attention of both sides on the substantive issues and clears the debate of mere opinions—which are so often colored. Implementation of the marketing program then proceeds in an informed but flexible fashion.

2
Winging It in Foreign Markets

Martin van Mesdag

What do hamburgers, hot dogs, soft cheeses, portion-packed yogurt, and Scotch whisky have in common besides that they're all edible or drinkable? They all sell like mad in global markets, and one strategy is responsible for their success. As marketers, we have three—and only three—available strategies for taking a product across national boundaries. The method behind these successful products is one of these three:

Phased internationalization appeals enormously to marketing people. It is what we all learned when we became marketers. You go to a foreign country with knowledge of your manufacturing capabilities but with no presuppositions about products. Next, you buy research to find out exactly what people there want within a product area you can cater to. Finally, you come home and get your development people to put together a product with which you can compete in that foreign market.

Global marketing is the trendiest and seemingly most promising approach. From a marketing point of view, it is a highly responsible strategy. Ignoring frontiers, you go out into a part of the world and try to discover newly emerging needs you might respond to with your manufacturing capabilities. You are particularly alert to consumer typology and to the behavior patterns into which your product offering will have to fit. You do a conscientious market segmentation job.

The shot-in-the-dark method is the seemingly crude, even sloppy, process of picking a product that is already successful in the home market and taking it abroad in the hope that it will sell there. It is an "unmarketing" approach since it makes what may be unwarranted assumptions about the behavior of a new and unfamiliar group of customers.

While we marketers are usually most comfortable with the first two approaches, the last—the shot-in-the-dark—is the one we use most often. Phased internationalization and formal global strategies are far less risky, but marketers who use them often miss the golden opportunities for taking products across national borders that may be right on our doorstep.

Constraints Abroad

When transcending national borders, marketers and product development people in all industries face a host of constraints. Some of these are obvious. People in different countries speak different languages. Rules and regulations differ across national borders: in most countries you drive on the right, but in some you drive on the left. Then there are climate, economic conditions, race, topography, political stability, and occupations. The most important source of constraints by far, and the most difficult to measure, is cultural differences rooted in history, education, economics, and legal systems.

Because of all these differences, the international convertibility of products and services varies enormously from one product category to another. Pocket calculators, credit card facilities, and lubricating oils need few international adaptations, whereas toilet soap, phonograph records, and candy require rather more adjustment. I am intrigued by how slow simple services like retailing and retail banking are to globalize and yet how standardization in some international hotel chains has gone so far that, as long as you stay inside the hotel, you cannot tell whether you are in Vancouver, Kuala Lumpur, Stockholm, or Torremolinos.

Of all the products I can think of, food and drink are probably the hardest to take global. Two constraints make globalizing food products especially difficult. The first, which is virtually unique to food products, is recognizability. People want to know what their food is made of, and they usually want to know how it's processed. They require recognizability in the appearance, the taste, and—in most cases—the texture of foods. Consumers impose no such requirements when they buy durables (except for textiles to some extent), personal care products, or household goods.

The recognizability constraint means that a food or a beverage product won't sell in countries where the people aren't familiar with its ingredients. It means that the amount of engineering and processing that companies can apply to food is limited. The recognizability requirement also means that extensive processing is more acceptable in countries where the product is not traditional than in countries where it is. Instant coffee is unpopular in Germany, France, and Italy, where people drink a lot of coffee and want it freshly brewed; it is more popular in non-coffee-drinking countries like Britain and Ireland.

The second main constraint on globalizing food products is what I call the age symptom. The more a product is associated with long-standing usage habits, the less internationally marketable it is. Conversely, the more recent the usage pattern, the more likely it is that the product will be marketable in a variety of countries.

The age symptom does not apply just to food products, of course. Garden spades, which have been in use for ages, look quite different in Switzerland, England, and Holland. But gardeners in those countries use identical motor diggers. And although styles do evolve slowly, men's formal clothing is made in response to long-established usage habits. You don't need to be a tailor to tell a German, a Frenchman, and a Briton apart by the suits or the shoes they wear. But with the recent emergence of casual clothing, everybody wears the same jeans, T-shirts, and sneakers.

The reason for this phenomenon is not mysterious. Products that have been around a long time respond to long-established usage patterns because people in different countries, and indeed different regions, used to live in isolation. Our modern international communications have proliferated: we can look at each other daily on TV, so our newly emerging usage patterns converge and thereby enhance the globalizability of the new products that respond to those patterns. Some products that respond to long-established usage patterns are natural cheese, popular cuts of meat, and varieties of beers, wines, and spirits. Products that respond to more recent usage patterns are portion-packed yogurts, hamburgers, hot dogs, soft drinks, and light beers. These products have more global potential than those that respond to older usage patterns. Global products like these have often come from the needs or wishes of a new stratum of customers, or—it doesn't matter which way you put it—a new stratum of customers has come along as suppliers have produced low-cost, universally available, integrated products.

Even though a food or a drink product that sells successfully in one country theoretically will not sell in another unless research explicitly predicts otherwise, many food products are, in fact, big successes globally. Moreover, I would argue that their success is overwhelmingly due to a shot-in-the-dark marketing approach.

Look, for example, at British food consumption patterns over the past 20 years. The United Kingdom has a massive debit balance of trade in food. My estimate of the consumer value of products that were new to the U.K. market in the past 20 years is $4.5 billion—more than 10% of total consumer spending on food. Further estimates show that 85% of those new products have either been imported or based on existing product concepts in other countries. Evidently, Britons like to try foods they're unfamiliar with.

By far the most important source of new product ideas in Britain has been, and is likely to remain, existing products in other countries. In 1985, for example, Britons ate $90 million worth of steaklets and grillsteaks—food products that, 20 years ago, were practically unheard of in Britain. The concept originated in America and is now meeting an enthusiastic response overseas. In the same year, Britons ate $260 million worth of yogurt—a product idea that came from Europe. Other nonindigenous foods popular in Britain now are low-fat cheeses, breakfast cereals, mineral water, pasta, and cookies.

Some of these products came to Britain through phased internationalization and through the formal global approach. Most of them, however, came by the shot-in-the-dark method. True, they were extensively researched and tested before their launch onto the British market. But the important fact is that they were products that had already established themselves in their respective home markets and were brought to Britain with a "let's try and see" attitude.

What Doesn't Work . . .

Phased internationalization works best with a single product in a particular market—the Dutch sell feta cheese in the Middle East, the Danes sell British-style bacon in Britain, and the Swiss chocolate makers carefully formulate their products to sell in America. Heinz and Unilever, among many others, have largely built their international business on this approach.

Phased internationalization, though, has a number of disadvantages. Because of the low international convertibility of food products, a product formulated for a single foreign country is unlikely to be salable in another. The Dutch do not sell their feta cheese outside the Middle

East, nor do the Danes sell British-style bacon outside Britain. The North American Swiss chocolate recipes are unsuitable for other areas. Consequently, this strategy implies a country-by-country approach to international expansion.

Moreover, the foreign supplier in a market may also have difficulty matching the value/price framework established by the indigenous competition. Finally, the foreign supplier may have difficulty establishing credibility. While some German cheese makers produce a very good Camembert, I imagine they'd have trouble selling it to the French. And despite their status as the world's largest producer of Scotch-type whisky, the Suntory Company in Japan considers it unwise to sell its product in Britain.

To all appearances the global marketing approach solves all these problems. It looks, without a doubt, like the worthiest of the three strategies. It promises all the benefits of economies of scale without the concessions dictated by the need to maximize market penetration. You can afford to skim the cream off your markets. You sell not what the greatest number of consumers finds acceptable; instead you sell what a minority of consumers is very keen on. Some products that were deliberately developed to sell in global markets are margarine (though the originators of the product curiously never adopted a global brand strategy for it), IDV's Bailey's Irish Cream liqueur, Ferrero's Tic Tac candy, and Rocher chocolates. Some global brands have global strategies. Others—Coca-Cola, Kellogg's cornflakes, Heineken beer, and McDonald's hamburgers, for example—have not. In the food and drink arena, brands that succeed in using the global marketing approach are few and far between. The reasons are the low international convertibility of food and drink products mentioned earlier and the increasing difficulty of finding brand names for international use.

. . . And What Does

I have described the shot-in-the-dark strategy of selling abroad what you happen to be selling in your home market as a sloppy way to approach international marketing. Especially in food and drink products, with their notoriously low levels of international convertibility, you'd think that no responsible marketer would ever employ this strategy. But wait. This strategy, which may look casual, has resulted in an enormous worldwide export business. Practically all the world's wine export businesses and most of the exports of beer and spirits were built on this shot-in-the-dark approach. Dispatching nearly 340,000 tons of cheese per year, Holland is the largest exporter of cheese in the world; nearly all of that volume is in indigenous varieties. West Germany has been building a sizable food and drink export business. In the United Kingdom alone, Germany sold $2 billion of unfamiliar, expensive, high-quality products straight from its home market—a sixfold increase, in real terms, in 12 years. And there's more.

Earlier, I mentioned Bailey's Irish Cream and some Ferrero products as having been deliberately developed for a global market—and they were. Then I mentioned Coca-Cola, Kellogg, Heineken, and McDonald's as other global brands—which they are. Or, strictly speaking, which they became. Those brands and products were not deliberately developed for global markets. They were developed and, for many years, sold only in their home markets. Marketers did not take these domestically successful products to foreign markets willy-nilly. They did extensive research, testing, and reformulation before the international rollout of all these brands, but the product concepts had domestic origins. It follows inescapably that the shot-in-the-dark strategy prompted the global growth of these brands. And when you think about it, the same applies to most global and international products and brands.

So while the shot-in-the-dark strategy is wholly reprehensible in theory, it has proved to be the most successful in practice. And the global marketing strategy—while the most laudable in theory—has proved the most difficult to implement.

Shots in the Not-So-Dark

While the shot-in-the-dark approach may be the most successful, marketers cannot afford to be lax about their planning and research methods. It is still important for marketers to examine and assess all three strategies since this choice will govern the entire product development process.

Once they've chosen a strategy, marketers can use the knowledge of their available technological resources to assess target markets not only for size and growth rate but also for age-of-usage and recognizability characteristics. A target market sector characterized by long-established usage habits will require a product offering that is closely tailored to expectations about domestic product attributes, and marketers will have to choose a country-by-country development route. The shot-in-the-dark and the global approaches are unlikely to work in this instance.

If, on the other hand, the company aspires after a global strategy, it will need to make a wide geographical sweep to ascertain whether it can discover any newly emerging need patterns that the company can respond to with its technological resources.

While the shot-in-the-dark approach has a high chance of failure, it can form the groundwork for either a phased internationalization or a global strategy; and it should certainly be tested against these possibilities.

No matter what strategy you choose, a rigorous knowledge-gathering program is in order. The resource investment in any serious sales expansion attempt is considerable, and appropriate knowledge can protect the investment. Getting ahold of that knowledge requires several types of inquiry skills:

Scanning, which is the collection of data, trends, judgments, and values that will—directly or indirectly—affect any envisaged marketing operation.

"Inferencing," which is speculating about customer responses to environmental influences and about responses to related influences.

"Propositioning," which is proposing a product offering in response to a particular customer need—whether assumed or ascertained—and measuring customers' assessment of that product offering.

Clearly, a formal global effort will initially concentrate on scanning and inferencing; a phased internationalization approach will start with a scanning exercise, soon to be followed by propositioning-type tests. The shot-in-the-dark approach will go straight to propositioning inquiries.

What About Brands?

Of all the marketing mix elements, the product is the most restrictive when a global strategy is considered. Some brands are intrinsically linked with particular products: what applies to the product applies to the brand. Coca-Cola and Kaffee HAG are good examples. In these cases, the globalizability of the brand is confined to the product. Other brands are associated with broad ranges of products: all private-label brands and brands like Hero and Kraft are in that category. In these cases, the brand can be globalized to cover product ranges that are internationalized—that is, product ranges are formulated to local needs, country by country; brands are global.

In the case of food and drink, the opportunities for globalizing products are much more limited than the opportunities for globalizing brands—provided those brands leave enough latitude to encompass product ranges formulated to suit the needs of specific markets.

I have said that products that have actually been designed for global markets are very rare (especially in the food and drink sectors) and that many of today's "global" products were originally intended for, and confined to, their home markets. The success rate of the shot-in-the-dark approach—on top of the fact that it requires the least amount of imagination, time, and development effort—suggests that it will remain a popular strategy. If we evaluate products in *one* market for their ability to answer newly emerging trends and needs in *other* markets, we are, in fact, using a shot-in-the-dark approach to build a global strategy. All sorts of food—and other—products have become global in this way. They have turned out to be shots in the not-so-dark.

3
Customizing Global Marketing

John A. Quelch and Edward J. Hoff

In the best of all possible worlds, marketers would only have to come up with a great product and a convincing marketing program and they would have a worldwide winner. But despite the obvious economies and efficiencies they could gain with a standard product and program, many managers fear that global marketing, as popularly defined, is too extreme to be practical. Because customers and competitive conditions differ across countries or because powerful local managers will not stand for centralized decision making, they argue, global marketing just won't work.

Of course, global marketing has its pitfalls, but it can also yield impressive advantages. Standardizing products can lower operating costs. Even more important, effective coordination can exploit a company's best product and marketing ideas.

Too often, executives view global marketing as an either/or proposition—either full standardization or local control. But when a global approach can fall anywhere on a spectrum from tight worldwide coordination on programming details to loose agreement on a product idea, why the extreme view? In applying the global marketing concept and making it work, flexibility is essential. Managers need to tailor the approach they use to each element of the business system and marketing program. For example, a manufacturer might market the same product under different brand names in different countries or market the same brands using different product formulas.

The big issue today is not whether to go global but how to tailor the global marketing concept to fit each business and how to make it work. In this article, we'll first provide a framework to help managers think about how they should structure the different areas of the marketing function as the business shifts to a global approach. We will then show how companies we have studied are tackling the implementation challenges of global marketing.

How Far to Go

How far a company can move toward global marketing depends a lot on its evolution and traditions. Consider these two examples:

Although the Coca-Cola Company had conducted some international business before 1940, it gained true global recognition during World War II, as Coke bottling plants followed the march of U.S. troops around the world. Management in Atlanta made all strategic decisions then—and still does now, as Coca-Cola applies global marketing principles, for example, to the worldwide introduction of Diet Coke. The brand name, concentrate formula, positioning, and advertising theme are virtually standard worldwide, but the artificial sweetener and packaging differ across countries. Local managers are responsible for sales and distribution programs, which they run in conjunction with local bottlers.

The Nestlé approach also has its roots in history. To avoid distribution disruptions caused by wars in Europe, to ease rapid worldwide expansion, and to respond to local consumer needs, Nestlé granted its local managers considerable autonomy from the outset. While the local managers still retain much of that decision-making power today, Nestlé headquarters at Vevey has grown in importance. Nestlé has transferred to its central marketing staff many former local managers who had succeeded in their local Nestlé businesses and who now influence country executives to accept standard new product and marketing ideas. The trend seems to be toward tighter marketing coordination.

To conclude that Coca-Cola is a global marketer and Nestlé is not would be simplistic. In Exhibit I, we assess program adaptation or standardization levels for each company's business functions, products, marketing mix elements, and countries. Each company has tailored its individual approach. Furthermore, as Exhibit I can't show, the situations aren't static. Readers can themselves evaluate their own *current* and *desired* levels of program adaptation or standardization on

Exhibit I. Global Marketing Planning Matrix: How Far to Go

		Adaptation		Standardization	
		Full	Partial	Partial	Full
Business functions	Research and development			▨	▨ Coca-Cola
	Finance and accounting			▨	▨
	Manufacturing		▨	▨	
	Procurement	▨		▨	
	Marketing		▨		▨
Products	Low cultural grounding High economies or efficiencies				▨
	Low cultural grounding Low economies or efficiencies				
	High cultural grounding High economies or efficiencies		▨		
	High cultural grounding Low economies or efficiencies				
Marketing mix elements	Product design			▨	▨
	Brand name			▨	▨
	Product positioning		▨		▨
	Packaging			▨	
	Advertising theme		▨		▨
	Pricing		▨	▨	
	Advertising copy	▨			▨
	Distribution	▨	▨		
	Sales promotion	▨	▨		
	Customer service	▨	▨		
Countries Region 1	Country A			▨	▨
	Country B			▨	▨
Region 2	Country C		▨		▨
	Country D		▨		▨
	Country E	▨			▨

▨ Nestlé   ▨ Coca-Cola

these four dimensions. The gap between the two levels is the implementation challenge. The size of the gap—and the urgency with which it must be closed—will depend on a company's strategy and financial performance, competitive pressures, technological change, and converging consumer values.

FOUR DIMENSIONS OF GLOBAL MARKETING

Now let's look at the issues that arise when executives consider the four dimensions shown in Exhibit I in light of the degree of standardization or adaptation that is appropriate.

BUSINESS FUNCTIONS.   A company's approach to global marketing depends, first, on its overall business strategy. In many multinationals, some functional areas have greater program standardization than others. Headquarters often controls manufacturing, finance, and R&D, while the local managers make the marketing decisions. Marketing is usually one of the last functions to be centrally directed. Partly because product quality and accounting data are easier to measure than marketing effectiveness, standardization can be greater in production and finance.

PRODUCTS.   Products that enjoy high scale economies or efficiencies and are not highly culture-bound are easier to market globally than others.

1. Economies or efficiencies. Manufacturing and R&D scale economies can result in a price spread between the global and the local product that is too great for even the most culture-bound consumer to resist. In addition, management often has neither the time nor the R&D resources to adapt products to each country. The markets for high-tech products like computers are not only very competitive but also affected by rapid technological change.

Most packaged consumer goods are less susceptible than durable goods like televisions and cars to manufacturing or even R&D economies. Coca-Cola's global policy and Nestlé's interest in tighter marketing coordination are driven largely by a desire to capitalize on the marketing ideas their managers around the world generate rather than by potential scale economies. Nestlé, for example, manufactures its packaged soups in dozens of locally managed plants around the world, with some transference of engineering know-how through a headquarters staff. Products and marketing programs are also locally managed, but new ideas are aggressively transferred, with local managers encouraged—or even prodded—to adapt and use them in their own markets. For Nestlé, global marketing does not so much yield high manufacturing economies as high efficiency in using scarce new ideas.

2. Cultural grounding. Consumer products used in the home—like Nestlé's soups and frozen foods—are often more culture-bound than products used outside the home such as automobiles and credit cards, and industrial products are inherently less culture-bound than consumer products. (Products like personal computers, for example, are often marketed on the basis of performance benefits that share a common technical language worldwide.) Experience also suggests that products will be less culture-bound if they are used by young people whose cultural norms are not ingrained, people who travel in different countries, and ego-driven consumers who can be appealed to through myths and fantasies shared across cultures.

Exhibit I lists four combinations of the scale economy and cultural grounding variables in order of their susceptibility to global marketing. Managers shouldn't be bound by any matrix, however; they should find creative ways to prepare a product for global marketing. If a manufacturer develops a new version of a seemingly culture-bound product that is based on new capital-intensive technology and generates superior performance benefits, it may well be possible to introduce it on a standard basis worldwide. Procter & Gamble developed Pampers disposable diapers as a global brand in a product category that intuition would say was culture-bound.

MARKETING MIX ELEMENTS. Few consumer goods companies go so far as to market the same products using the same marketing program worldwide. And those that do, like Lego, the Danish manufacturer of construction toys, often distribute their products through sales companies rather than full-fledged marketing subsidiaries.

For most products, the appropriate degree of standardization varies from one element of the marketing mix to another. Strategic elements like product positioning are more easily standardized than execution-sensitive elements like sales promotion. In addition, when headquarters believes it has identified a superior marketing idea, whether it be a package design, a brand name, or an advertising copy concept, the pressure to standardize increases.

Marketing can usually contribute to scale economies most significantly by creating a standard product design that will sell worldwide, permitting savings through globalized production. In addition, scale economies in marketing programming can be achieved through standard commercial executions and copy concepts. McCann-Erickson claims to have saved $90 million in production costs over 20 years by producing worldwide Coca-Cola commercials. To ensure that they have enough attention-getting power to overcome their foreign origins, however, marketers often have to make worldwide commercials expensive productions.

To compensate local management for having to accept a standard product and to fit the core product to each local market, some companies allow local managers to adapt those marketing mix elements that aren't subject to significant scale economies. On the other hand, local managers are more likely to accept a standard concept for those elements of the marketing mix that are less important and, ironically, often not susceptible to scale economies. Overall, then, the driving factor in moving toward global marketing should be the efficient worldwide use of good marketing ideas rather than any scale economies from standardization.

In judging how far to go in standardizing elements of the marketing mix, managers must also be mindful of the interactions among them. For example, when a product with the same brand name is sold in different countries, it can be difficult and sometimes impossible to sell them at different prices.

COUNTRIES. How far a decentralized multinational wishes to pursue global marketing will often vary from one country to another. Naturally, headquarters is likely to become more involved in marketing decisions in countries where performance is poor. But performance aside, small markets depend more on headquarters assistance than large markets. Because a standard marketing program is superior in quality to what local executives, even with the benefit of local market knowledge, could develop themselves, they may welcome it.

Large markets with strong local managements are less willing to accept global programs. Yet these are the markets that often account for most of the company's investment. To secure their acceptance, headquarters should make standard marketing programs reflect the needs of large rather than small markets. Small markets, being more tolerant of deviations from what would be locally appropriate, are less likely to resist a standard program.

As we've seen, Coca-Cola takes the same approach in all markets. Nestlé varies its approach in different countries depending on the strength of its market presence and each country's need for assistance. In completing the Exhibit I planning matrix, management may decide that it can sensibly group countries by region or by stage of market development.

Too Far Too Fast

Once managers have decided how global they want their marketing program to be, they must make the transition. Debates over the size of the gap between present and desired positions and the speed with which it must be closed will often pit the field against headquarters. Such conflict is most likely to arise in companies where the reason for change is not apparent or the country managers have had a lot of autonomy. Casualties can occur on both sides:

Because Black & Decker dominated the European consumer power tool market, many of the company's European managers could not see that a more centrally directed global marketing approach was needed as a defense against imminent Japanese competition. To make his point, the CEO had to replace several key European executives.

In 1982, the Parker Pen Company, forced by competition and a weakening financial position to lower costs, more than halved its number of plants and pen styles worldwide. Parker's overseas subsidiary managers accepted these changes but, when pressed to implement standardized advertising and packaging, they dug in their heels. In 1985, Parker ended its much heralded global marketing campaign. Several senior headquarters managers left the company.

If management is not careful, moving too far too fast toward global marketing can trigger painful consequences. First, subsidiary managers who joined the company because of its apparent commitment to local autonomy and to adapting its products to the local environment may become disenchanted. When poorly implemented, global marketing can make the local country manager's job less strategic. Second, disenchantment may reinforce not-invented-here attitudes that lead to game playing. For instance, some local managers may try bargaining with headquarters, trading the speed with which they will accept and implement the standard programs for additional budget assistance. In addition, local managers competing for resources and autonomy may devote too much attention to second-guessing headquarters' "hot buttons." Eventually the good managers may leave, and less competent people who lack the initiative of their predecessors may replace them.

A vicious circle can develop. Feeling compelled to review local performance more closely, headquarters may tighten its controls and reduce resources without adjusting its expectations of local managers. Meanwhile, local managers trying to gain approval of applications for deviations from standard marketing programs are being frustrated. The expanding headquarters bureaucracy and associated overhead costs reduce the speed with which the locals can respond to local opportunities and competitive actions. Slow response time is an especially serious problem with products for which barriers to entry for local competitors are low.

In this kind of system, weak, insecure local managers can become dependent on headquarters for operational assistance. They'll want headquarters to assume the financial risks for new product launches and welcome the prepackaged marketing programs. If performance falls short of headquarters' expectations, the local management can always blame the failure on the quality of operational assistance or on the standard marketing program. The local manager who has clear autonomy and profit-and-loss responsibility cannot hide behind such excuses.

If headquarters or regions assume much of the strategic burden, managers in overseas subsidiaries may think only about short-term sales. This focus will diminish their ability to monitor and communicate to headquarters any changes in local competitors' strategic directions. When their responsibilities shift from strategy to execution, their ideas will become less exciting. If the field has traditionally been as important a source of new product ideas as the central R&D laboratory, the company may find itself short of the grassroots creative thinking and marketing research information that R&D needs. The fruitful dialogue that characterizes a relationship between equal partners will no longer flourish.

How to Get There

When thinking about closing the gap between present and desired positions, most executives of decentralized multinationals want to accommodate their current organizational structures. They rightly view their subsidiaries and the managers who run them as important competitive strengths. They generally do not wish to transform these organizations into mere sales and distribution agencies.

How then in moving toward global marketing can headquarters build rather than jeopardize relationships, stimulate rather than demoralize local managers? The answer is to focus on means as much as ends, to examine the relationship between the home office and the field, and to ask what level of headquarters intervention for each business function, product, marketing mix element, and country is necessary to close the gap in each.

As Exhibit II indicates, headquarters can intervene at five points, ranging from informing to directing. The five intervention levels are cumulative; for headquarters to direct, it must also inform, persuade, coordinate, and approve. Exhibit II shows the approaches Atlanta and Vevey have taken. Moving from left to right on Exhibit II, the reader can see that things are done increasingly by fiat rather than patient persuasion, through discipline rather than education. At the far right, local subsidiaries can't choose whether to opt in or out of a marketing program, and headquarters views its country managers as subordinates rather than customers.

When the local managers tightly control marketing efforts, multinational managers face three critical issues. In the sections that follow, we'll take a look at how decentralized multinationals are working to correct the three problems as they move along the spectrum from informing to directing.

INCONSISTENT BRAND IDENTITIES. If headquarters gives country managers total control of their product lines, it cannot leverage the opportunities that multinational status gives it. The increasing degree to which consumers in one country are exposed to the company's products in another won't enhance the corporate image or brand development in the consumers' home country.

LIMITED PRODUCT FOCUS. In the decentralized multinational, the field line manager's ambition is to become a country manager, which means acquiring multiproduct and multifunction experience. Yet as the pace of technological innovation increases and the likelihood of global competition grows, multinationals need worldwide product specialists as well as executives willing to transfer to other countries. Nowhere is the need for headquarters guidance on innovative organizational approaches more evident than in the area of product policy.

Exhibit II. Global Marketing Planning Matrix: How to Get There

		Informing	Persuading	Coordinating	Approving	Directing
Business functions	Research and development					
	Finance and accounting					
	Manufacturing					
	Procurement					
	Marketing					
Products	Low cultural grounding High economies or efficiencies					
	Low cultural grounding Low economies or efficiencies					
	High cultural grounding High economies or efficiencies					
	High cultural grounding Low economies or efficiencies					
Marketing mix elements	Product design					
	Brand name					
	Product positioning					
	Packaging					
	Advertising theme					
	Pricing					
	Advertising copy					
	Distribution					
	Sales promotion					
	Customer service					
Countries Region 1	Country A					
	Country B					
Region 2	Country C					
	Country D					
	Country E					

Nestlé   Coca-Cola

SLOW NEW PRODUCT LAUNCHES. As global competition grows, so does the need for rapid worldwide rollouts of new products. The decentralized multinational that permits country managers to proceed at their own pace on new product introductions may be at a competitive disadvantage in this new environment.

WORD OF MOUTH

The least threatening, loosest, and therefore easiest approach to global marketing is for headquarters to encourage the transfer of information between it and its country managers. Since good ideas are often a company's scarcest resource, headquarters efforts to encourage and reward their generation, dissemination, and application in the field will build both relationships and profits. Here are two examples:

Nestlé publishes quarterly marketing newsletters that report recent product introductions and programming innovations. In this way, each subsidiary can learn quickly about and assess the ideas of others. (The best newsletters are written as if country organizations were talking to each other rather than as if headquarters were talking down to the field.)

Johnson Wax holds periodic meetings of all marketing directors at corporate headquarters twice a year to build global esprit de corps and to encourage the sharing of new ideas.

By making the transfer of information easy, a multinational leverages the ideas of its staff and spreads organizational values. Headquarters has to be careful, however, that the information it's passing on is useful. It may focus on updating local managers about new products, when what they mainly want is information on the most tactical and country-specific elements of the marketing mix. For example, the concentration of the grocery trade is much higher in the United Kingdom and Canada than it is in the United States. In this case, managers in the United States can learn from British and Canadian country managers about how to deal with the pressures for extra merchandising support that result when a few powerful retailers control a large percentage of sales. Likewise, marketers in countries with restrictions on mass media advertising have developed sophisticated point-of-purchase merchandising skills that could be useful to managers in other countries.

By itself, however, information sharing is often insufficient to help local executives meet the competitive challenges of global marketing.

FRIENDLY PERSUASION

Persuasion is a first step managers can take to deal with the three problems we've outlined. Any systematic headquarters effort to influence local managers to apply standardized approaches or introduce new global products while the latter retain their decision-making authority is a persuasion approach.

Unilever and CPC International, for example, employ world-class advertising and marketing research staff at headquarters. Not critics but coaches, these specialists review the subsidiaries' work and try to upgrade the technical skills of local marketing departments. They frequently visit the field to disseminate new concepts, frameworks, and techniques, and to respond to problems that local management raises. (It helps to build trust if headquarters can send out the same staff specialists for several years.)

Often, when the headquarters of a decentralized multinational identifies or develops a new product, it has to persuade the country manager in a so-called prime-mover market to invest in the launch. A successful launch in the prime-mover market will, in turn, persuade other country managers to introduce the product. The prime-mover market is usually selected according to criteria including the commitment of local management, the probabilities of success, the credibility with which a success would be regarded by managers in other countries, and its perceived transferability.

Persuasion, however, has its limitations. Two problems recur with the prime-mover approach. First, by adopting a wait-and-see attitude, country managers can easily turn down requests to be prime-mover markets on the grounds of insufficient resources. Since the country managers in the prime-mover markets have to risk their resources to launch the new products, they're likely to tailor the product and marketing programs to their own markets rather than to global markets. Second, if there are more new products waiting to be launched than there are prime-mover markets to launch them, headquarters product specialists are likely to give in to a country manager's demands for local tailoring. But because of the need for readaptation in each case, the tailoring may delay roll-outs in other markets and allow competitors to preempt the product. In the end, management may sacrifice long-term worldwide profits to maximize short-term profits in a few countries.

MARKETING TO THE SAME DRUMMER

To overcome the limits of persuasion, many multinationals are coordinating their marketing programs, whereby headquarters has a structured role in both decision making and performance evaluation that is far more influential than person-to-person persuasion. Often using a matrix or team approach, headquarters shares with country managers the responsibility and authority for programming and personnel decisions.

Nestlé locates product directors as well as support groups at headquarters. Together they develop long-term strategies for each product category on a worldwide basis, coordinate worldwide market research, spot new product opportunities, spark the field launch of new products, advise the field on how headquarters will evaluate new product proposals, and spread the word on new products' performance so that other countries will be motivated to launch them. Even though the product directors are staff executives with no line authority, because they have all been successful line managers in the field, they have great credibility and influence.

Country managers who cooperate with a product director can quickly become heroes if they successfully implement a new idea. On the other hand, while a country manager can reject a product director's advice, headquarters will closely monitor his or her performance with an alternative program. In addition, within the product category in which they specialize, the directors have influence on line management appointments in the field. Local managers thus have to be concerned about their relationships with headquarters.

Some companies assign promising local managers to other countries and require would-be local managers to take a tour of duty at headquarters. But such personnel transfer programs may run into barriers. First, many capable local nationals may not be interested in working outside their countries of origin. Second, powerful local managers are often unwilling to give up their best people to other country assignments. Third, immigration regulations and foreign service relocation costs are burdensome. Fourth, if transferees from the field have to take a demotion to work at headquarters, the costs in ill will often exceed any gains in cross-fertilization of ideas. If management can resolve these problems, however, it will find that creating an international career path is one of the most effective ways to develop a global perspective in local managers.

To enable their regional general managers to work alongside the worldwide product directors, several companies have moved them from the field to the head office. More and more companies require regional managers to reach sales and profit targets for each product as well as for each country within their regions. In the field, regional managers often focus on representing the views of individual countries to headquarters, but at headquarters they become more concerned with ensuring that the country managers are correctly implementing corporatewide policies.

Recently, Fiat and Philips N.V., among others, consolidated their worldwide advertising into a single agency. Their objectives are to make each product's advertising more consistent around the world and to make it easier to transfer ideas and information among local agency offices, country organizations, and headquarters. Use of a single agency (especially one that bills all advertising expenditures worldwide) also symbolizes a commitment to global marketing and more centralized control. Multinationals shouldn't, however, use their agencies as Trojan horses for greater standardization. An undercover operation is likely to jeopardize agency-client relations at the country level.

While working to achieve global coordination, some companies are also trying to tighten coordination in particular regions:

Kodak recently experimented by consolidating 17 worldwide product line managers at corporate headquarters. In addition, the company made marketing directors in some countries responsible for a line of business in a region as well as for sales of all Kodak products in their own countries. Despite these new appointments, country managers still retain profit-and-loss responsibility for their own markets.

Whether a matrix approach such as this broadens perspectives rather than increases tension and confusion depends heavily on the corporation's cohesiveness. Such an organizational change can clearly communicate top management's strategic direction, but headquarters needs to do a persuasive selling job to the field if it is to succeed.

Procter & Gamble has established so-called Euro Brand teams that analyze opportunities for greater product and marketing program standardization. Chaired by the brand manager from a "lead country," each team includes brand managers from other European subsidiaries that market the brand, managers from P&G's European technical center, and one of P&G's three European division managers, each of whom is responsible for a portfolio of brands as well as for a group of countries. Concerns that the larger subsidiaries would dominate the teams and that decision making would either be paralyzed or produce "lowest common denominator" results have proved groundless.

STAMPED AND APPROVED

By coordinating programs with the field, headquarters can balance the company's local and global perspectives. Even a decentralized multinational may decide, however, that to protect or exploit some corporate asset, the center of gravity for certain elements of the marketing program should be at headquarters. In such cases, management has two options: it can send clear directives to its local managers or permit them to develop their own programs within specified parameters and subject to headquarters approval. With a properly managed approval process, a multinational can exert effective control without unduly dampening the country manager's decision-making responsibility and creativity.

Procter & Gamble recently developed a new sanitary napkin, and P&G International designated certain countries in different geographic regions as test markets. The product, brand name, positioning, and package design were standardized globally. P&G International did, however, invite local managers to suggest how the global program could be improved and how the nonglobal elements of the marketing program should be adapted in their markets. It approved changes in several markets. Moreover, local managers developed valuable ideas on such programming specifics as sampling and couponing techniques that were used in all other countries, including the United States.

Nestlé views its brand names as a major corporate asset. As a result, it requires all brands sold in all countries to be registered in the home country of Switzerland. While the ostensible reason for this requirement is legal protection, the effect is that any product developed in the field has to be approved by Vevey. The head office has also developed detailed guidelines that suggest rather than mandate how brand names and logos should appear on packaging and in advertising worldwide (with exceptions subject to its approval). Thus the country manager's control over the content of advertising is not compromised, and the company achieves a reasonably consistent presentation of its names and logos worldwide.

DOING IT THE HEADQUARTERS WAY

Multinationals that direct local managers' marketing programs usually do so out of a sense of urgency. The motive may be to ensure either that a new product is introduced rapidly around the world before the competition can respond or that every manager fully and faithfully exploits a valuable marketing idea. Sometimes direction is needed to prove that global marketing can work. Once management makes the point, a more participative approach is feasible.

In 1979, one of Henkel's worldwide marketing directors wanted to extend the successful Sista line of do-it-yourself sealants from Germany to other European countries where the markets were underdeveloped and disorganized as had once been the case in Germany. A European headquarters project team visited the markets and then developed a standard marketing program. The country managers, however, objected. Since the market potential in each country was small, they said, they did not have the time or resources to launch Sista.

The project team countered that by capitalizing on potential scale economies, its pan-European marketing and manufacturing programs would be superior to any programs the subsidiaries could develop by themselves. Furthermore, it maintained, the already developed pan-European program was available off the shelf. The European sales manager, who was a project team member, discovered that the salespeople as well as tradespeople in the target countries were much more enthusiastic about the proposed program than the field marketing managers. So management devised a special lure for the managers. The project team offered to subsidize the first-year advertising and promotion expenditures of countries launching Sista. Six countries agreed. To ensure their commitment now that their financial risk had been reduced, the sales manager invited each accepting country manager to nominate a member to the project team to develop the final program details.

By 1982, the Sista line was sold in 52 countries using a standard marketing program. The Sista launch was especially challenging because it involved the extension of a product and program already developed for a single market. The success of the Sista launch made Henkel's field managers much more receptive to global marketing programs for subsequent new products.

Motivating the Field

Taking into account the nature of their products and markets, their organizational structures, and their cultures and traditions, multinationals have to decide which approach or combination of approaches, from informing to directing, will best answer their strategic objectives. Multinational managers must realize, however, that local managers are likely to resist any precipitate move toward increased headquarters direction. A quick shift could lower their motivation and performance.

Any erosion in marketing decision making associated with global marketing will probably be less upsetting for country managers who have not risen through the line marketing function. For example, John Deere's European headquarters has developed advertising for its European country managers for more than a decade. The country managers have not objected. Most are not marketing specialists and do not see advertising as key to the success of their operations. But for country managers who view control of marketing decision making as central to their operational success, the transition will often be harder. Headquarters needs to give the field time to adjust to the new decision-making processes that multicountry brand teams and other new organizational structures require. Yet management must recognize that even with a one- or two-year transition period, some turnover among field personnel is inevitable. As one German headquarters executive commented, "Those managers in the field who can't adapt to a more global approach will have to leave and run local breweries."

Here are five suggestions on how to motivate and retain talented country managers when making the shift to global marketing:

1. Encourage field managers to generate ideas. This is especially important when R&D efforts are centrally directed. Use the best ideas from the field in global marketing programs (and give recognition to the local managers who came up with them). Unilever's South African

subsidiary developed Impulse body spray, now a global brand. R.J. Reynolds revitalized Camel as a global brand after the German subsidiary came up with a successful and transferable positioning and copy strategy.

2. Ensure that the field participates in the development of the marketing strategies and programs for global brands. A bottom-up rather than top-down approach will foster greater commitment and produce superior program execution at the country level. As we've seen, when P&G International introduced its sanitary napkin as a global brand, it permitted local managers to make some adjustments in areas that were not seen as core to the program, such as couponing and sales promotion. More important, it encouraged them to suggest changes in features of the core global program.

3. Maintain a product portfolio that includes, where scale economies permit, local as well as regional and global brands. While Philip Morris's and Seagram's country managers and their local advertising agencies are required to implement standard programs for each company's global brands, the managers retain full responsibility for the marketing programs of their locally distributed brands. Seagram motivates its country managers to stay interested in the global brands by allocating development funds to support local marketing efforts on these brands and by circulating monthly reports that summarize market performance data by brand and country.

4. Allow country managers continued control of their marketing budgets so they can respond to local consumer needs and counter local competition. When British Airways headquarters launched its £13 million global advertising campaign, it left intact the £18 million worth of tactical advertising budgets that country managers used to promote fares, destinations, and tour packages specific to their markets. Because most of the country managers had exhausted their previous year's tactical budgets and were anxious for further advertising support, they were receptive to the global campaign even though it was centrally directed.

5. Emphasize the general management responsibilities of country managers that extend beyond the marketing function. Country managers who have risen through the line marketing function often don't spend enough time on local manufacturing operations, industrial relations, and government affairs. Global marketing programs can free them to focus on and develop their skills in these other areas.

4
Local Memoirs of a Global Manager

Gurcharan Das

There was a time when I used to believe with Diogenes the Cynic that "I am a citizen of the world," and I used to strut about feeling that a "blade of grass is always a blade of grass, whether in one country or another." Now I feel that each blade of grass has its spot on earth from where it draws its life, its strength; and so is man rooted to the land from where he draws his faith, together with his life.

In India, I was privileged to help build one of the largest businesses in the world for Vicks Vaporub, a hundred-year-old brand sold in 147 countries and now owned by Procter & Gamble. In the process, I learned a number of difficult and valuable lessons about business and about myself. The most important lesson was this: to learn to tap into the roots of diversity in a world where global standardization plays an increasingly useful role.

"Think global and act local," goes the saying, but that's only half a truth. International managers must also think local and then apply their local insights on a global scale.

The fact is that truths in this world are unique, individual, and highly parochial. They say all politics is local. So is all business. But this doesn't keep either from being global. In committing to our work we commit to a here and now, to a particular place and time; but what we learn from acting locally is often universal in nature.

This is how globalization takes place. Globalization does not mean imposing homogeneous solutions in a pluralistic world. It means having a global vision and strategy, but it also means cultivating roots and individual identities. It means nourishing local insights, but it also means reemploying communicable ideas in new geographies around the world.

The more human beings belong to their own time and place, the more they belong to *all* times and places. Today's best global managers know this truth. They nourish each "blade of grass."

Managerial basics are the same everywhere, in the West and in the Third World. There is a popular misconception among managers that you need merely to push a powerful brand name with a standard product, package, and advertising in order to conquer global markets, but actually the key to success is a tremendous amount of local passion for the brand and a feeling of local pride and ownership.

I learned these lessons as a manager of international brands in the Third World and as a native of India struggling against the temptation to stay behind in the West.

On Going Home

I was four years old when India became free. Before they left, the British divided us into two countries, India and Pakistan, and on a monsoon day in August 1947 I suddenly became a refugee. I had to flee east for my life because I was a Hindu in predominantly Muslim West Punjab. I survived, but a million others did not, and another 12 million were rendered homeless in one of the great tragedies of our times.

I grew up in a middle-class home in East Punjab as the eldest son of a civil engineer who built canals and dams for the government. Our family budget was always tight: after paying for milk and school fees, there was little left to run the house. My mother told us heroic stories from the *Mahabharata* and encouraged in us the virtues of honesty, thrift, and responsibility to country.

I grew up in the innocence of the Nehru age when we still had strong ideals. We believed in secularism, democracy, socialism, and the U.N.; and we were filled with the excitement of building a nation.

I came to the United States at the age of 12, when the Indian government sent my father to Washington, D.C. on temporary assignment. When my family returned to India a few years later, I won a scholarship to Harvard College and spent four happy years on the banks of the Charles River. My tutor taught me that the sons of Harvard had an obligation to serve, and I knew that I must one day use my education to serve India.

In 1964, in the towering confidence of my 21 years, I returned home. Some of my friends thought I had made a mistake. They said I should have gone on to graduate school and worked for a few years in the West. In fact, I missed the West in the beginning and told myself that I would go back before long; but I soon became absorbed in my new job with Richardson-Vicks in Bombay, and like the man who came to dinner, I stayed on.

From a trainee, I rose to become CEO of the company's Indian subsidiary, with interim assignments at Vicks headquarters in New York and in the Mexican subsidiary. When I became CEO, the Indian company was almost bankrupt, but with the help of a marvelous all-Indian organization, I turned it around in the early 1980s and made it one of the most profitable companies on the Bombay Stock Exchange. In 1985 we were acquired by Procter & Gamble, and so began another exciting chapter in my life. We successfully incorporated the company into P&G without losing a single employee, and we put ourselves on an aggressive growth path, with an entry first into sanitary napkins and then into one of the largest detergent markets in the world.

At three stages in my life, I was tempted to settle in the West. Each time I could have chosen to lead the cosmopolitan life of an expatriate. Each time I chose to return home. The first after college; the second when I was based in the New York office of Vicks, where I met my Nepali wife with her coveted Green Card (which we allowed to lapse); the third when I was in Mexico running our nutritional foods business, when once again I came home to earn a fraction of what I would have earned abroad.

Apart from a lurking wish to appear considerable in the eyes of those I grew up with, I ask myself why I keep returning to India. I have thrice opted for what appeared to be the less rational course in terms of career and money. The only remotely satisfying answer I have found comes from an enigmatic uncle of mine who once said, "You've come back, dear boy, because as a child you listened to the music of your mother's voice. They all say, 'I'll be back in a few years,' but the few years become many, until it is too late and you are lost in a lonely and homeless crowd."

Yet I think of myself as a global manager within the P&G world. I believe my curious life script has helped to create a mind-set that combines the particular with the universal, a mind-set rooted in the local and yet open and nonparochial, a mind-set I find useful in the global management of P&G brands.

On One-Pointed Success

I first arrived on the island of Bombay on a monsoon day after eight years of high school and college in America. That night, 15-foot waves shattered thunderously against the rocks below my window as the rain advanced from the Arabian sea like the disciplined forward phalanx of an army.

The next morning I reported for duty at Richardson-Vicks' Indian headquarters, which turned out to be a rented hole-in-the-wall with a dozen employees. This was a change after the company's swank New York offices in midtown Manhattan, where I had been interviewed. That evening my cousin invited me for dinner. He worked in a big British company with many factories, thousands of employees, and plush multistoried marble offices. I felt ashamed to talk about my job.

"How many factories do you have?" he wanted to know.

"None," I said.

"How many salesmen do you have?" he asked.

"None," I said.

"How many employees?"

"Twelve."

"How big are your offices?"

"A little smaller than your house."

Years later I realized that what embarrassed me that night turned out to be our strength. All twelve of our employees were focused on building our brands without the distraction of factories, sales forces, industrial relations, finance and other staff departments. Our products were made under contract by Boots, an English drug company; they were distributed under contract by an outside distribution house with 100 salesmen spread around the country; our external auditors had arranged for someone to do our accounting; and our lawyers took care of our government work. We were lean, nimble, focused, and very profitable.

All my cousin's talk that night revolved around office politics, and all his advice was about how to get around the office bureaucracy. It was not clear to me how his company made decisions. But he was a smart man, and I sensed that with all his pride in working for a giant organization, he had little respect for its bureaucratic style.

If marketing a consumer product is what gives a company its competitive advantage, then it seems to me it should spend all its time building marketing and product muscle and employ outside suppliers to do everything else. It should spin off as many services as someone else is willing to take on and leave everyone inside the company focused on one thing—creating, retaining, and satisfying consumers.

There is a concept in Yoga called one-pointedness (from the Sanskrit *Ekagrata*). All twelve of us were one-pointedly focused on making Vicks a household name in India, as if we were 12 brand managers. I now teach our younger managers the value of a one-pointed focus on consumer satisfaction, which P&G measures every six months for all of its major brands.

Concentrating on one's core competence thus was one of the first lessons I learned. I learned it because I was face-to-face with the consumer, focused on the particular. Somehow I feel it would have taken me longer to learn this lesson in a glass tower in Manhattan.

As so often in life, however, by the time I could apply the lesson I had learned, we had a thousand people, with factories, sales forces, and many departments that were having a lot of fun fighting over turf. I believe that tomorrow's big companies may well consist of hundreds of small decentralized units, each with a sharp focus on its particular customers and markets.

On the Kettle That Wrote My Paycheck

For months I believed that my salary came from the payroll clerk, so I was especially nice to her. (She was also the boss's secretary.) Then one day I discovered the most important truth of my career—I realized who really paid my salary.

Soon after I joined the company, my boss handed me a bag and a train ticket and sent me "up-country." A man of the old school, he believed that you learned marketing only in the bazaar, so I spent 10 of my first 15 months on the road and saw lots of up-country bazaars.

On the road, I typically would meet our trade customers in the mornings and consumers in the evenings. In the afternoons everyone slept. One evening I knocked on the door of a middle-class home in Surat, a busy trading town 200 miles north of Bombay. The lady of the house reluctantly let me in. I asked her, "What do you use for your family's coughs and colds?" Her eyes lit up, her face became animated. She told me that she had discovered the most wonderful solution. She went into the kitchen and brought back a jar of Vicks Vaporub and a kettle. She then showed me how she poured a spoon of Vaporub into the boiling kettle and inhaled the medicated vapors from the spout.

"If you don't believe me, try it for yourself," she said. "Here, let me boil some water for you."

Before I could reply she had disappeared into the kitchen. Instead of drinking tea that evening we inhaled Vicks Vaporub. As I walked back to my hotel, I felt intoxicated: I had discovered it was she who paid my salary. My job also became clear to me: I must reciprocate her compliment by striving relentlessly to satisfy her needs.

The irony is that all the money a company makes is made *outside* the company (at the point of sale), yet the employees spend their time *inside* the company, usually arguing over turf. Unfortunately, we don't see customers around us when we show up for work in the mornings.

When I became the CEO of the company I made a rule that every employee in every department had to go out every year and meet 20 consumers and 20 retailers or wholesalers in order to qualify for their annual raise. This not only helps to remind us who pays our salaries, we also get a payoff in good ideas to improve our products and services.

The idea of being close to the customer may be obvious in the commercial societies of the West, but it was not so obvious 20 years ago in the protected, bureaucratic Indian environment. As to the lady in Surat, we quickly put her ideas into our advertising. She was the first consumer to show me a global insight in my own backyard.

Of Chairs, Armchairs, and Monsoons

Two years after I joined, I was promoted. I was given Vicks Vaporub to manage, which made me the first brand manager in the company. I noticed we were building volume strongly in the South but having trouble in the North. I asked myself whether I should try to fix the North or capitalize on the momentum in the South. I chose the latter, and it was the right choice. We later discovered that North Indians don't like to rub things on their bodies, yet the more important lesson was that it is usually better to build on your strength than to try and correct a weakness. Listen to and respect the market. Resist the temptation to impose your will on it.

We were doing well in the South partially because South Indians were accustomed to rubbing on balms for headaches, colds, bodyaches, insect bites, and a host of other minor maladies. We had a big and successful balm competitor, Amrutanjan, who offered relief for all these symptoms. My first impulse was to try to expand the use of

Vaporub to other symptoms in order to compete in this larger balm market.

My boss quickly and wisely put a stop to that. In an uncharacteristically loud voice, he explained that Vaporub's unique function was to relieve colds.

"Each object has a function," he said. "A chair's function is to seat a person. A desk is to write on. You don't want to use a chair for writing and a desk for sitting. You never want to mix up functions."

A great part of Vaporub's success in India has been its clear and sharp position in the consumer's mind. It is cold relief in a jar, which a mother rubs tenderly on her child's cold at bedtime. As I thought more about balms, I realized that they were quite the opposite. Adults rub balms on themselves for headaches during the day. Vaporub was succeeding precisely because it was not a balm; it was a rub for colds.

Every brand manager since has had to learn that same lesson. It is of the utmost importance to know who you are and not be led astray by others. Tap into your roots when you are unsure. You cannot be all things to all people.

This did not prevent us from building a successful business with adults, but as my boss used to say, "Adult colds, that is an armchair. But it is still a chair and not a desk."

When I took over the brand we were spending most of our advertising rupees in the winter, a strategy that worked in North America and other countries. However, my monthly volume data stubbornly suggested that we were shipping a lot of Vaporub between July and September, the hot monsoon season. "People must be catching lots of colds in the monsoon," I told my boss, and I got his agreement to bring forward a good chunk of our media to the warm monsoon months. Sure enough, we were rewarded with an immediate gain in sales.

I followed this up by getting our agency to make a cinema commercial (we had no television at that time) showing a child playing in the rain and catching cold. We coined a new ailment, "wet monsoon colds," and soon the summer monsoon season became as important as the winter in terms of sales.

Another factor in our success was the introduction of a small 5-gram tin, which still costs 10 cents and accounts for 40% of our volume. At first it was not successful, so we had to price it so that it was cheaper to buy four 5-gram tins than a 19-gram jar. The trade thought we were crazy. They said henceforth no one would buy the profitable jar; they would trade down to the tin. But that didn't happen. Why? Because we had positioned the tin for the working class. We were right in believing that middle class consumers would stay loyal to the middle-class size.

Moves like these made us hugely successful and placed us first in the Indian market share by far. But instead of celebrating, my boss seemed depressed. He called me into his office, and he asked me how much the market was growing.

"Seven percent," I said.

"Is that good?"

"No," I replied. "But *we* are growing twenty percent, and that's why we're now number one in India."

"I don't give a damn that we are number one in a small pond. That pond has to become a lake, and then an ocean. We have to grow the market. Only then will we become number one in the world."

Thus I acquired another important mind-set: when you are number one, you must not grow complacent. Your job is to grow the market. You always must benchmark yourself against the best in the world, not just against the local competition. In the Third World this is an especially valuable idea, because markets there are so much less competitive.

Being receptive to regional variations, tapping the opportunity that the monsoon offered, introducing a size for the rural and urban poor, and learning to resist complacency and grow the market—all are variations on the theme of local thinking, of tapping into the roots of pluralism and diversity.

On Not Reinventing the Wheel

We could not have succeeded in building the Vicks business in India without the support of the native traders who took our products deep into the hinterland, to every nook and corner of a very large country. Many times we faced the temptation to set up an alternative Western-style distribution network. Fortunately, we never gave in to it. Instead, we chose each time to continue relying on the native system.

Following the practice of British companies in India, we appointed the largest wholesaler in each major town to become our exclusive stock point and direct customer. We called this wholesaler our stockist. Once a month our salesman visited the stockist, and together they went from shop to shop redistributing our products to the retailers and wholesalers of the town. The largest stockist in each state also became our Carrying-and-Forwarding Agent (in other words, our depot) for reshipping our goods to stockists in smaller towns. Over time, our stockists expanded their functions. They now work exclusively on P&G business under the supervision of our salesmen; they hire local salesmen who provide interim coverage of the market between the visits of our salesmen; they run vans to cover satellite villages and help us penetrate the interior; they conduct local promotions and advertising campaigns; and they are P&G's ambassadors and lifeline in the local community. The stockists perform all these services for a five percent commission, and our receivables are down to six days outstanding.

In our own backyard, we found and adopted an efficient low-cost distribution system perfected by Indian traders over hundreds of years. Thank God we chose to build on it rather than reinvent the wheel.

On Taking Ancient Medicine

We learned our most important lesson about diversity and tapping into roots shortly after I became head of the company in the early 1980s. We found ourselves against a wall. The chemists and pharmacists had united nationwide and decided to target our company and boycott our products in their fight for higher margins from the entire industry. At the same time, productivity at our plant was falling, while wages kept rising. As a result, our profitability had plummeted to two percent of sales.

Beset by a hostile environment, we turned inward. The answer to our problems came as a flash of insight about our roots, for we suddenly realized that Vicks Vaporub and other Vicks products were all-natural, herbal formulas. All their ingredients were found in thousand-year-old Sanskrit texts. What was more, this ancient *Ayurvedic* system of medicine enjoyed the special patronage of the government. If we could change our government registration from Western medicine to Indian medicine, we could expand our distribution to food shops, general stores, and street kiosks and thus reduce dependence on the pharmacists. By making our products more accessible, we would enhance consumer satisfaction and build competitive advantage. What was more, a new registration would also allow us to set up a new plant for Vicks in a tax-advantaged "backward area," where we could raise productivity dramatically by means of improved technology, better work practices, and lower labor costs.

I first tested the waters with our lawyers, who thought our solution to the problem quite wonderful. We then went to the government in Delhi, which was deeply impressed to discover all the elements of Vaporub's formula in the ancient texts. They advised us to check with the local FDA in Bombay. The regulators at the FDA couldn't find a single fault with our case and, to our surprise and delight, promptly gave us a new registration.

Lo and behold, all the obstacles were gone! Our sales force heroically and rapidly expanded the distribution of our products to the nondrug trade, tripling the outlets which carried Vicks to roughly 750,000 stores. Consumers were happy that they could buy our products at every street corner. At the same time we quickly built a new plant near Hyderabad, where productivity was four times what it was in our Bombay plant. Our after-tax profits rose from 2% to 12% of sales, and we became a blue chip on the Bombay Stock Exchange.

Finally, we decided to return the compliment to the Indian system of medicine. We persuaded our headquarters to let us establish an R&D Center to investigate additional all-natural, Ayurvedic therapies for coughs and colds. When I first mooted this idea, my bosses at the head office in the United States practically fell off their chairs. Slowly, however, the idea of all-natural, safe, and effective remedies for a self-limiting ailment sold around the world under the Vicks name grew on them.

We set up labs in Bombay under the leadership of a fine Indian scientist who had studied in the United States. They began by creating a computerized data bank of herbs and formulas from the ancient texts; they invented a "finger-printing" process to standardize herbal raw materials with the help of computers; and they organized clinical trials in Bombay hospitals to confirm the safety and efficacy of the new products. We now have two products being successfully sold in the Indian market—Vicks Vaposyrup, an all-natural cough liquid, and Vicks Hotsip, a hot drink for coughs and colds. The lab today is part of P&G's global health-care research effort and has 40 scientists and technicians working with state-of-the-art equipment.

Of Local Passions and Golden Ghettos

The story of Vicks in India brings up a mistaken notion about how multinationals build global brands. The popular conception is that you start with a powerful brand name, add standardized product, packaging and advertising, push a button, and bingo—you are on the way to capturing global markets. Marlboro, Coke, Sony Walkman, and Levis are cited as examples of this strategy.

But if it's all so easy, why have so many powerful brands floundered? Without going into the standardization vs. adaptation debate, the Vicks story demonstrates at least one key ingredient for global market success: *the importance of local passion.* If local managers believe a product is theirs, then local consumers will believe it too. Indeed, a survey of Indian consumers a few years ago showed that 70% believed Vicks was an Indian brand.

What is the universal idea behind Vicks Vaporub's success in India? What is it that made it sell? Was it "rubbing it on the child with tender, loving care?" Could that idea be revived in the United States? Some people argue that the United States has become such a rushed society that mothers no longer have time to use a bedtime rub on their children when they've got a cold. Others feel that Vaporub could make its marketing more meaningful by striking a more contemporary note.

The Vicks story shows that a focus on the particular brings business rewards. But there are also psychic rewards for the manager who invests in the local. Going back to my roots reinvigorated me as a person and brought a certain fullness to my life. Not only was it pleasant to see familiar brown faces on the street, it also was enormously satisfying to be a part of the intense social life of the neighborhood, to experience the joys and sorrows of politics, and to share in the common fate of the nation. But at another level I also began to think of my work as a part of nation building, especially training and developing the next generation of young managers who would run the company and the country. It discharged a debt to my tutor at Harvard and a responsibility that we all have to the future.

Equally, it seems to me, there are powerful though less obvious psychic rewards for an international manager on transfer overseas who chooses to get involved in the local community. When such people approach the new country with an open mind, learn the local language, and make friends with colleagues and neighbors, they gain access to the wealth of a new culture. Not only will they be more effective as managers, they also will live fuller, richer lives.

Unfortunately, my experience in Mexico indicates that many expatriate managers live in "golden ghettos" of ease with little genuine contact with locals other than servants. Is it any surprise that they become isolated and complain of rootlessness and alienation in their new environment? The lesson for global companies is to give each international manager a local "mentor" who will open doors to the community. Ultimately, however, it is the responsibility of individual managers to open their minds, plunge into their local communities, and try to make them their own.

On Global Thinking

It would be wrong to conclude from the Vicks story that managing a global brand is purely a local affair. On the contrary, the winners in the new borderless economy will be the brands and companies that make best use of the richness of experience they get from their geographical diversity. Multinational companies have a natural advantage over local companies because they have talented people solving similar problems for identical brands in different parts of the world, and these brand managers can learn from each other's successes and failures. If a good idea emerges in Egypt, a smart brand manager in Malaysia or Venezuela will at least give it a test.

The Surat lady's teakettle became the basis of a national campaign in India. "One-pointedness" emerged from a hole-in-the-wall in Bombay, but it became the fulcrum on which we built a world-class business over a generation. Advertising for colds during the hot monsoon months seems highly parochial, but it taught us the importance of advertising year round in other places. The stockist system found applicability in Indonesia and China. Even the strange Ayurvedic system of medicine might plausibly be reapplied in the form of efficacious herbal remedies for common ailments in Western countries.

Business truths are invariably local in origin, but they are often expressions of fundamental human needs that are the same worldwide. Local insights with a universal character thus can become quickly global—though only in the hands of flexible, open-minded managers who can translate such ideas into new circumstances with sensitivity and understanding. My admonition to think local is only half the answer. Managers also must remember to think global. The insights we glean from each microcosm are ultimately universal.

Organizational specialists often express a fear that companies will demotivate their local managers by asking them to execute standardized global marketing packages. If they impose these standardized marketing solutions too rigidly, then this fear may be justified. However, this does not happen in successful companies. In fact, the more common disease in a global company is the "not invented here" syndrome, which especially afflicts subsidiaries and managers whose local triumphs have left them arrogant and unwilling to learn from successes in other parts of the world.

We in India were no different. But slowly and painfully we learned that useful lessons can emerge anywhere. For all our efforts to tap into the roots of Indian pluralism, we were dealing with a global brand. The product itself, the positioning, and the packaging were basically the same everywhere. Global brands are not free-for-alls, with each subsidiary doing its own thing. It took us six months, for example, to persuade our marketing people to try a new advertising idea for Vaporub that came from Mexico. It asked the consumer to use Vaporub on three parts of the body to obtain three types of relief. When we finally tried "Three-by-Three" in our advertising, it worked brilliantly.

It is deeply wrong to believe that going global is a one-stop, packaged decision. Local managers can add enormous value as they tap into local roots for insights. But it is equally wrong to neglect the integrity of the brand's core elements. Smart global managers nourish each blade of grass without neglecting the garden as a whole.

On Karma

Although the principles of managing a business in the Third World are the same as in the West, there are still big differences between the two. For me, the greatest of these is the pervasive reality of poverty.

I have lost the towering confidence of my youth, when I believed that socialism could wipe away poverty. The problem of socialism is one of performance, not vision. If it worked, we would all be socialists. Ironically, the legacy of the collectivist bias in Indian thinking has been the perpetuation of poverty. We created an over-regulated private sector and an inefficient public sector. We did not allow the economy to grow and produce the surplus that might have paid for direct poverty programs. We created an exploitative bureaucracy that fed on itself. Today, happily, we are righting the balance by liberalizing the economy, reducing state control, and restoring legitimacy to the market. I am confident that these changes will foster the entrepreneurialism and economic vitality India needs to create prosperity and eliminate the destitution of so many of its people.

Despite the problems, I find managers in India and other poor countries more optimistic than their counterparts in rich nations. The reason is that we believe our children will be better off than our parents were, and this idea is a great source of strength. We see our managerial work as nation building. We are the benign harbingers of technology and modernity. As we learn to manage complex enterprises, we empower people with the confidence they need to become responsible, innovative, and self-reliant.

It seems to come down to commitment. In committing to our work we commit to a here and now, to a particular place and time. The meaning in our lives comes from nourishing a particular blade of grass. It comes from absorbing ourselves so deeply in the microcosm of our work that we forget ourselves, especially our egos. The difference between subject and object disappears. The Sanskrit phrase *nishkama karma* describes this state of utter absorption, in which people act for the sake of the action, not for the sake of the reward from the action. This is also the meaning of happiness.

5

From Complacency to Competitiveness: An Interview with Vitro's Ernesto Martens

Nancy A. Nichols

As Canada, the United States, and Mexico continue to debate the North American Free Trade Agreement, companies are scrambling to position themselves to take advantage of the emerging North American market. Many have come to focus on Mexico. With its plentiful and inexpensive labor force and expanding middle class, Mexico presents ample opportunities both as a manufacturing site and as a vast new market for competitors to exploit.

Those searching for a way to navigate the many changes in Mexico would do well to study Vitro, Sociedad Anónima, an 84-year-old Mexican company. No organization exemplifies the newly revived spirit of Mexican competition better than this holding company with roughly $3 billion in sales and 44,000 highly trained and well-educated employees. Through subsidiaries like Anchor Glass Container Corporation and joint ventures with Ford, Corning, Samsonite, and Whirlpool, the company manufactures everything from glass bottles and plastic yogurt containers to suitcases and washing machines. Some of these products are destined for the Mexican market, and some are exported to the United States and overseas.

One of the largest companies in Mexico today, Vitro is run by Ernesto Martens-Rebolledo, a charismatic executive who was first brought in to head the company's container division in 1977. A chemical engineer by training, Martens studied in Canada and Germany and was CEO of Union Carbide Mexico before joining Vitro. In a major break with tradition, Martens became Vitro's first nonfamily CEO in 1985.

During his eight years in office, Martens has made some controversial decisions, including laying off 3,000 workers in 1992—a first for a company that used to claim that it wasn't giving workers a job but was giving them a way of life. And while Martens excels in a culture that values consensus building, he also led the only hostile takeover of a U.S. company by a Mexican company when Vitro took over the Anchor Glass Container Corporation in November 1989. Martens is a rare example of a new breed of manager in Mexico, one who is equally versed in tradition and technology, culture and competition.

HBR: *How has NAFTA helped shape your strategy?*

Ernesto Martens: NAFTA has never really shaped our strategy; it simply confirms the trends we have seen coming for some time. We started to implement our market-oriented strategy in 1985, when the Mexican market began to change from one that did not allow any imports to a market that is open and competitive. NAFTA will make that change permanent and, in that sense, stabilize our strategy, but NAFTA does not change our strategy. The course for Mexico is set with or without NAFTA, and Vitro has few options if it wants to survive.

What are the challenges Vitro faces?

In 1988, when Mexico's economy was still mostly closed, exports to Mexico from the United States of float glass, the large sheets of glass used in the construction and automobile industries, totaled $900,000. In 1991, exports of float glass to Mexico totaled $30 million. So in four years, exports grew 30-fold. In the wake of NAFTA, it is possible that exports to Mexico will grow even faster.

There are more furnaces to make float glass in Texas alone than there are in all of Mexico. If U.S. producers decide to ship only the last 10% of their production to our country, they can flood our market and drive us out of business. Sometimes I think that they break more glass in the United States than we make in Mexico.

In the wake of these changes in the Mexican economy, our growth, indeed our survival, will depend on two things: how successfully we penetrate the U.S. market and how fast the Mexican market grows. Right now, for example, only 60% of the Mexican population has washing machines. In the United States, that number is closer to 97%. More than 50% of the Mexican population is under 20. Now, if their income grows and their purchasing power increases, we will have a significant market to serve.

How are you preparing Vitro to compete?

One of the most difficult things to do in a successful company is to convince people that they must change. My challenge is to convince the people here that we can no longer be complacent in the face of world competition, that we must change and we must do it swiftly.

So Vitro continues to change, making many transitions at once. We used to be a closely held company, but now we are a publicly held company listed on the Mexican Bolsa, and we recently began trading on the New York Stock Exchange. We have transformed ourselves from a Mexican company to an international company, and from a complacent competitor to an aggressive one.

Vitro is a study in paradoxes. It is a company caught between the demands of Mexico's emerging free-market economy and a corporate culture steeped in tradition. It has one foot in the old world of Mexico and the other in the new competitive global environment.

For example, our workers use the most advanced German machinery under the watchful eye of Our Lady of Guadalupe. And here in our corporate headquarters, you see the heavy dark woods and white-washed walls that were common in eighteenth-century Mexico, but our mind-set is twentieth-century capitalism.

We don't want to lose our identity as a Mexican company with a unique culture and relationship with our employees, but we don't want to be battered in the world marketplace either. And that is the tightrope that Vitro must walk. Our challenge is to change who we are without losing sight of what we are all about. (For a brief history of Vitro see "The Monterrey Group: a Mexican Keiretsu.")

The Monterrey Group: A Mexican Keiretsu

Some of the best economic thinkers of our day have stopped focusing on countries and started focusing on regions as the most important vehicle for economic development. New York City has long been known for its financial acumen; Milan and Paris dominate the fashion industry; and Silicon Valley is famous for its concentration of high-tech equipment makers.

Vitro, Sociedad Anónima, sits in the middle of a region that is well-known for its industrial and entrepreneurial capabilities. Based in Monterrey, Vitro is commonly included in the "Monterrey Group," an informal collection of independent companies in northern Mexico engaged in various businesses, such as beer, steel, and chemicals.

Monterrey began to bloom in the late nineteenth century, when Francisco Sada started a brewery, known as Cervecería Cuauhtemoc, to make Carta Blanca beer, now one of the most popular brands in Mexico. Sada invited his brother-in-law, an accountant named Isaac Garza, to join the company. This partnership marked the beginning of a dynasty that endured for nearly a century.

But in the early days, Garza and Sada were short on both capital and materials. So the two entrepreneurs, in conjunction with other local families, turned adversity into advantage by integrating their company vertically. If the brewery couldn't import bottle caps, they would start a steel company to make them. If they couldn't get bottles for their beer, they would form a company to make the bottles.

Toward that end, in the early 1900s a group of 60 investors from different areas of the country, including merchants, bankers, landholders, and small manufacturers, gathered the 600,000 pesos needed to purchase bottle-making machinery. Vidriera Monterrey was born. It was run by the grandson of the brewery founder, Don Roberto G. Sada, an MIT-trained engineer who carried on the legacy of the Sada family.

As the glass business grew during the 1950s and 1960s, the company diversified and began making flat glass, dinnerware, and household glass products, followed by fiberglass. All those divisions are now consolidated into Vitro.

Other local companies also expanded during this period. Throughout the mid-1970s, the steel and beer industries grew together under the auspices of one holding company named Visa. This company, together with other Monterrey-based businesses, was a dominant force in Mexico until 1973, when industrialists became a target for Mexico's leftist movement. Guerrillas assassinated the acknowledged leader of the Monterrey Group, Eugenio Garza Sada, during a botched kidnapping attempt. In the wake of the tragedy and as part of Visa's transition from a parochial Mexican company to a global competitor, his descendants split the company in two. Alfa, a company that started out making bottle caps, grew into Mexico's largest private steel producer, while the brewery—still operating under the banner of Visa—became one of the largest beer producers in Latin America. Today the Monterrey companies continue to share many common business and community interests and more than a few board members.

Vitro is traded publicly on the Bolsa Mexicana de Valores and now on the New York Stock Exchange. Currently, some of its directors, which include a number of Francisco Sada's descendants (one of whom is the present chairman of the board), own approximately 20% of the common shares outstanding, and a consortium of international investors owns another 20%.

However, the transition from a closely held company to a publicly traded company has not come easily. Vitro did not escape the insider trading violations that were common during the takeover transactions of the late 1980s. During Vitro's acquisition of Anchor Glass Container Corporation, one Vitro executive was accused of insider trading violations. The executive's dismissal demonstrated to the world that Vitro had completed the transition from a closely held Mexican company to a publicly traded global company ready to uphold international standards.

—Nancy A. Nichols.

How are you making the transition from the old world to the new world?

Both very quickly and not fast enough. When I came here in 1977, Vitro had about $1 billion in sales. While we did export some to the Caribbean and to Central and South America, we were primarily making bottles and plastic containers for the Mexican market. Since the market was closed at that time, demand was fairly steady.

In a closed economy, it was possible to do everything for everybody, to make everything to satisfy everyone. Just being competitive was not very relevant because the market was right there for you. In an open economy, you can't do everything for everybody. The Mexican market doesn't have the volume to make a company as cost competitive as it needs to be in order to compete against foreign companies that come into Mexico. We needed to go out and acquire Anchor and form joint ventures like the ones with Whirlpool and Corning.

If you look at our company today, more than 50% of our sales and more than 30% of our assets are located outside of Mexico, and we are beginning to position ourselves to take advantage of the emerging North American market.

So Vitro wasn't well positioned when you came to the company?

When I first joined the company, we were well positioned to serve Mexico's closed economy. It was the height of the oil boom, and we were growing by leaps and bounds. We doubled capacity in a couple of years, and we branched out into plastic containers and pharmaceutical glass. We were trying to satisfy a market that appeared to have endless growth possibilities; the Mexican economy was growing by 6% to 8% every year. Like many other Mexican companies, we borrowed heavily—about $750 million—to expand.

Then, in late 1981, there was a significant slowdown in demand for our containers. We couldn't understand why. It was the first signal that something was wrong. We talked to the best economists in the country, and they said, "Well, you are just nervous because you have expanded." We said, "No, there is something wrong." And that's when we decided to start looking into other markets for our products.

What were the major challenges you faced in entering the U.S. market?

The physical border dividing the two countries was one thing, but there was also a huge psychological barrier for us to jump over. We had to prove that we were not *mañana* Mexican managers and that we could produce a consistent, high-quality product. To do this, we had to get our processes under control, install the proper machinery, and find distributors in the United States who would help us get orders. We had to give samples to these distributors, but, most important, we had to prove that they should buy from us. And we had to do it all without creating too much of a stir in the United States.

Why did Vitro need to be so cautious?

U.S. glass producers are huge compared with Mexican producers, and they were intent on keeping imports out of their market. When we started producing glass for the U.S. market, a few of the American producers, including Anchor, waged a "Don't Buy Mexican Glass" campaign.

Instead of taking on the U.S. producers in head-to-head competition, we decided to go into returnable soft drink bottles, a dying market that U.S. glass manufacturers were abandoning. In 1960, 94% of the soft drinks sold in the United States came in returnable bottles, but by the time we were looking at the market, that number was down to around 6%. Aluminum cans and nonreturnable bottles accounted for the rest.

Not surprisingly, U.S. manufacturers weren't interested in making returnable bottles. They wanted to make single-serving bottles, which you use once and then throw away. But even though we knew that the returnable market was dying, it was an opportunity for us to get into the United States without making waves. It was a niche where we could go in and still not be a dramatic threat to the major glass producers. And we could get a reasonable price on what was, for us, a huge volume.

So this was a major launch?

It was a major learning process. We knew that if we wanted Vitro to be a growing company that was not completely dependent on a closed market, we had to have competitive products, competitive costs, and a small image outside of Mexico.

But all this didn't come easily. Bottles were broken during shipment, and products were held up at the border. Most important, we didn't know how to communicate with our customers about product specifications. We had a whole combination of challenges, including finding warehouses. But our real problems began in 1982.

What happened then?

Overnight the peso went kaboom. It went from 25 pesos to 70 pesos against the dollar. Instead of needing $18.7 billion in pesos to pay our bankers in the United States, we needed nearly three times that number, or roughly $52.5 billion. We had the pesos, but because of currency controls, we couldn't get them out of the country. We couldn't pay our suppliers either. We had an executive studying at MIT, and we couldn't pay his tuition. It was traumatic because we hadn't failed in running our company, our country had failed.

Many Mexican companies went bankrupt during this period. How did Vitro survive?

The difference between Vitro and other companies was that when we borrowed the $750 million I mentioned earlier, we invested it in fixed assets to increase our capacity. A glass furnace burning day-in and day-out at 1,200° to 1,500° centigrade lasts 10 to 12 years before it literally burns out and must be replaced. So we invested in plant and equipment when others might have borrowed for working capital or to diversify.

The other key element is that we never allowed our holding company to be in debt. Holding companies have only one source of income: dividends from their operating companies. But if the operating companies aren't making money and paying large dividends, then there's no way to service the debt on the holding company.

Luckily, we weren't in that position. We were able to refinance our bank debt within 2 to 3 weeks of the devaluation. That gave us the financial flexibility to acquire Anchor in 1989.

Why did you acquire Anchor?

We were a strategic buyer, not a financial player. Anchor has a 24% participation in the U.S. glass container market. We saw this acquisition as an excellent opportunity for us to expand. We paid $900 million for Anchor in 1989 in a heavily contested hostile takeover that took more than four months.

I can remember a group of us standing on the 54th floor of the World Trade Center at 6:00 A.M. on the morning we were going to launch our bid. We were surrounded by lawyers, bankers, and accountants. We looked out over the canyons of Wall Street and started to laugh. Wall Street, after all, is a long way from Monterrey.

Both psychologically and physically?

Psychologically, it was an enormous step for us. In general, business in Mexico is done on a consensus basis, very genteel and sometimes slow by U.S. standards. But there we were sitting across from the Anchor management team, and they wouldn't even say good morning.

Just six years before Vitro bought the company, these very same managers had heavily leveraged Anchor's assets in a buyout. As a result, when we acquired Anchor, the company was $500 million in debt.

Glass is a commodity product differentiated only by price. Because of the leverage, Anchor's cost structure had gotten way out of line, so it was no longer the lowest cost producer. The company's previous owners didn't invest in the machinery necessary to keep its cost structure competitive. These were the same managers who wouldn't say good morning to us.

What did you do to make Anchor's cost structure competitive?

The first thing we did was a sort of triage. We had to decide which plants were most productive, had the best quality, and were the most cost conscious. Then we had to decide which facilities could be fitted with new technologies. Some of this came down to determining which plants had access to the least expensive energy—making glass is very energy intensive—and which were closest to our customers. After studying this for some months, we decided to close four plants and lay off 2,055 workers. Then we decided to upgrade the existing technology in the remaining 17 plants.

How did you do that?

One of our earliest strategies was to team up with people who had equity to invest as well as the best technology. In glass, that meant getting state-of-the-art technology from Owens-Illinois. As a rule, our licensing agreements allow us to use these technologies in Mexico only. But in this case, we were able to put Owens-Illinois technology into our Anchor plants and actually compete against them using their technology. This joint venture was a major opportunity to make Anchor more competitive, but it also represented over $300 million in sales for Fabricación de Máquinas. FAMA is our subsidiary that makes the machinery and molds used in making glass containers. This venture was just one way in which being vertically integrated paid off. Overall, we took Anchor from a $44 million loss in 1989 to a $20 million profit in 1990.

This was a successful turnaround, but it was still just one piece of your strategy to go from a closed economy to an open one.

Absolutely. The acquisition of Anchor was important for Vitro, but the most difficult and probably the most crucial thing we needed to do was change the mind-set of the managers, which is next to impossible to do in a successful company. We needed to get them to understand that this was a dramatic change and that we would have many challenges as we went forward. It was like trying to tell Little Red Riding Hood that she is in trouble. I kept running around saying, "The wolf is coming! The wolf is coming!" And Little Red Riding Hood just went merrily on her way.

It wasn't until the economy opened up, the peso began appreciating in value, and imports became cheaper that the realization came, "My God, that isn't grandma; that's a wolf." You could actually feel it sweep through the company, this realization that the world was becoming a different place. That awareness really hit home last year when we laid off 3,000 people. Now everyone knows this isn't a child's game, that world competition will have an effect on everyone in this company.

One of the things we are now working on is an incentive compensation plan that makes that concept concrete. In a closed economy, a variable compensation plan doesn't work. We used to have one, but since no particular manager was responsible for any of our gains, it was almost impossible to know whom to compensate. Now we are trying to create a compensation plan that works for all our managers and really drives home the point that we are competing in a new environment.

What else has to change in order for the company to make the transition from a closed economy to an open economy?

In a closed economy, you become complacent, and you forget how to do many things. For example, in a closed economy, you don't sell, people buy. You eventually forget how to sell and market your products, and you start overstaffing like crazy. You forget that your company needs to have the proper structure. But most important, managers' mind-sets become distorted. For example, one manager called me at 7:00 A.M. and said, "I have a fantastic idea that will make us lots of money." So the gentleman came up to my office and explained his idea, which revolved around my giving him two secretaries and three telephones. He thought that all you needed to do to sell glass containers was answer the phones. He wasn't going to take any initiative. Indeed, he didn't think it was necessary for him to call on customers. It was only necessary for him to have the correct number of secretaries to answer customers' calls.

Today we know that we can no longer take our customers for granted. Traditionally, a glass plant in the United States will run one color and one bottle style for 5 to 6 years. Here at Vitro, however, we do smaller runs and work with different colors to meet our customers' needs.

We've had one huge success already with the Clearly Canadian bottle. Clearly Canadian is the ultimate North American product: it is made of Mexican glass, filled with Canadian water, and sold to consumers in the United States, where it has been a big seller.

So part of the strategy is to become a niche player?

No. Our decision to enter the returnable market in the United States was a decision to become a niche player. Our strategy today is to get as close as possible to our customers and learn as much as possible from them. For example, because we worked with the Clearly Canadian people, we learned a lot about working with colored glass. Getting close to the customer allows us to exploit the market for specialized glass. The customers and the intelligence we gather from them drive the strategy. The strategy doesn't drive what we offer our customers. That is the main difference between competing in a closed economy and in an open one. In a closed economy, you make what you want and develop a strategy to get rid of it. In an open economy, you listen to the customers and let them dictate your strategy.

Since the walls have come down, we've had to reevaluate the way we do business in almost every way—culturally, strategically, and structurally. The only constant has been the customer's needs. Our currency has fluctuated wildly; the technology has changed rapidly; and 50-year-old barriers that separated us from fierce competition have fallen. But our focus on the customer has remained constant.

How have you changed Vitro's structure to allow it to operate in a competitive environment?

The mind-set of the manager who wants three phones and two secretaries can create overstaffing problems. One of the small ways I am trying to change the company is by creating pools of secretaries, which are very common in the United States but almost unheard of in Mexico, where there is a tradition of personal service. I hear from my managers that secretaries who have joined the pools are being taunted by the other secretaries, who say, "Why are you working for seven people and getting paid for serving only one?" So I must tell these new secretaries not to get coffee for anyone, write checks for managers' wives, or type their children's homework. I tell them they are professionals.

It is all part of changing the mind-set of the people in our company from one of loyalty to a particular manager to one of loyalty to the customer. I have had to convince each and every one of our employees that it is the customer who feeds them and it is the customer to whom they owe their loyalty. And, by the way, this isn't something that only Vitro must accomplish; it is something that every Mexican company must do.

Part of the challenge for Vitro, however, is completing the change from a traditional Mexican company, run mainly by family members until the 1960s, to a publicly run company.

Yes, in part. Many of the people here are second- or third-generation employees whose loyalty is to particular individuals or managers. Part of making Vitro competitive is going to be teaching these people how to work in an environment where their allegiance must be to the customer, not just to certain individuals or businesses. For example, it used to be very difficult for me to get managers to do succession planning, to sit in a room and say that one person is doing well and another person isn't. It just wasn't considered polite or politic in Mexican society to criticize people openly or even talk about their weaknesses. We've changed that, and we now do succession planning once a year in a room with all our division presidents. We no longer hide our talent or our problems from each other.

For years, we were very secretive around here. We used to hide our mission statement among confidential papers. Can you imagine that? What good does it do to hide your mission statement from the people who must carry out the mission? Now we've had our mission statement printed on large cards and placed on easels in the front entrance of our building where everyone can see them.

Can Vitro change faster than Mexico?

We must change faster than Mexico. We must change Mexico's infrastructure. We must change its railroads. Railroads are more expensive in Mexico than in the United States, but they run at one-third the speed of U.S. railroads. This won't change overnight, but now that the economy is open, we must overcome that setback and still compete.

But hasn't your country put you in a very difficult situation by forcing you to compete without adequate infrastructure?

That's right. There are a number of problems in Mexico that affect our ability to compete: high interest rates, the unavailability of long-term debt, and the premium that we must pay to borrow dollars because Mexico is still considered a high risk. There is a four-hundred basis point surcharge for us to borrow in dollars, and that is still cheaper than trying to borrow in pesos. When the Swiss lend to a Mexican company, for example, they have to put 65% of the money they lend into a special reserve. As a result, our cost of capital is outrageously high.

Still, if we make the most of Mexico's competitive advantages, we should be able to find a significant number of products with which we can increase our exports to other parts of the world. One logical market is the United States.

What are Mexico's competitive advantages?

I would say that Mexico's key advantage is being close to the largest market in the world. It is very expensive to ship glass bottles, since what you are really doing is shipping air. Most of the major glass producers are within 200 miles of a major brewery and population center. That's why our company was built in Monterrey, after all: to be as close as possible to the brewery.

In addition, Mexican workers are highly productive. You can talk to General Motors, and they'll tell you that their most productive plant is in Saltillo. If you talk to Ford, you'll discover the very same phenomenon. Ford's plant in Hermosillo is one of the most, if not *the* most, productive facilities that they have. This is because Mexican workers know no limits.

I remember when I was at Union Carbide overseeing the production of carbon for batteries. Headquarters thought we should be making 45 units per shift, but our workers didn't know that. Soon they were producing 118 in each shift. They didn't know that they weren't supposed to make that many.

Productive, however, is different from cheap. You'll notice that I'm not counting labor costs as a competitive advantage for Mexico. That is only a temporary element. In time, wage rates in Mexico will get close to the rates in Japan and Germany.

But it isn't just a question of wages. There are many unique benefits that you give your workers.

Yes. Many of our workers are very poor by U.S. standards; 90% do not own cars. As a consequence, we give our workers access to wholesale food goods delivered directly to their homes, and we also subsidize their midday meals at the plants. And as I've said, Mexican workers are extremely family oriented. The mobility of Mexican workers is very limited, because they do not want to go far from their families. So we have created a club where 14,000 families can come together and swim or play tennis. And we also provide cultural facilities, such as a glass museum.

During this transition period, when we are trying to move from the way we have done things in the past to the way we will do things in the future, one of the most critical decisions we must make is what elements of our culture we must respect and which we must try to change. There is a great deal of value in the moral and spiritual way in which business is conducted in Mexico. So there are a number of important cultural elements that we must be sure to carry into the future. Our strategy for many years has been to grow from what we know. And our knowledge is not just technical, it is linked to very strong beliefs about how to conduct ourselves in the world.

There is no question that a significant number of Mexican companies will not be able to make this transition. They will need to change the way they operate, or change the products that they create, or both. I think that there are many Mexican companies that will not survive. They will disappear just like foam in beer. Indeed, one trade association estimates that only 30% of Monterrey's plastics companies will still be viable in 5 years.

What roles have joint ventures played in your survival strategy?

We started our joint ventures about 30 years ago. When Mexico's economy was closed, we wanted to make sure we had the best technology. Naturally, we looked for companies that were either number one or number two in the world. For example, we have the right to use British technology from Pilkington Brothers to create float glass.

Then, over time, our strategy changed. In 1979, we joined forces with Ford to gain access to technology and to be close to the markets. Not only did we learn how to make auto glass, but also we learned a lot about the U.S. markets.

Most recently, we have created joint ventures with Corning and Whirlpool. In these ventures, we are producing both for the domestic market and for export, but we are also using these alliances to import products for the growing Mexican market.

So instead of manufacturing products to sell in the United States, the purpose of the joint ventures is to bring products into Mexico to sell?

It's a two-winged concept. First of all, we take advantage of Mexico's productive labor force to create economical products for world markets. But at the same time, we use these joint ventures to bring high-end products to the growing Mexican market. So we are also fulfilling a need in Mexico. Then, when the demand in Mexico is large enough for this type of product—say top-of-the-line refrigerators and washing machines—we can justify manufacturing them here. That's why we need a country with a healthy economy, where people can grow into more significant jobs with more earning power. We can come up with modern marketing techniques to get people to buy our products, but we cannot increase the purchasing power of the Mexican people by ourselves.

Are these the kinds of strategies that have made people say that you were on the road to NAFTA before there was a NAFTA?

We have been anticipating the NAFTA agreement for some time. The one thing that has become clear to me throughout this transition is that the competitive forces shaping the world's markets are now stronger than any government policy. In that way, the transition that Vitro is going through is hardly unique. In an open economy, everything is driven by global competitive forces, and very little is driven by a country's policies. All that managers can do is respond quickly and efficiently to the competitive forces shaking their companies and their countries.

Afterword:
What "Thinking Globally" Really Means

Rosabeth Moss Kanter

As this collection of *Harvard Business Review* articles illustrates, globalization is transforming business in powerful ways. It is forcing companies to rethink strategies, redesign their organizations, seek new partnerships, and open minds as well as boundaries. Not too long ago, "export markets" meant dumping excess production or obsolete inventory in countries not yet accustomed to the standards of the home market. "Offshore production" meant cheap, unskilled labor. "International management" meant a separate division, an unconnected afterthought. And "overseas rotation" meant relegating a manager to career obscurity, or uncomfortable status, as an expatriate abroad who would return with "foreign" ideas to be expunged.

For some U.S. companies and regional economic development programs, the search for international markets still reflects this old-fashioned mind-set: finding foreign buyers for products already developed for the home market rather than creating products with many countries in mind.

But the companies showcased here—from Whirlpool to Unilever— as well as a growing number of companies around the world, are defining "global strategy" to consider all the company's markets and operations together, viewing them through an integrated framework. For some companies, this simply means that international sources and markets are part of the company's thinking from the beginning. For others, it means standardizing product formulas and rationalizing production to create economies of global scale, even if product features and marketing are handled on a country-by-country basis. And for a handful of leaders, it means transformation from domestic or even multinational players to a single global entity operating seamlessly in every function, anywhere in the world.

Consider Gillette, an international company that has recently become a truly global one. Gillette had operated in foreign markets almost since its founding before World War I, at a time when there were only a handful of companies doing so. It developed and introduced new products sequentially country by country, with long lags between them—first in the United States, then in other industrialized countries, and finally, many years later, offered the same products to the developing world. The company's international manufacturing strategy was similar. Each country used manufacturing technology appropriate to its presumed stage of development, receiving equipment from other Gillette factories moving on to more advanced technology.

Many experiences caused Gillette to rethink this strategy in the 1980s. One involved a joint venture in China for local manufacturing of the razor and blade products considered appropriate for that market's stage of evolution. While the joint venture did well, Gillette sold even larger numbers of its more advanced products in China through imports. Meanwhile, cost pressures dictated a rationalization of world manufacturing, which meant discarding aspects of the company's evolutionary theory. And retail customers—first in the United States and then Europe—were increasingly consolidating into more powerful forces demanding special treatment.

By the 1990s, the company was operating as a model global company. It reorganized into broad regional units: the North Atlantic shaving products division integrated all functions in North America and Europe. Large investments were made in innovation of the core product as well as in advanced manufacturing technology. New products were rolled out worldwide within months rather than years and decades. Manufacturing was consolidated into fewer plants. Operations were standardized so that production could be moved from place to place rapidly. Computers and faxes significantly increased the efficiency of global scheduling. Human resource policies were standardized globally (with exact compensation determined by local market rates) to facilitate personnel transfers. Global advertising was consolidated through fewer agencies that would design world campaigns, to be translated and adapted to local markets.

Gillette executives likened their new global system to operating across "500 states," the same way companies operate across 50 states in America. They recognized that Kansas City and Kuala Lumpur are different just as New York and New Orleans are; but these differences could be taken into account by local sales offices, without challenging the company's global strategy.

This model of the fully globalized company has been realized by a mere handful of giant companies. But in many ways such companies set the tone for international competition today.

Indeed, to some analysts, this model is associated with market dominance so great that it transcends the efforts of the nation-state to control economic life. Richard Barnet and John Cavanaugh propose in *Global Dreams* that giant global companies have already lost their national identities and have replaced national sovereignty. They argue that a few hundred giant "imperial corporations" control the flow of money, goods, and information across the world: Sony, Bertelsmann, Philips, Time Warner, Matsushita, Disney, dominating a "global cultural bazaar" for information and entertainment; Philip Morris, RJR Nabisco, Nestlé, Sara Lee, and Heinz, dominating a "global shopping mall" for consumer products; Citibank, creating a "global financial network."

But other observers, noting fragmentation in the European Community and the success of smaller, entrepreneurial high-technology firms operating through networks of partners, see the opposite. Futurist John Naisbitt, for example, argues that smaller is better, more able, more competitive in the global economy. Indeed, it is not hard to find examples of competent local, or regional, niche players outcompeting global giants even in industries once considered prime targets for global consolidation. The success of such niche competitors as Southwest Airlines, for example, challenged the common wisdom that only a few large international airlines would survive. Deep knowledge of a local or regional market (and a cost structure appropriate to it) can provide advantages against global companies.

This controversy itself reflects the paradoxical nature of the global economy: the co-existence of globalizing consumption and localized distribution.

Globalism leads in information and communication, and that, in turn, supports convergence of tastes. Protected markets dominated by national champions are disappearing. Nearly every industry is being opened up to some form of competition from outside the traditional territory, even if it is only "theoretical" competition from knowledge of the existence of better products in other markets. In any country of the world, there is a growing pool of more sophisticated customers with access to the best the world has to offer. They no longer have to choose the local product or service as the only alternative. Among the many problems of EuroDisney, the theme park outside of Paris, for example, was the fact that European tourists could almost as easily, and sometimes more cheaply, go to sunnier Disney World in Orlando, Florida.

Localism prevails in politics and distribution—the differences in infrastructure and logistics to get goods and services to customers. Even if people accept, and sometimes even prefer, foreign products (why else would McDonald's be one of the best-known American brands worldwide?), they support local sovereignty. Local jurisdictions set the rules. Local distribution channels require specific, differentiated relationships within a country. When Kenichi Ohmae exhorts companies to undergo "insiderization" in order to be globally effective, he is referring to relationship building with local officials, distributors, and opinion leaders.

Countries can be grouped into regions for administrative convenience, but that often masks great differences. One American company worked on an "Asian strategy" without seeming to acknowledge the vast differences that existed between Hong Kong and Malaysia or Indonesia and India. Even the assumption that laws in Europe would be harmonized by 1992 has not been realized. Companies gain efficiencies by creating "Eurobrands," but they still have to deal with many jurisdictions and local distributors. For some purposes, "Europe" exists; for other purposes, it is a chimera.

The competing forces of globalism and localism make it almost impossible for companies to operate effectively alone. Hence, globalization encourages the formation of alliances and partnerships—cooperative relationships that extend each partner's global reach while each contributes its local competence, as Perlmutter and Heenan suggest. Some countries require local partners in order for companies to do business there. But even where this is not required, many companies recognize the benefits of establishing alliances to combine technologies or develop market access quickly. Connection to a global network allows smaller companies to gain the purchasing power or market clout of larger ones. Cohen & Wilks International, a small British apparel supplier to large retailers such as BhS (British Home Stores), benefits from a partnership with the Japanese trading company, Mitsui. Mitsui invested in Cohen & Wilks in the late 1960s, helping the company develop relationships with Japanese textile factories. Today Cohen & Wilks has access to Mistui's 189 offices worldwide, most of which employ textile managers who can offer on-site support. The Mitsui connection gives Cohen & Wilks immediate credibility when it seeks foreign manufacturing partners in Korea or Indonesia. Mistui also introduces Cohen & Wilks to other resources which enhance Cohen & Wilks' offerings to its British customers.

Globalization, therefore, requires new relationships both across companies and in companies. To compete effectively in the global economy, companies must strengthen their internal unity as well as become more adept at external learning.

Only strong companies can be effective global competitors and effective partners for others. Strength comes from both excellence in each line of business and the combined power of the whole. Lippo Group, one of Southeast Asia's fastest-growing financial conglomerates, active in China, evolved from a domestic company in Indonesia, with independent lines of business, to a strong regional competitor through explicitly tapping synergies among diverse product lines and geographic territories. San Miguel, the largest company in the Philippines, realizes that it cannot become a global competitor while its highly decentralized divisions operate separately; they must work together effectively to gain regional and then global scale. Consumer marketing companies such as Colgate-Palmolive, Nestlé, and Disney Consumer Products with traditions of strong country managers are discovering the benefits of greater synergies and transfer of learning across countries in a region, uniting their European operations in a common quest for excellence, even before there are common Euro-products. Only if all markets are considered together can managers determine the opportunities for sharing or the need to maintain differences. Thus, global competitiveness often requires greater internal cooperation.

At the same time, global competitiveness involves watching, listening, and learning outside the company. Openness to learning from foreign markets and external partners is often a key to success. Partnerships provide a way to absorb knowledge, stimulate innovation, and become an insider in new markets. This was the Japanese strategy for making inroads in China, as Peter Williamson illustrates in *Managing the Global Frontier*. One Japanese auto company allied with a car-leasing company in China well before it considered manufacturing in China or even exporting there, as a way to learn about the use and repair of cars in the market. In 1989 three leading food retailers, Ahold in the Netherlands, Argyll in the United Kingdom, and Casino in France, formed the European Retail Alliance to develop joint projects as well as to learn about new products and markets in anticipation of greater European integration.

Global strategy brings new skill requirements for companies and their managers. They must balance deep local knowledge with breadth of perspective. They must juggle many variables simultaneously, organizing along several dimensions. In *Managing Across Borders* Christopher Bartlett and Sumantra Ghoshal have shown that worldwide product managers, worldwide functional managers, and regional geographic managers must each maintain focus on their dimension of the business while coordinating closely with the others. They must celebrate cultural diversity while building shared values—common companywide disciplines and perspectives that permit communication and teamwork across areas.

The balancing acts required for effective execution of global strategies represent one more force for organizational change. The global competitor of the future will be characterized by less bureaucracy and more communication. Vertical control and a hierarchy of command will be replaced by more horizontal, peer-oriented relationship building across borders and boundaries. The ultimate challenge for global business success, then, is to develop new organizational capabilities and managerial mind-sets. Without these capabilities, even the best global strategy will fail.

What global strategy really means is to think in an integrated way about all aspects of the business—its suppliers, production, markets, and competition. The true meaning of "global" is holistic, not international. Union Pacific Resources of Fort Worth, Texas, for example, has grown aggressively by pursuing what it calls a "home-alone" strategy—to concentrate on oil and gas exploration in the western United States while all its competitors roam the world. But unlike myopic, parochial domestic companies of the past, Union Pacific Resources scanned the world for opportunities, noted where its competition was strong, and considered the areas in which it could best deploy new technology.

Global thinking is what's important for companies today, not international operations. Global strategy involves focusing on areas of excellence against a backdrop of global possibilities.

About the Contributors

Christopher A. Bartlett is a professor of general management at the Harvard Business School and served as chairman of the International Senior Management Program there from 1990 to 1993. Recent books by Professor Barlett and Professor Ghoshal include *Managing Across Borders: The Transnational Solution* (Harvard Business School Press) and *Transnational Management: Text, Cases, and Readings in Cross-Border Management.*

Percy Barnevik is president and chief executive officer of ABB Asea Brown Boveri Ltd., in Zurich, Switzerland, which was formed by the merger of the Swedish ASEA and Swiss Brown Boveri in the late 1980s. Mr. Barnevik is also chairman of the board of Sandvik AB and Skanska AB of Sweden and serves on the Board of Directors of E.I. Du Pont de Nemours & Co. He was profiled in a *Harvard Business Review* interview in 1991.

Formerly chairman and managing director of Procter & Gamble India, **Gurcharan Das** is vice president and managing director of worldwide strategic planning for health and beauty care at Procter & Gamble. He is the author of a novel, *A Fine Family,* and three plays.

Sumantra Ghoshal is an associate professor who teaches business policy and international management at INSEAD in Fontainebleau, France. He is co-author, with Christopher Bartlett, of *Managing Across Borders: The Transnational Solution* and *Transnational Management: Text, Cases, and Readings in Cross-Border Management.*

Gary Hamel is a professor of strategic and international management at London Business School, where each spring he directs an executive program that attracts managers from all over the world. As a consultant, Professor Hamel has worked in many of the world's leading companies. He is also a member of the editorial board of the *Strategic Management Journal* and co-author, with C.K. Prahalad, of the forthcoming *Competing for the Future* (Harvard Business School Press).

David A. Heenan is chairman, president, and CEO of Theo. H. Davies & Co., the North American Holding company for the Hong Kong–based Jardine Matheson. He is the author of *The Re-United States of America* and the co-author of *Multinational Organizational Development;* his most recent book is *The New Frontier: The Big Move to Small Town, USA.*

When his article appeared in the *Harvard Business Review,* **Edward J. Hoff** was a graduate student in business economics at Harvard University. Before that he was an instructor in marketing at the Harvard Business School, which awarded him a Dean's Doctoral Fellowship to complete his Ph.D.

Richard W. Hoole is a director in the Weston, Massachusetts, office of Pittiglio Rabin Todd & McGrath, an international management consulting firm that specializes in operations management.

Thomas Hout is a vice president in the Boston office of The Boston Consulting Group and head of the firm's worldwide operational effectiveness practice. He is co-author, with colleague George Stalk, of *Competing Against Time,* the critically acclaimed book on time-based competition.

Rosabeth Moss Kanter holds the Class of 1960 Chair as Professor of Business Administration at the Harvard Business School. Her many books include the best-selling, award-winning *When Giants Learn to Dance* and *The Change Masters.* An advisor to leading companies worldwide, she also served as editor of the *Harvard Business Review* from 1989 to 1992 and hosts "Rosabeth Moss Kanter on Synergies, Alliances, and New Ventures" in the Harvard Business School Video Series.

Kamran Kashani wrote his article as a professor of marketing at the International Management Development Institute (IMEDE) in Lausanne, Switzerland. Previously he worked for Coca-Cola, General Tire, and Continental Can International.

Floris A. Maljers recently retired from Unilever, the Anglo-Dutch consumer goods group, where he was chairman of Unilever N.V. and vice-chairman of Unilever PLC, as well as a member of the Special Committee.

Regina Fazio Maruca is an associate editor at the *Harvard Business Review.*

Michael E. McGrath is a director in the Weston, Massachusetts, office of Pittiglio Rabin Todd & McGrath, an international management consulting firm that specializes in operations management.

When his article appeared in the *Harvard Business Review,* **Martin van Mesdag** was the acting president of Halliday Associates, a British consulting firm focusing on policy-making, planning, and marketing management. He was previously marketing director at Van Houten, the Dutch chocolate company.

Nancy A. Nichols is a senior editor at the *Harvard Business Review.* A former reporter for the MacNeil/Lehrer Newshour, she has written articles for *HBR, Working Woman, The Christian Science Monitor, The Chicago Tribune,* and *Inc.* She is editor of *Reach for the Top* (Harvard Business School Press), a recently published collection of *Harvard Business Review* articles examining the challenges and opportunities faced by professional women.

Kenichi Ohmae is a partner in McKinsey's Tokyo office. He is the author of *The Mind of the Strategist: The Art of Japanese Business, Triad Power: The Coming Shape of Global Competition, Beyond National Borders,* and most recently, *The Borderless World.*

Howard V. Perlmutter is a professor at the Wharton School at the University of Pennsylvania where he teaches courses on global strategy and cross-cultural management. He has served on the boards of several multinational companies in Europe and the United States and advised over one hundred multinationals. His article is based on part of his book, *On the Rocky Road: The First Global Civilization.*

Michael E. Porter is the C. Roland Christensen Professor of Business Administration at the Harvard Business School and a leading authority in the field of competitive strategy. He is the author of fourteen books, including *The Competitive Advantage of Nations,* as well as the co-editor of the *Harvard Business Review* collection *Strategy: Seeking and Securing*

Competitve Advantage (Harvard Business School Press). Twice he has been awarded the McKinsey award for best *HBR* article of the year.

C.K. Prahalad is the Harvey C. Fruehauf Professor of Business Administration and professor of corporate strategy and international business at the University of Michigan. He is co-author, with Gary Hamel, of *Competing for the Future* (Harvard Business School Press).

John A. Quelch is the Sebastian S. Kresge Professor of Marketing at the Harvard Business School, where he teaches in the International Senior Managers Program and the International Marketing Management course in the MBA program.

When her article appeared in the *Harvard Business Review,* **Eileen Rudden** was a manager at The Boston Consulting Group's Boston office.

Nan Stone is the editorial director of the *Harvard Business Review.* Previously she was the Program Executive of the Harvard Business School Publishing Corporation's Management Production Group.

INDEX